T0354799

SOCIAL HOUSING FOUND

By
Robert B. Whittlesey

November 2013

authorHOUSE®

2

AuthorHouse™
1663 Liberty Drive
Bloomington, IN 47403
www.authorhouse.com
Phone: 1 (800) 839-8640

Published by AuthorHouse   01/20/2016

ISBN: 978-1-5049-3298-1 (sc)
ISBN: 978-1-5049-3297-4 (e)

Library of Congress Control Number: 2015913661

Print information available on the last page.

Any people depicted in stock imagery provided by Thinkstock are models, and such images are being used for illustrative purposes only. Certain stock imagery © Thinkstock.

This book is printed on acid-free paper.

Because of the dynamic nature of the Internet, any web addresses or links contained in this book may have changed since publication and may no longer be valid. The views expressed in this work are solely those of the author and do not necessarily reflect the views of the publisher, and the publisher hereby disclaims any responsibility for them.

This book is dedicated to Louise Allen Whittlesey,
who was with me for 70 years. She was a wonderful mother,
determined supporter, a kind and generous person, whose
cheerful personality radiated through her ever present smile.
She is cherished by all who knew her.

Preface

I received a lot of help bringing this opus to print. Partnership directors drafted pieces for the profiles. There was help running down photos of projects. I was taken about to see projects. There were interesting discussions with directors, their staffs and residents. Tom Bledsoe was generous with his time and there were numerous others who gave their time and attention. John MacKinnon, our printer, was always helpful. My daughter Prudence and her husband, Leighton Pierce, did the cover with an artistic touch. I am indebted to Governor Dukakis, William Edgerly and my old friend Langley Keyes for their opinions that appear on the cover. Many others, including all the actors who worked with me over the years, were great. And not the least was Peter Richardson, who did the redlined book review, my son Rob and his wife Cindy Soule for picture scanning and proofreading. I also want to thank the National Association of Housing and Redevelopment Officials for granting me approval to use and edit my article on the Boston Housing Authority which first appeared in their *Journal of Housing*, June 1980.

There are several reasons for writing this book. I want to illustrate the role of mission-driven nonprofit organizations, the ways in which they may be created and developed, and how they can serve as special players in society. I hope to illustrate the satisfaction that one can have in achieving the goal of establishing and working for institutions that provide social benefits to those in need in an effective and productive way. My story may encourage others to follow. Lastly, I want to explain to my children just what I did during those long hours working for a "not-for-profit" company.

They all have my thanks and my recognition that without them, this tale would never have been told.

6

Photo Acknowledgements

The photos in this book are largely copies from my own collection. The housing directors were good enough to provide photos of their organization's leaders and projects. I am indebted to Amos Williams for his permission to use the photos of Beth Smith and Anna Faith Jones; to Ms Bethany Versoy for her permission to use photos of three group photos taken at Metropolitan Boston Housing Partnership third annual meeting. Thanks to the File Photo, POUA, Inc. for permission to use the photo of Father Groden. Thanks also to the New Settlement Community Center for allowing use of the photo of the Center.

Cover: Author in front of Rollins Square, South End.

TABLE OF CONTENTS

TABLE OF CONTENTS

Introduction

Shelter is a basic human need. It is satisfied in a variety of forms from a homeowner's own creation to the work of an urban developer. Most people desire private shelter and the separation is as important as protection from the elements. Ownership is considered important and there are all sorts of institutional arrangements that flow from the production and marketing of housing. Housing costs money, the amount of which is a barrier to many. One can spread out the costs by borrowing money to pay for the housing or one can rent. It is necessary in the operation of a housing market that there exist a system which defines rights to property and establishes a set of procedures for the transfer of these rights. In most developed nations such as the US, the production, management and distribution of housing is a blend of private enterprise and government regulation. Within that context, there has been a history of the U.S. Government supporting programs that are intended to provide affordable housing to people within their means. Today, about 5 percent of housing in the U.S. has government limitations on the costs to the consumer.

Social housing is a term used around the world to describe housing that receives some form of direct public assistance, financial or otherwise. In turn, it is regulated to some degree and is required to provide homes for certain eligible groups, such as families whose breadwinner works in low-paid employment or is unemployed, as well as families with elderly or handicapped members.

I have been involved in pursuing social housing through several private nonprofit corporations. Social housing is one of the activities in the national economy in which private nonprofit enterprises play a significant role. These private agencies, which address social issues and meet consumer needs, are initiated in the U.S. in a number of ways consistent with our cultural tradition of innovation. These institutions benefit more often than not from being more focused and effective managers than government agencies. They partner more easily with private supporters and other groups, be they for-profit or nonprofit organizations. I was a practitioner for fifty years at a time when the federal government was experimenting with programs for the nonprofit sector. I was the founder of several nonprofit institutions which are models in our social housing system. My work has persuaded me that our efforts in creating a nonprofit sector are not finished but that we have institutions now that are key corporations which if recognized and supported could provide the basis for addressing among other things the need of a good home in a decent environment for all Americans. This goal has been promised for decades.

I grew up during the Franklin Roosevelt years and acquired progressive attitudes about societal issues and the role of government. I encountered public enterprise during two short stints with government agencies and three years in the U.S Army. For ten years I worked for a private for-profit building construction company, which I regarded as the best in the country. These experiences gave me business judgment and skills that were beneficial when I changed careers to social enterprise.

A decision to redirect my work from for-profit industry to nonprofit enterprise was made possible by a fellowship from the Sears Roebuck Foundation for graduate study in City Planning at the University of Pennsylvania. At the time, I was thirty seven years old with a wife and four children. Penn's City Planning department was endowed with a number of distinguished people. It was a wonderful learning opportunity. After receiving a degree in City Planning and a stay in Washington, DC working as a senior planner for a nonprofit organization, I was recruited to come to Boston and direct a new housing and community development corporation. The corporation was the centerpiece in a proposal that I had prepared with Charles Liddell and the staff of the United South End Settlements in Boston and filed with the predecessor agency of the U. S. Department of Housing and Urban Development. The plan was to build social housing for low and moderate income families in the South End Renewal Area. This was the beginning of a fifty year career in which I had the opportunity to create with the help of others three charitable nonprofit housing institutions that were and are still successful. This began during the Great Society years of Lyndon Johnson's Administration, the civil rights movement, and the national poverty programs. There was considerable focus at the time on urban problems, the women's movement, and increased participation by private business in public actions programs. I had the good fortune to work at the cutting edge of new federal welfare and community development programs with top-flight, dedicated individuals, young and old, who were both energetic and capable of getting things done. I am indebted to hundreds of associates and supporters who made things possible.

Private social enterprise comes out of the tradition of charity that has been with us since the beginning of man. But as practiced in the 20th and 21st centuries, it is of a different magnitude. Today, charities are increasingly associated with business practices and performance standards. They work in conjunction with government to achieve publicly set goals. While philanthropic organization receive both funding and tax benefits, they must comply with regulations as to their organizational structure, administrative practices and distribution of any revenue or earnings to private individuals. They benefit from being private. Although they need financial help from government, they make their own decisions about what they will and will not do.

Governments today face the daunting task of administering comprehensive social programs that are designed to benefit all eligible members of society. Only in the last century or so have we had the administrative tools to do this. Involving private agencies in the implementation of social programs has been a real challenge. The effectiveness of private organizations has been enhanced through their ability to set up networks through which to share administrative practices and influence program regulations and funding. In turn, interaction improves program performance and political support for continuation.

A social enterprise is born when a group of citizens decide to do something together under an organizational structure to accomplish an activity or goal. It is generally local, unique and frequently innovative. It could be a baseball league for eighth graders. It could be a community garden. It could be a soup kitchen, or a charter school, or a health clinic or a wellness center. It could be housing for the homeless. There are now in the United States 3.5 million charitable and educational organizations that are operating on a not-for-profit basis.

Social enterprises can vary in the scale of the operations and in the complexity of their governance and management. They can have limited goals or be part of a larger network that serves as a whole component in a delivery system. This book is about social housing enterprises that develop and manage housing and serve as an increasingly important component in our national housing system. The endeavors involve private organizations focused on providing housing to individuals and families that cannot afford free market prices.

Private non-profit enterprise over the last fifty years has played an increasing role in social housing. This is particularly true in Europe and other developed countries around the world. These entities can operate with greater flexibility and more direct engagement with consumers. This was argued in the nineteenth century when the capacity of voluntary organizations was much lower. Today, these organizations are demonstrating that they can manage large scale operations. There are numerous social housing enterprises here and in Europe that own over 10,000 dwellings. They operate in large municipal areas, in multi-jurisdiction regions and nationally. They have economies of scale and substantial assets to support the financing of their activities.

Social housing is not socialism. Socialism is generally thought of as political and economic systems under which land and farming, commerce and industry are either owned and/or managed by the State. I remember on a visit to Budapest in 1986, speaking with the government official in the Hungarian Department of Commerce who controlled the manufacture of furniture. She was the person who decided how many lawn chairs would be built the next year by the 13 State furniture enterprises. There were regulations at the time that an individual could only employ up to five other individuals. Any business that had more than five employees was taken over by the State. If you were a furniture maker and prospered, you might have to turn your chair business over to the State and concentrate on making only the seats. That was socialism.

It is interesting to note Theodore Roosevelt's remark after his defeat in the 1912 election and was asked to write about current socialism. "I am against the kind of Socialism of Debs and that kind of applied Socialism ...which means the break-up of the family. But as you say, I am not to be frightened in the least by the word Socialism, or of ideas because they are called Socialistic." [1]

Currently, the politically correct term in the U. S. is "affordable housing," not "low income" or "social housing." But they are fundamentally the same. Affordable housing implies developments that include at least some units reserved for low- and moderate-income households. It is a political term which has to be clarified in law and regulations. When the playwright George Kaufman saw Rockefeller's mansion in upstate New York he described it as "what God would have built if he had the money." One can believe that it was "affordable" by Mr. Rockefeller.

Social housing is one of the primary building blocks of a modern civil society. It functions in conjunction with other programs that collectively provide a safety net for the less fortunate citizens of the country. The other primary programs involve economic security including unemployment insurance, workman's compensation and retirement programs. There is also education and job training; health care and public health; security and a criminal justice system; the physical infrastructure, including roads, transportation, utilities, public spaces and facilities; protection of the environment; and, as recently demonstrated, a financial system.

Individuals in a society require social, economic, and security programs in various degrees. Education and healthcare are universal needs. Security needs vary. Some neighborhoods are very safe and people don't lock their doors at night and in other areas people are afraid to walk to the store or even go into their apartment hallway. Most Americans are well housed at standards higher than any other country in the world but there are still thousands of Americans families living in substandard housing. Many are overcrowded, and too many are homeless.

The fact that in America social housing is only needed by a minority of citizens makes political support for its public funding tenuous. This is true of any social program but housing is particularly denied because housing markets separate the population along economic lines into affluent and low-income communities. There is often a social disconnect between those in need and the general population that must bear the costs. Poor families and individuals are frequently in separated locations such as the other side of town or in rural settings where they can be overlooked. Convincing a majority of the public to support a particular program over time is not easy.

Comprehensive programs that reach everyone are difficult to design and administer. They are also complex and contentious. They are prone to have operating problems that fuel criticism and introduce regulatory burdens. There are multiple constituencies and special interests that are hard to manage and satisfy. Social housing, along with other programs, requires that the public decide between benevolence and individual responsibility, between social inequities and spending tax money, between private initiative and government action.

This book is about my discovery of private nonprofit social enterprise and its role in providing a decent home in a suitable environment. This is the commitment first promised in the National Housing Act of 1949. My work in housing and community development started in 1960 and I had direct experience as a practitioner with the changes in the housing system that followed.

This book follows a chronological order.

Chapter One presents some personal background: my family heritage, my formative years, and how I became a progressive. It includes episodes from the time I spent in the U.S. Army in World War Two, which interrupted my pursuit of a college education.

Chapter Two recalls my ten years in the building construction business and graduate studies in City Planning. The skills learnt during these years were crucial to my success in the direction of nonprofit social enterprises.

Chapter Three is a brief history of the government's role in social housing through the Franklin D. Roosevelt Administration and the Housing Act of 1949 that promised every American a decent home in a suitable environment. Along with the Social Security Act of 1935, this comprehensive legislation transformed the relationship between the federal government and the American family.

Chapter Four describes a federal demonstration carried out by South End Community Development, one of the first community development corporations in the Country.

Chapter Five describes the work of Greater Boston Community Development, renamed from South End Community Development, as a provider of technical assistance to other nonprofit community organizations to develop and own social housing.

Chapter Six describes my work as the Court-Appointed Master working for reform of the Boston Housing Authority.

Chapter Seven describes my work as the Executive Director and President of the Boston Housing Partnership, an early public/private housing partnership that became a national model for others.

Chapter Eight covers profiles of a number of high-performing public/private housing partnerships that were formed in states around the country.

Chapter Nine describes the creation and development of the Housing Partnership Network (HPN). HPN is a national network with 100 members from 37 states. It is now one of the major institutions in social housing in the USA.

Chapter Ten describes social housing in the UK and the Netherlands. Both countries provided grants to nonprofit enterprises which contributed materially to the growth of their social housing sectors.

Chapter Eleven looks to the future and the further growth of non-profit social housers, the increasing role of residents, and the contributions to the well-being of the communities of which they are a part.

Whittlesey, 21 years old, at Princeton University

Robert Bruere,
Chairman of the Maritime Labor Board, 1937

Henry Bruere, Presidential advisor, 1934

Whittlesey in jeep during war

Whittlesey with comrades at Gladbeck, Germany, 1945

Robert and Louise at Evelyn Place, Princeton, 1946

Bureau of Reclamation, Big Thompson site

Chapter One

Background

My father, Walter Lincoln Whittlesey, was born in California in 1878. His ancestors go back to John Whittlesey, who was born on July 4, 1623, in Cambridgeshire near Whittlesey, England. He was one of a complement of young men who, in 1635, came to America with Robert Lord Brooks and his business associates of the Lord Say and Seal Company. Records indicate that John and William Dudley received a contract from the town of Saybrook in 1662 to run the ferry across the Connecticut River. In 1664 John married Ruth Dudley of famous Scottish ancestry. They were the parents of eleven children, the eighth of whom was named Eliphalet. He was my ancestor. My grandfather Albert, five generations after Eliphalet, was born in 1843 in Cleveland. He served in the 41st Ohio Infantry in Sherman's Army during the Civil War. His family had been prominent in Cleveland in the newspaper and real estate businesses. Albert's father died during the War and his real estate holdings were sold. When Albert returned from the Army and discovered that there was no estate, he traveled west. He settled in Colorado and became a cattle and sheep farmer. His herd was wiped out over night by hoof and mouth disease and he moved on to California as so many other Americans. He met my grandmother, Lucy Wright, also from Cleveland, and they were married in December 1873. After several years in Los Gatos, where Father was born on March 13, 1878, the family moved to Portland, Oregon, where Grandfather had a job in the lumber business.

Father was educated in the Portland schools and graduated from the University of Oregon Phi Beta Kappa in 1901. After teaching a few years at the University, he came East in 1905 to study economics and history at Cornell University. There, in 1906, he was recruited by Woodrow Wilson to be one of the famous forty new preceptors at Princeton University. He left Princeton in 1910 to take a position with the Atlantic Telephone and Telegraph Company. Father and Mother were married on April 1, 1911 and took up residency at 400 Riverside Drive in New York City.

My mother's forebears came from Germany and Poland. Her grandfather, born in 1805, was an architect who spent much of his professional career away from home on building projects, including the Cologne Cathedral. He married Wilhelmina Yaeger in St.Goar, Germany, in 1829. They moved to Darmstadt where Wilhelmina ran a girls school. Wilhelmina opposed Emperor Frederick's policy of conscription into the Army and she sent her boys to America when they had reached sixteen years of age. Johan, born in 1836, was sent to America with an older brother Gustave in 1853. He worked for a time as a carpenter and then had an opportunity to study with a local St. Charles doctor and later at the St. Louis Medical School. In 1858 he went to Europe to further his training and was fortunate to train with some of the best doctors at the time including Doctor Rudolph Virchow. He returned to America in 1861 better trained than most of his American colleagues. He served as a surgeon with the Missouri State Militia Calvary in 1862-3. After his service in the Army he opened his practice with another doctor in St. Charles.

My mother was named Louise Jeanne Bruere. Her mother married Johan in St. Charles in 1862. They had nine children. Grandfather was determined the children be well educated. All four boys and the oldest two girls attended college even though money was scarce. My mother was born in St. Charles on Christmas Day 1883. At the age of 12, she became a serious student of music and singing. Her father bought for her one of the famous Steinway grand pianos that had been on display at the Chicago Exposition of 1893. That piano would be with us throughout our childhood. At the age of 16 Mother traveled to Wales by herself to study with Franken Davies, a renowned baritone well known in England and the Continent. She returned from Europe in 1904. She needed an audition with an agent to launch a professional career, but the family baulked at paying the fee. On a visit to her brother Gustave in Portland, Oregon, she met my Father. She found Father interesting and admired his keen intellect and immense knowledge of history and literature.

Throughout her life Mother was always in search of ways to use her intellectual talents and be independent. In 1916 she became interested in farming for the purpose of supporting the War effort as a food producer. She attended agricultural school in Farmingdale, Long Island, and then bought a 70-acre farm in New Preston, Connecticut. Mother was in constant difficulties managing erratic and sometimes drunken farmhands and trying not to be cheated by her neighbors and suppliers. She did some teaching at a local girls private school. The collapse of farm prices in 1920 was devastating. The farm was sold in 1922 and the family moved to Princeton, New Jersey, on Father's reappointment to the Princeton faculty as an Instructor and later Professor in Politics and History.

I was born on the farm in Connecticut. The story goes that my brother John jumped off a feed bin and my pregnant mother caught him in her arms, starting labor that led to my being born five minutes before midnight on that Thursday, September 22, 1921. The only person on hand was the maid. The doctor did not appear until after my arrival. It would not be the last time that professional medical help would fail my family.

In Princeton the family owned a house on Ober Road. In 1926, Mother decided to move to England of which she had fond memories. In a letter to her sister Alice she wrote that her reason for going was "to find a more cultured and enjoyable environment in which she could raise her children." We lived in Bournemouth on the Southern coast for three years. Mother received a substantial portion of Father's salary and she had help from several of her sisters. Mother had a number of English friends including Sir Dan Godfery, the Conductor of the Bournemouth Symphony. She performed several times with the Symphony until the day a bobby showed up at our front door to invite Mother to come down to the station. She was told that her passport did not allow her to perform. These were hard times for the British, and there was unemployment everywhere, including musicians. In time her sisters withdrew their support and we returned to the United States in February 1929, six months before the stock market crash.

After a year and a half in Fleetwood, New York, Mother returned to Princeton. A prime reason was in seeing that Father obtained tenure. She had been very popular in her previous stays in Princeton and was admired by the President of the University. My brother, two sisters, and I enjoyed Princeton and its university amenities – tennis courts, skating rink, the campus to ride our bikes and interesting events like concerts, sports and famous visitors to the University. Mother was interested in a variety of social causes such as early child care, health care and home education. While Mother voted for the socialist candidate Norman Thomas in the 1932 election, she welcomed the election of FDR who was known personally by her brothers Robert and Henry and sister Wilhelmina.

Father received tenure in 1933. Mother then picked up and moved to Washington, DC, with the election of Franklin Delano Roosevelt. My brother John stayed with Father. We lived in a third floor two-bedroom apartment in a small four-story red brick building on 17th Street next to the Tally-Ho restaurant. The first floor was occupied by a real estate office. A small top attic apartment was occupied by a very elderly black woman named Rosa, the daughter of slaves freed during the Civil War. She was a very pleasant person who always said hello on her way up and down the stairway. We visited with her briefly on several occasions but never learned much about her background. On the second floor was a charming toy store with all sorts of interesting things, many from foreign countries. We enjoyed visiting the shop and discussing items with the proprietor on our trips up and down to our apartment. The toy store gave us an opportunity to say hello to Mrs. Roosevelt who came in occasionally to purchase toys for her grandchildren. She became one of the people we most admired.

Our playground was the sidewalk around Farragut Square. I became acquainted with the newspaper man who sold papers on 17th and K Streets and became an unpaid helper. The Evening Star was the evening paper that many picked up on the way home. I remember well the edition that reported on a "communist cell" in the Administration. Among the accused in the picture on the front page was my Uncle Robert, for whom I am named. He and others had been accused of being "communist brain trusters." The fuss had started when on March 23, 1934 James H Rand, Chairman of the Remington Rand Company and Chairman of the Committee for the Nation, stated that the Administration's Bill for Regulation of the Stock Exchange would "push the nation along the road from democracy to communism". To back this up, Rand referred to a paper written by Dr. William Wirt, a member of the Committee and Superintendent of Schools in Gary, Indiana, for the past 25 years. Wirt asserted the existence of a group of inside brain trusters "who proposed overthrow of the social order" and saw Roosevelt as a transitional figure, a Kerensky in the revolution. These ideas were revealed at a Virginia dinner party put on by a Miss Alice Barrows. I recall the day Uncle Bob came by our apartment on 17th Street to pick up a Bible to be sure he had it handy when he testified at the House of Republicans. When he did testify, Bruere described Wirt's comments as irresponsible and outrageous. He did acknowledge, when asked whether he had been a member of the Socialist Party, that he had been a member for a year in 1910. But he said he had withdrawn when he became "convinced that the Marxian revolution theory was not appropriate to the conditions of American life." The whole affair went down in history as a foolish performance on Wirt's part. The Wirt affair did, however, contribute to the emergence of political opinion on the part of some that the New Deal contained subversive elements and needed to be watched. It reflected the fears that some people had of communism and radical groups and individuals. The bonus March on Washington had been put down by the army and there were leaders of major trade unions that were active members of the Communist Party. Russian communism was being exported around the world and National Socialism was emerging in Germany. Other countries, such as the Scandinavian countries, had model socialistic societies. They were admired at a distance, but were regarded as contrary to the American free enterprise system. Many Americans saw the Depression as a failure of the capitalist system. However, there was never a threat that socialism would take hold in America. Its culture of individual enterprise would not only bar socialism, it would impede social action vital to the country's progress.

My uncle Robert Bruere had attended the Washington University of St. Louis and studied at the University of Berlin and University of Chicago from 1899 until 1904. It was here that he became involved in social policy issues with Jane Addams at Hull House and was increasingly interested in the living and working conditions of the poor. He moved to New York City in 1905 to be a writer and teacher at the Rand School of Social Science and the General Agent for the New York Association for the Conditions for the Poor. In the 1912 election Robert Bruere served as an advisor to Theodore Roosevelt on labor and social policy issues. He was an investigator in the infamous Triangle Building fire in 1911 in which one hundred and forty workers perished. He made a survey of factory conditions and issued a critical report that was endorsed by his friend Francis Perkins, then Secretary of the Committee of Safety. He became a labor arbitrator and was involved in the lockout of 60,000 garment workers in New York City. During the War, he was a mediator in labor disputes involving the International Workers of the World and he defended the International Workers of the World in their dispute with Colorado Coal and Iron over union rights and wages. He later became Associated Editor of the Survey Graphic and a contributor in labor issues, regional electricity and planning. After conversations with his friend Benton McKaye, the environmentalist, Uncle Bob organized a special edition of the Survey. That edition became a hallmark for regional planning in the country with contributors such as Lewis Mumford, Stuart Chase, Clarence Stein and others. He was on the Rockefeller study group that went to China and Japan in 1929-30. He served in FDR's Administration as the mediator for the Textile Industry Code. He was appointed by FDR as a member of the Camden Board of Arbitration and was a delegate to the Geneva Labor Conference in 1936 and 1937. In 1937 he was appointed by the President to be Chairman of the Maritime Labor Board. The dockworkers, both on the East and West Coast, had been on strike for nine months. Union leaders such as Bill Ryan on the East Coast and Harry Bridges on the West Coast, were determined union leaders.

The story goes that on one occasion, Uncle Bob was called by the White House and asked to visit with the President on his Potomac launch. Roosevelt would on occasion invite officials to visit with him as they traveled down and back on the river. Bruere dutifully came at the appointed time and sat in the forward waiting area of the boat. After some time he was ushered into the President's section and to his surprise learned that FDR was looking for Henry, not Robert Bruere. As they were well down the river, the President welcomed him, and they spent a pleasant hour talking about a variety of issues with which FDR was concerned.

Henry Bruere had a much deeper engagement with FDR as part of an interesting career that took him from social worker to bank president to presidential advisor. Henry was involved with social organizing in Boston and Chicago. He came to New York City in 1905 to be the Director of the Bureau of Publicity and Investigations for The Citizens Voice, later to be the Bureau of Municipal Research (BMR). His work at the BMR centered on municipal reform and budgeting. He backed John Purrow Mitchel for mayor and on Mitchel's victory became Chamberlain. He led the reform in city administration, abolished the pork-barrel system of appropriations and brought the City its first budget system. Henry was involved in addressing unemployment and relicf programs. Frances Perkins, who would become FDR's Secretary of Labor, worked with Henry on these issues and later stated that this was her first experience with unemployment issues. Henry was famous for having recommended that his office be abolished when he left.

Henry Bruere's friend Paul Wilson, an economist, came with him from Chicago to work at BMR. Wilson was involved with the Mitchel campaign and became chief of staff to the Mayor. Mother got to know Wilson through Henry and he was one of two witnesses at her wedding in 1911. Several years later Wilson married Frances Perkins on September 26, 1913. From 1918 on Wilson suffered from a recurring illness that burdened Frances Perkins until his death in 1952.

Leaving the city, Henry did consulting work that led to an appointment as a senior executive of American Metals Company, a Vice Presidency of the Metropolitan Life Insurance Company and the 1927 appointment as a Vice-President of the Bowery Savings Bank. He became President of the Bank in 1931 and Chairman in 1949. When he retired in 1952, he was made an honorary Chairman for Life. During his career from social worker to bank executive, he never overlooked the social and civic sides of his work. For example, he was the Treasurer of the New York City Public Library for 25 years.

Henry had been an advisor to FDR while FDR was Governor of New York State. He headed a State Commission on relieving unemployment, an appointment recommended to FDR by Frances Perkins. President Roosevelt's selection for Secretary of the Treasury in 1933 was his friend and contributor William Woodin, President of American Car and Foundry Company. Unfortunately, Woodin became seriously ill shortly after his appointment and was progressively absent during the year. He was forced to resign in December and died in the following January. This situation resulted in Henry Bruere being called in to help on a number of occasions. He was consulted during the "Bank Holiday" days during which time the banks were ordered closed and told not to open until the federal examiners had declared them financially sound. The plan required the banks to augment their capital assets position through loans from the Reconstruction Finance Corporation secured by preferred stock. The banks were slow to take out the loans which interfered with their qualifying for FDIC insurance. There was criticism of how Jesse Jones, head of RFC, was handling the program. Some in the Administration were critical and were proposing that the loans be made by a new agency. FDR called a meeting to iron out the difficulties. Present were Jones; Eugene Black, Governor of the Federal Reserve Board; Lewis Douglas, Director of the Budget; and Henry Bruere of the Bowery Savings Bank, who had been offered and turned down the position of Coordinator of Federal Credit Agencies. After a lengthy discussion, Roosevelt said "Boys, I am going to back Jess. He has never failed me yet. Henry, you and Lew and Jess get together and work out a plan." The plan resulted in the recapitalization of 6105 banks; all but two redeemed their securities with a loss to the government of only $5,000,000.[2]

I returned to Princeton, New Jersey, to attend Lawrenceville School. I lived at home with Father and went to school as a day student. I was surrounded by political talk. Father ran for Congress in 1936 and was beaten by an incumbent Republican. I was a reader of the New York Times and was aware of the unfolding of FDR's presidency and new programs that his Administration initiated. As a staunch Democrat, I encountered opposite views from my Republican friends at Lawrenceville and defended Eleanor Roosevelt, who was subject to boorish remarks about her appearance and speaking voice. I spent a summer traveling with a pediatrician in Waynesboro, Virginia. Uncle Bob set up a meeting with Doctor Parran, Surgeon General in Washington, DC and I went down to discuss going into medicine. He recommended that I not try when he understood my interest in transforming the medical profession and our system of care.

After finishing high school in June 1939, I spent a summer working for the U. S. Forestry Service in Maine. Most the men in the camp had been in the Citizens Conservation Corp. A majority had worked for lumber companies, either cutting and hauling logs or in the mills. Most had not finished high school and had a narrow view of the world. Our job was to cut fire trails through the forests. I enjoyed the forestry work and developed a friendship with many of my associates. I would hear stories of their experiences. One friend had a large scar down the calf of this leg which he got when his father threw a hatchet at him because he came home with no money. Many followed the custom of accumulating some money and then going out and blowing the whole amount on liquor and girls. The U.S. Forestry Department's supervisor in charge was both capable and conscientious. My stay gave me an opportunity to consider working for the government in a civil service position. I was paid $75 a month less $22 for room (a cot in a tent) and board.

Like many others Americans of my generation, I did not appreciate the military threat presented by Hitler and the Nazis regime in Germany. I did not learn of the full horrors of the Nazi regime in Germany until late in the 1930s when I read news reports and magazines articles about the arrest and persecution of the Jews. Books were being burned in town squares across Germany and distinguished Jewish writers and professionals were coming to America. The concentration camps were less well understood and had not yet been recorded as the killing machines we would discover later. My father was a field judge at the Track and Field events at Princeton University and became acquainted with Jesse Owens, the great sprinter. I became a fan. When we heard about the way Hitler snubbed Owens on his Olympic victories in Germany in 1936, I was furious. I had an acquaintance in the graduate school at Princeton who spent some time in Berlin in 1938 and he described to me the destruction of the synagogues, the smashing of the store fronts of shops owned by Jewish proprietors and the arrest of thousands of Jewish men in November 1938. Apartments of Jewish families were looted and smashed and families were driven from their homes. It was the beginning of the Nazis program to force all Jews to emigrate, leaving all their possessions behind.

My friend also described the famous purge of 1938. He was living in Berlin at the time. Everybody in the city sensed that something was about to happen. Hitler went off to Berchesgarden and left Goering in charge of murdering a selected group of distrusted leaders. Hitler was careful to take Goebbels with him for fear that he would not survive. It was a demonstration of the ruthless tactics of the Nazis and the nature of the Nazi leadership.

The New York Times which my father and I read diligently reported the steps that Hitler took on his road to war. Following the plebiscite mandated by the League of Nations held in January 1935, in which

32

the mainly German speaking Saarlanders voted to return to Germany, Hitler made his first move to take over Europe. In March 1936 he remilitarized the Rhineland and intervened in the Spanish Civil War in 1936 -1937. German troops marched into Austria on March 12, 1938 and made it part of Germany. Czechoslovakia was swallowed up to cheering crowds in September 1938. Germany attacked Poland on September 1, 1939. The British were finally duty bound by its Treaty with Poland to declare war on Germany on September 3, 1939.

I entered Princeton University in the fall of 1939. My faculty tuition scholarship paid the bill and I worked a variety of jobs including being the Music Department's record librarian. After my freshman year I traveled with my friend Dimi Barton to the West Coast and back. The day we left, Germany invaded Russia. The draft was passed and signed by President Roosevelt on September, 10, 1940. I was with Dimi Barton on December 6, 1941, when we heard over the radio the report of the attack on Pearl Harbor. In the following week, I investigated the Navy V-seven program. It allowed enrollees to complete college prior to active duty. The Navy turned me down for being too light. As things worked out, my weight of 120 pounds was quite good enough for the Infantry. I transferred to civil engineering thinking that an engineering degree would prove be more useful. In September I signed up with the enlisted reserves. I told them I was a member of no religion and was told my tags would be marked capital P. It was the beginning of the U.S. Army telling me what to think and do. In the following June 1943, I was called up for active service.

Every young man had a draft number, and joining the armed services was the usual thing to do. Timing was, however, important. Assignment priorities when one arrived at the gate were always shifting and one could not predict what the services were thinking week to week. What happens in the Army is all luck. Where you are assigned as well as your survival is just chance.

The new recruits over the next several weeks ended up doing both hard labor like kitchen patrol and soft make-work assignments that accomplished almost nothing. I thought that my three years of college engineering might mean something but it did not. The Army Specialized Training Program (ASTP) had priority over all classifications except Air Force pilots training. After a three-week stay, I was shipped out with a contingent of ASTP solders for basic training at Camp Hood near Waco, Texas. Sixteen weeks of basic training was new to all of us. The trainers were seasoned non-commissioned officers (noncoms) and some were disdainful of college type recruits. We went off to training sessions dealing with how the Army operated, how to use fire arms, and how to protect ourselves and take care of wounded buddies. We had time on the rifle range. When using the bayonet, we were ordered to growl and grunt. I suppose that it was an attempt to make new recruits, who since infancy had been told not to harm anyone, to be a more willing killers.

After completing sixteen weeks of basic training, I returned to the ASTP program at Pratt Institute in New York City, studied mechanical engineering and lived with my contingent in the new Fort Greene Housing Project in Brooklyn. I had Wednesday afternoons off and went to Manhattan. My sister was living with her friend Louise Allen, whom I got to know and love. We decided to marry. We got the certificate, took the blood tests and were scheduled to go to City Hall on Saturday. However, the ASTP program was shut down on that very day. We were all loaded onto railroad cars, shipped to the woods and swamps of Louisiana and told that we were privates in the 75th Infantry Division. Louise had no idea where I had gone. I was just a no-show. The marriage had to wait.

After about sixty days, the Division was sent to Camp Breckenridge in Kentucky for training. There it was discovered that I could paint names on helmets. This led to my staying in the Company area during the day, and in time I was appointed mail clerk. Dropping the ASTP recruits into a combat infantry division as privates was a questionable use of resources but infantry solders were needed. It is striking to see how the quality of leadership makes a difference. Some of the officers and noncoms in the 75th were good leaders and trainers, others were not.

I was assigned to Company A, 290th Regiment. The 289 and 291 were the other regiments in the Division. Exercises at Breckinridge were serious and organized. A full complement of officers and non-coms meant that there was always someone in charge. One gets to know most of one's comrades and special friendships develop. My role as mail clerk contributed to my knowing every one of the 200 men and officers in the Company.

After I had been in Breckinridge about eight weeks, Louise was brave enough to come to Kentucky so that we could get married. Her friends at her job in New York had a good laugh about sensible Louise doing such a foolish thing. Her parents did not approve. Yet she had made up her mind. She came down on a crowded train to Terre Haute where I met her. We went to the USO and found her a room for the night. I stayed overnight in the USO. The following day we took the "cattle car" type bus out to Morganfield, Kentucky, which was the town adjacent to the Camp. I had arranged for a room at a house owned by a Mrs. Young. The latter was put out when she discovered that we were not married. However, she did allow Louise to stay provided I returned to camp before dark. On the following Wednesday I got a day pass, took the camp bus out to Morganfield, picked up Louise and we went to the town hall where we were married by a Judge Richards. The license cost $2 and the town clerk and a secretary were our witnesses. We spent the night at Mrs. Young's. I left at 4:00 am in the morning to be able to get back by reveille. Thereafter, I would return on weekends or on overnight passes which were allowed provided you returned to the base in time to attend reveille. Louise got a job working for a lawyer and put up with misfortunes of being a military wife.

Late in the summer the division received orders to move out. Preparing for the move required that we be fully equipped. Inordinate amounts of supplies were ordered. Everybody received new clothes and a duffle bag with our identification number on it. Every supply sergeant had ordered an ample supply of clothing and where this was overdone, the excess was burned in the supply room pot stove. The smoke over the supply rooms was quite apparent. Our departure also required some new officers. Our company commander, who was widely admired, had been transfered out for overseas assignment. A new company commander was assigned and there was little time to get to know him. He looked pretty tough but did not turn out to be so.

Louise on hearing that we would be leaving Camp Breckinridge, quit her job, gathered her things and took the train back to Princeton. We packed up our stuff in our duffle bags and marched off to the rail siding. I had the scoop from the kitchen crew that we would go east and not west but one could never be sure. We were blessed on seeing the train after a day head eastward toward Europe rather than the Pacific. Our destination turned out to be Camp Shanks, 15 miles north of New Your City. After several days of spreading our stuff out in our bunks for inspection and then packing it away, we were told that we would have the following evening off for a visit to New York City if we wished. I called Louise and told her I would meet her in at the Pennsylvania Station at 6:00 o'clock the next day. However, orders came down the next afternoon that we were to ship out. We were confined to our barracks and told that we should not speak to anyone about it. The next day we were put on trains to Weehawken, maybe Hoboken, and marched up the gangway of our ship for Europe. Louise came as promised to the station, waited all night for me and then had to go back to Princeton not knowing what had happened. She would not hear from me for several weeks.

The weather was good for the trip but the conditions were less than luxurious. We were stacked in bunks four or five deep, waited in lines for hours for meals and were allowed only five minutes to eat standing up. I spent a lot of time out on the deck winning $56 dollars in poker and then losing it all. There were fierce crap games going all the time in the bunk areas. About half way across we picked up a destroyer escort. German subs were in business in the Atlantic and we occasionally heard depth charges going off. The ship, the SS Pacific, was about 29,000 tons and had been a cruise ship modified to serve as a troop ship. The trip took about nine days. The mail that I later received indicated that our destination had been changed several times. We finally landed at Swansea on the Coast of Wales and a ceremony was planned for our arrival. A gangway had been setup between the ship's lower level and the dock and several American and English officials were waiting on the dock. As our Regimental Commander walked down the gangway, several blown up condoms floated down on the ceremony from one of the top decks above us. The colonel lost his cool, stormed back onto the ship and ordered everybody back to quarters. There were speeches over the loudspeakers about conduct and soldiering. In time, we all disembarked.

We traveled by train to Porthcawl, a pleasant seaside town, further east on the coast. It was a pleasant seaside town. Company A was housed in a resort hotel overlooking the golf course along the beach. The hotel had a minimum number of baths. The Army had constructed a toilet and bath facility at the back of the building that cut down but did not eliminate the waiting lines. Our main activities for the month that we were there were formations, marching up and down on the golf course, and laying out our stuff on the bed and packing it up again. We had weekends off and I was able to visit some of the nearby villages and take a sightseeing trip to Cardiff. I received mail from several different European locations indicating that our destination had been revised. I encountered one unusual personnel situation. Several days before we left, a soldier named McHugh, was transferred into the Company. He told me that he had made money running a business in London, had been arrested and had served six months in a military jail. He indicated that he had little interest in staying with the Company. Just before we shipped out he disappeared. He was to turn up months later.

On December 1, 1944, we were moved by train to Southampton where we boarded a troop ship. On nearing the coast of France, we had to climb down rope nets into landing crafts. We were carrying our rifles, usual gear and duffle bags. The only odd item was the mailbox that each mail-clerk had. They were wooden boxes about a foot square and two feet tall. They had rope handles on the side. The person behind me had the additional burden of taking one of the handles when going down the ladder. It was a bit much for me but I made it. We motored ashore and disembarked. By that time it was dark and each company was ordered to gather at a certain location. We were also told to put our duffle bags nearby in a pile. It would be the last time we would see them. All the business about having the correct number of shirts and underwear was history. We moved in-land and found ourselves in a bivouac area near Yvetot. The weather had been sunny and we put up our pup-tents and waited. The weath-er changed and several days of rain turned the field into a quagmire. Standing at reveille and moving about was frightful. The pup-tents slowly sank into the mud. We were off to a wet beginning.

The reputation of the Division was mixed. A lot of the officers were new, had been reassigned into the Company and were inexperienced. The new Company A Commander lasted just three days in combat. The talk in Kentucky had been that we were likely to do military duty somewhere. Our first order in Europe was to go up to Holland and support an English air-drop. But the German offensive on December 16, 1944 changed all that. Rather than traveling 300 miles north, we were ordered off the train in Belgium and moved into a position in front of the advancing German assault. There was incredible vehicle traffic and confusion in the area among troops, artillery units and supply vehicles. We would hear all sorts of stories from passing GIs. Each infantry company had a two and a half ton truck with a three-quarter ton trailer and two jeeps, one with a mounted 50 caliber machine gun. The three cook stoves and supplies were moved on the truck. The trucks of each regiment with attached trailers moved in convoys and hopefully were in contact with their companies. This was a time when the commanding officers were not sure where the enemy was. On the 21st of December, the 290th, was attached to an armored division and saw action with the Germans. The weather was cloudy and the Air Force could not see or attack the enemy. Christmas, however, was a beautiful sunny day and the skies opened up and were crowded incessantly with waves of Allied planes. Within days the 75th was fully engaged in combat.

The Battle of the Bulge has been well recorded. The 75th was an untried division but it acquitted itself quite well. It started at the point of the furthest advance of the Germans attack and participated in the campaign that drove the Germans back to their original starting point, thereby eliminating the Bulge. This was accomplished by the end of January. The weather was bitterly cold and casualties were high. We had to live in our overcoats. Some had a blanket but others had lost theirs. I was fortunate that I had some nights in the kitchen tent when I was not in a house or under a folded tarp on the ground. The fighting was fierce. One takes away pictures of what happened for the rest of their lives. I remember the morning when we were positioned along the edge of an open snow-covered field facing the Germans. After they had been riddled with machine gun and artillery fire, the Americans crossed the field. When I got to the other side, I looked down into a foxhole at the edge of the woods and saw a Germen soldier slumped down, his helmet had been knocked off, he had a white handkerchief in his hand and a bullet hole right in the middle of his forehead. He had given his all for his country. He might have hated Hitler and the War for all I knew. I recall the evening when eight or ten new replacements arrived at the kitchen area. They had been through only basic training in the States when sent overseas. They seemed young and apprehensive. I had a few words with them before they moved up to the front line. The next morning I saw one of them lying dead in the middle of the road. He received some mail, all of which I had to return.

Mail clerks were the link to the folks back home. There were no telephones or email. Each company had a personnel clerk but he was fifty miles behind the lines at Division headquarters. I would hear about the letter that brought news of trouble at home. I recognized letters from girlfriends. It was ordered that all outgoing mail be read to check that the position of the troops was not revealed and that casualties were not reported to people back home. The Army did not want reports of deaths to reach families before the official notice. In the absence of any officer who could do this, I took on the task. I was anxious that the mail go out promptly. So it was necessary that I read through each letter under the kitchen lanterns, stamp them and deliver them to the Army mail post, which often was not easy to locate. Getting the mail to the soldiers was also not easy. It was not unusual for the kitchen convoy to stop and be ordered to have a meal ready to take up to the men in two hours. The kitchen crew was composed of a mess sergeant, two cooks and a helper. When the meal was ready, a kitchen detail would take the food up to the front line, find the company, often in the dark, and pass out the food. On occasions a meal would be ready, but the order would come down to dump the meal and move out. Our men would then have to survive on C rations which were handed out periodically or that they had hung onto. The C ration was a four by eight inch waxed box with a can of meat, some biscuits, powdered drink, plastic utensils and napkins. I would go to the mail pick-up at some location behind the lines and take it up to the Company with the meals. I preferred to hand mail directly to the individual to make sure mail got to the right person. I had to manage the mail for those not present or killed or injured. Some of the wounded would be away for short periods and return. I recall a package that had been sent to a soldier named Behrens. It had broken and the contents were obviously cookies. I gave it to the platoon sergeant for delivery to Behrens. It turns out that Behrens had been injured and was no longer with the platoon. It was useless to return broken packages. The sergeant gave out the cookies and discovered that an inscribed bracelet had been enclosed among the cookies. He sent it back to me via a messenger. Believe it or not, the messenger was hit before he could get to me. The brace-let was lost. When Behrens came back to the Company he asked about the bracelet his girl had sent him. I pleaded innocence until I was able to reconstruct what had happened. Behrens agreed that it was not smart putting the bracelet in the cookies.

We had an inordinate number of non-battle casualties. When we left the States, we all wore the standard Army boot. As we passed through the UK, we saw a lot of people with the new style combat boot. Belgium was bitterly cold that winter and the snow was deep. GI's had their feet in snow for hours. We needed better footwear. So what did the Army provide in the middle of the campaign - galoshes. GI's feet would swell and they could not get their boots on. So they would remove their boots and rely on the goulashes. Water would get into the galoshes. Standing in a foxhole all night with galoshes full of frozen wet socks was a calamity. Frozen feet were common. At the start of the campaign we had about 205 men. By the end of the campaign thirty days later, only about 45 of the original number were still with us. The strain on the men was heavy. There were occasions of deaths and injury from friendly fire, which is haunting to those who saw or knew of it. In one situation we had a soldier who clearly should not have been in the Company in the first place. He had a minimum IQ. At one point, he was in a foxhole near another adjacent foxhole of a soldier named Sills, who had a cold and was coughing frequently. During the night, he crawled across the snow, pointed his rifle at Sills, and said "if you cough again, I will shoot you." I heard of that incident the next day. I was driving the jeep and after a short discussion with others, I loaded him onto the jeep and drove him away. I left him at a medical station and told the people there not to send him back but to transfer him out of the area.

Normally when a division has been on the line for 30 days, they would have some relief time. However, our division was immediately reassigned to support the American Seventh and the French First Armies in the Strasbourg area. The task was to drive the Germans in the Colmar area across the Rhine. This was accomplished. The Americans were thoughtful and after pushing the German back, would have the French capture Colmar and the towns along the River. They were an excited crowd, not only for the victories but for the wine they had enjoyed. The campaign resulted in driving the Germans out of eastern France. One of the anomalies of the Colmar campaign was that the Army caught up to the need for better boots. We were issues shoepacks. These are for use in places like Alaska or the North Pole. They are heavy boots with felt padding inside. The weather in the Colmar region was milder than in Belgium and shoepacks were a joke. As the men moved around, one could see shoepacks lying along the roads where they had been discarded in favor of the regular boot.

After seven weeks on the line, the Division was due a rest. We moved back to a camp near Luneville, France, where we had showers and some recreation. We lined up on the shower, took everything off, had three minutes in the shower, got out and picked up new clothing. It was the first change of clothing since Porthcawl. Maybe some of the clothes might have been salvaged from the bags we left on the beach at Le Harve. Some supply guy undoubtedly got the wool socks that Louise had knitted for me in Kentucky.

Our next destination was to a position along the west side of the Maas River in Holland. During our travels I remember the occasion when we were in a woods about to get into trucks along the road at the edge of the woods. Just before the order to board the trucks, a plane swooped down and raked the trucks with fire. One or two of the drivers were killed and the truck beds, as we could see when boarding, were riddle with holes and marks from the attack. As best as we could see, the plane had British insignia on the sides. It was a near miss for many of us.

In the new assignment, the Division was in a defensive role. Most of the men occupied comfortable houses and were to observe the Germans from the tops of the houses. At one point our Company was designated to occupy a large mansion surrounded by servant quarters, stables and walls forming a courtyard. It had a mote with a drawbridge and gate tower. In the middle of the courtyard was a wooden building that had been used as a garage. It had a sunken pit for repair of cars. The Company arrived in the afternoon and the kitchen was set up in the garage building. The men occupied the mansion and some of the quarters. I was assigned to go to the supply depot in the jeep with trailer for food, supplies and pick up the mail if any. I left about five o'clock. It was dark by then and I could use only the peep lights. I found the depot, received the supplies and returned about six o'clock. As I crossed the drawbridge, I picked up the smell of burnt wood. There were no lights in the yard. Something was wrong. I stopped abruptly, jumped out of the jeep and ran up the stairs into the mansion. Inside I found my comrades crowded along the walls of the main hall. I was told that the men had lined up for the evening meal at five o'clock and that the Germans sent an artillery shell over the house and seconds later, a shell that hit the kitchen. When we came out and looked around, we discovered that the shell had killed the whole kitchen crew. We had the job of pulling the bodies out of the pit under the floor. These guys had been my constant companions. I also realized that if I had not been away, I would have been in that chow line. War is just a matter of luck.

After an incredible artillery barrage, the experienced divisions and commandos, both British and Americans, crossed the river on March 24, 1945. On the Third day, the 75th followed. I recall leaning back on the gasmasks and stuff piled high in our truck, holding myself from slipping into the Rhine by the heels of my boots as we rode over the rocking platoon bridge that the engineers had constructed. We were supporting the Eighth Armored Division. The plan was to advance 50 miles the first day. But there was heavy resistance and our gains were modest. The Division was active throughout in the campaign to win the Ruhr area. There were pockets of very stiff German counterattacks. German forces at the end of the War were frequently old men and boys.

When our Company reached Gladbeck, we took over a large home in a triplex building and drove the family out. It had been the home of a high official in one of the local industries, one could tell, by the pictures on the wall. I took possession of the well-furnished living room and moved in my mailbox. The others occupied other rooms in the house. I was not surprised when a woman, probably the wife of the owner, came back into the living room, gave me a look of hatred, grabbed up family pictures and left. Her husband was shortly thereafter chased out of the backyard as he protested our taking over. We stayed several days and I was shocked on our departure to see the

44

condition of the house. My room was as I had found it. However, the rest of the house was in ruins. Every drawer had been pulled out. Furniture had been overturned. Combat areas are scenes of destruction and chaos and soldiers are want to lose track of a need to protect property as well as people and to value an orderly environment.

One replacement to the Company was an anti-war dreamer. He had been in service in Europe for several years. He had been sick in England, then returned to France to a replacement unit, went AWOL and traveled about Southern France, was picked up and returned to the replacement pool and then assigned to Company A. He told me he was unhappy in the Services and mentioned he might travel around the World when he got out. He did in fact disappear. At some point I heard from him that he had his ticket and was about to leave from Marseille on his way to India.

Near the end of the War, there were pockets of Germans behind us as well as in front of us. Germans were changing into civilian clothes and surrendering. Unexploded bombs were lying in the streets. Once I went to a Battalion Medical Station and was asked to go pick up some wounded Germans. A medic joined me and we went as directed to a nearby school building. We were met at the door by a German woman and taken down into the basement. She then led us along a basement tunnel with walls about four feet high. Above and extending back from the walls was a dark earthen crawl space. Lying on the dirt were many wounded Germans wrapped in blankets. The woman helped one of the men out. He was clearly very sick. We helped him get up the stairs and on to the jeep. She was constantly indicating her thanks. Just as we were about to leave, a young soldier, who had followed us, came up from behind her. She knew him. He had one arm in a sling and appeared to be in some pain. She turned to me and indicated that she would like us to take the young man as well. I indicated we would and pointed to the hood of the jeep as the only place to sit. He came up and I made a move to help him. He wheeled on me and shoved me away. His eyes were full of hate. The woman fearing that he had struck me jumped between us. She was fearful that I would shoot him or something. I step back, let the soldier climb on the hood and then indicated to the woman that everything was OK. She shook my hand and expressed again her thanks. What remained with me was the look on the young soldier's face. His world had come crashing down and the dreams he had for a future Germany and a good life for himself were gone. He was now just a prisoner of war. We took both back to the medical station.

It took most of April to clear out the remaining German resistance. The War ended on May 8, 1945. For several months the Division was camped in tents near Rheims, France. We had the task of transferring equipment from divisions that were headed for the States and then to Japan. I was the Administrative first sergeant in the Company's headquarters. During this time I received my duffle bag and found two bars of soap in it. That's all! I received a call one day. It was the military police asking that we come and pick up a soldier named McHugh. I was the only person in the Company at the time who had any idea of who McHugh was. I went to the military police station, picked up McHugh and brought him back to our Company. As he was a deserter from Company A, we would have to charge him. He was tried and received a ten year sentence.

I had furloughs to Switzerland, England and Cannes and enjoyed them all. When I went to England, I went through Hyde Park on the way to my cousins' apartment. I heard the soapbox orators claiming that England should throw Churchill out. I mentioned this to my cousins who discounted my impression. As we know they did.

I finally got on a ship and came home in February 1946. I was discharged from the Army at Camp Dix where I had started. What a wonderful pleasure it was to see Louise come up the sidewalk to meet me. My parents and family were then living on Evelyn Place in Princeton.

Judgments about the conduct of war are not easily rendered. The 75th Division made major contributions to the victory in Europe in spite of its imperfections. It suffered 888 killed in action and 8000 total casualties, of which 4000 were non-battle casualties. Performance was a mix of good and bad management. Individual performance in almost every situation was the key. It is incredible how survival holds infantry solders together. They are there for each other. The record of the Company and its 94 days in combat was exemplary. As we gained experience, we did better. Company A had some wonderful Lieutenants such as Jenerette who survived and Swift who did not. Jenerette was awarded a medal by the British for leading the assault on Grandmenil. We had a great number of brave and remarkable solders, a number of whom I had known from our days at Camp Hood. Many were honored. Most were average Americans. Some however, were unusual. Anderson from Alabama could not read or write and had to mark an x for his name. But he could play a fiddle with the best of them. While we had a variety of people, we had no Afro-Americans.

47

Statler Hotel in Hartford under construction

48

River Ranch house at the flood peak in 1955

River Ranch house after flood

Travelers Office Building

*Louis Kahn, Robert Mitchell, William Wheaton, Ian McHarg and
other staff and graduate students at the University of Pennsylvania*

50

River Park houses under construction

Louise with Suzanne in courtyard at River Park

Louise and Robert in River Park living room

John F Kennedy Funeral

Charles Liddell

Chapter Two

Learning a Trade

One comes home a different person after spending a year and a half abroad in wartime military service. At times it was an incredible ordeal. Other times, you were just waiting around for something to happen. Most of the time was in the company of fellow soldiers who you didn't know very well, always aware that you were under the command of higher-ups whose job it was to tell you what to do. Coming home to Louise with whom I had not spoken since leaving the country, and the family was joyful. Louise and I had been to-gether for only four months in an unfamiliar Kentucky town, a time during which the Army had control of 90 % of my time. Returning to Princeton, Louise had obtained a new job and continued to stay with my family which was nice. I was anxious to get back to my uni-versity work so that I could finish the requirements for my degrees and start a career. My scholarship funding had been expended but the GI Bill provided enough for me to complete my work for both my Bachelor and Master's Degree in Civil Engineering. I reregis-tered at Princeton on March 1, 1946. I had become fully committed to civil engineering and found the courses interesting and informa-tive. I took courses through the summer of 1946, completing work for my Bachelor Degree by June 1947.

The summer of 1947 was an opportunity to have another look at engineering and government enterprise. I had heard good things about the Bureau of Reclamation and the projects they were build-ing out west. The Bureau was the best builder of earth-filled dams in the world. Visitors came from all over to see their projects. I was advised to visit them in Denver and apply for a position. Louise and I drove our new car to Denver. Bureau officials said that they had no positions open but suggested that I visit Professor Rader at the

University of Colorado at Boulder. He was great and uncovered a position as a P-1 Engineer with the Bureau on the Big Thompson Project at Grand Lake. The project involved impounding run-off on the western side of the Continental Divide and sending the water through a five-foot pipe to provide irrigation for hundreds of thousands of acres of farm lands in northern Colorado.

I worked as an engineer testing the material and compaction of the layers of fill installed by the contractor. The material was hauled in large earth movers from a gravel and sand plant a mile away. The mix was then dumped from the bellies of the movers, leveled to 14 inches and compacted. If we rejected a layer, it had to be scarified and compacted again. The contractor was from California and had recruited his crew from many localities. In one instant the company's work on a concrete key wall was rejected. He complained bitterly, put up a great fuss and then fired the whole crew. He was back at the local coffee shop in the morning rehiring them.

The Bureau provided us housing. They were 12-foot square wooden cabins that had been brought 150 miles from another site. A pit was dug in the gravel, two logs were placed across the pit and the cabins were set on the logs. The sink drained into the gravel. There was no water or light, but there was a bath house nearby. We furnished the house with a bed, a table and two chairs, all for about $25. The houses were lined up along a dirt road. The headwater of the Colorado River was a hundred feet away and trout was plentiful.

At one point I had the task of checking the temperatures of the water in the cooling pipes that ran through the nine-foot high concrete dam sections. I had to do this at night. I would take the Bureaus' pickup truck and drive to the dam site, then down the curving road to where the concrete had been poured. Outside temperatures reached as low as 34 degrees. In the meanwhile, stray wild horses would come up to our cabin windows and bray. Louise found such a strange sound unnerving in the middle of the night. She was pregnant with our first child. We had to drive 120 miles to Denver to visit a doctor.

I left the Bureau of Reclamation in late-August. It was a useful experience about public enterprise. My colleagues at the Bureau of Reclamation were both able and experienced. They were proud of the agency and supportive of its projects. They were reasonably good managers and well thought of in the local area. They were focused on their professional activities but did provide an economic stimulant to the local economy. I could not determine whether the Bureau's costs were well-budgeted and controlled, but they were a successful enterprise that was admired by local, national and international critics. Questions have arisen in the intervening decades about the environmental impacts of some of the Bureau's projects but these considerations should not diminish solid performance at the time of construction.

I returned to my studies at Princeton. I completed my course work for a Master's Degree by January 1948 and was awarded the Degree in June 1948. By January, I was ready to look for a job. I considered several teaching positions, as well as jobs with engineering firms. I consulted with Dean Condit of the Engineering School. He counseled that I not take a position in teaching or government before working in the private business sector. After a series of visits to engineering firms in New York, I settled on a position with M W Kellogg, an industrial plant designer and builder. But I was not satisfied that the position adequately met my interests in building construction. I visited Uncle Henry Bruere at his second floor office at the Bowery Savings Bank on 42nd Street across from the Grand Central Station. We discussed my choices, and he gave me an introduction to Dick Olds, a banker and relative of his acquaintance of long standing, Robert Moses. I visited Olds, who was very helpful.

He set up an appointment for me with Lou Crandall, President of the George A. Fuller Company. I met Mr. Crandall at his office on the following Saturday. Mr. Crandall had just come back from a four-day stay in Baltimore trying to win the building construction contract and arrange the financing for a new plant for the Baltimore Sun. It had been an arduous reworking of plans, re-estimating the work and negotiating with lenders. It had not worked out and he came back exhausted and empty handed. But that "was the nature of the building construction business" he explained, adding that "there would be other projects that Fuller would certainly win." Crandall was an admirer of Henry Bruere. He offered me a position in the estimating department at $65 dollars per week and I accepted.

We moved into our first house in Orangeburg, New York, with some trepidation. It was a one-room house with a massive fieldstone fireplace. Surrounded by porches, which had been incorporated and weatherized, the house was built in 1885 as a retreat with the only access through the adjoining cemetery. We had a local lawyer provide a title survey when we bought the house but he missed the kitchen porch which extended into the cemetery. We hired the Princeton student's moving agency to bring up our furniture. There was six inches of snow on the ground when we arrived at the house and the moving agency could not get their truck up the 700-foot driveway easement cut through to the town road. The result was that we had to use our 1940 station wagon to bring in the furniture piece-by-piece. They left at 11 o'clock that night and the three of us went to bed exhausted.

Commuting involved Louise dressing the baby and driving me to the station about a mile away and doing the same at the end of the day. The six-foot shallow well did not go dry and the furnace in the crawlspace provided heat. But on balance the house was a loser. We sold the house in September and moved into Louise's Aunt Carrie's house in Englewood, New Jersey. She had a big house, her husband had died, and her children had grown up and moved out. Louise had been a frequent visitor when she worked in New York City. Commuting was better. Louise would drive me to the station in the morning. When we were a bit late, the engineer could see us and I would have ten more seconds to go under the tracks and run up and catch the train. It was interesting to observe some of the commuter habits. There were bridge games at both ends of the cars. The conductors had the tables and decks of cards. The commuters would line up along the platform and as the train came in, they would swing themselves up on to the train. When it stopped, the card players were already in position.

We were going to take an apartment over Dan, Louise's brother, in a new building under construction. Getting an apartment in the New York City region was tough and the landlord required an eight months security deposit in advance. When we decided not to take the unit because of the delay in completing the building as promised, the landlord refused to return our deposit, complaining that he had a contract. Dan along with one of his New York University classmates struggled with the owner who finally agreed to return the money.

I started night law school at New York University in the fall of 1948. It made for a long day and I became annoyed with process over substance of the cases we studied. I switched to Public Administration and enjoyed courses with Clarence Stein and Sydney Hillman. Stein had interesting stories to tell of his designs and planning issues that he had faced. Hillman, who was counsel for the New York Housing Authority, taught a course in Zoning. The housing authority was the largest in the country with over 150,000 units and the flagship for the public housing program. The authority had a somewhat silent tenant selection plan, which allowed it to maintain a good percentage of working families in their apartments. The policy had made an important economic contribution to the economy of the city. The authority was also in the middle of the race relations issues. Hillman described how the children would get along fine until the middle years when the adults in the families would start to have an influence over the kids.

Large construction generally involves a bidding process under which a construction manager or lowest price builder is selected. Fuller generally was selected as a construction manager with an up-set price, but also competed for a lot of projects. I started in the es-timating department and we competed for jobs all over the country. Putting together a bid was an artful process and out-guessing the opposition was even more subtle. The first project I worked on in the field was the Lighthouse for the Blind on 61st Street in New York. Fuller won that job because we missed a requirement for a certain elevator manufacture. It caused our bid to be $15,000 lower that the other bidders. It was the margin that made us the low bidder.

The Lighthouse for the Blind staff were very special people. Most were blind. The project involved an addition to their present build-ing. It was simply incredible the way they could show poeple about their old building, knowing where every doorknob was and describ-ing every detail. The new building had some interesting building challenges such as a roof on which kids could skate safely and a theater stage with floor markers. Slattery was our excavating sub-contractor and he started excavating the hole before I knew it. I had to rush downtown and get a permit from the City. They were very helpful as I remember it.

Louise and I were anxious to have our own place. After looking around we found a two-bedroom townhouse in Hackensack in the fall of 1948. We bought some new furniture at Bloomingdale's in New York, and we were just getting settled in when I received a call on a Saturday afternoon from Vice President Clyde Roth. He asked if I could go to Pittsburgh. It was just three weeks into the Lighthouse job, and I told him not without Crandall's approval. He negotiated the deal with Crandall, and I was assigned to start the project for the Heinz Company. It was the renovation of the Heinz Service Building at their plant in Pittsburgh, all part of a major plan to rebuild most of their Pittsburgh manufacturing facilities. This was the initial job and Fuller put in an aggressive bid to finishing the job in eleven months, a good deal short of the twenty-five months it did take.

I picked up a roll of drawings and the three-inch specifications and went out on Wednesday of that week. I set up an office in the cloakroom of the auditorium in the building, arranged for phone service, put an ad in the newspaper for a secretary. Then I lined up cement company salespeople who offered to find me a house, and came home on Friday.

That was my last weekend in Hackensack. I left the house on Sunday evening and went to New York. I caught the overnight train to Pittsburgh and never returned. Louise, who was then pregnant with our second child, had to arrange for packers and movers (paid for by Fuller) and follow me out to Pittsburgh. Her brother George was nice enough to drive her to Pittsburgh after I found a place to live. We moved into 175 Highland Park on November 19, 1949

One of the cement salesmen found us a flat in a row house in Highland Park, about ten miles north of downtown Pittsburgh. The development was composed of a number of two-story apartment buildings and single homes. The developer had gone bankrupt, and the cement companies and building suppliers were second mortgage holders. Management was in disarray and every new renter negotiated a deal, taking into account any unfinished landscaping,

broken washing machines or other complaints they had. We negotiated a rent accordingly and moved in. Months later new management straightened things out and we accepted a final rent. We spent
Christmas at home. Our son Robert was born on January 19, 1950.
One of the reasons I had strong leverage with suppliers was the
planned start of the Alcoa Building. It was known that Fuller had
the contract. The US Steel Building, which was under construction
when I arrived, and the Alcoa Building were the biggest landmarks
to hit the city in decades. Not only were the suppliers looking at
Fuller, the trade unions were looking for a job by an out-of-town
contractor to resolve their jurisdictional disputes. The Heinz building would suffer accordingly.

The Service Building presented some difficult challenges. The
building was a Baroque landmark with an auditorium used primarily
for high school commencements. We were required to bring in and
assemble a 56-foot pile driver to drive concrete piling for the interior
structural steel columns that supported the new flooring. The pre-
sidium arch had to be cut free simultaneously by workmen at each
end of the arch and caught on cables rigged off the columns. The
lobby's 14-inch marble balustrade was stripped out to be replaced
by a stainless steel and glass railing. The lobby and much smaller
auditorium were paneled with side and book matched plywood.

There were all sorts of labor arguments. People wanted to protect
their jobs. There was a fight over setting the metal doorframes.
Work stopped and Fuller had to relay the problem to John Dunlap,
Committee Chair of the Joint Committee in the Labor Department
in Washington, DC. Carpenters won the setting of 16-gauge frames
and above; iron workers got the 14-gauge and heavier. An argument
arose among the carpenters, masons and plasters about who should
set acoustic ceiling tile. Mr. Dunlap's Joint Committee reviewed the
case and advised Fuller and the parties that the carpenters should

set the tile and the masons and plasters should share in putting the adhesive on the back of the tile. In another case there was an argument between electricians and pipe-fitters as to who would handle and install the combination electric circulating water pumps. The electricians took the motors off the pumps and hid them. The next morning, I saw ten or fifteen pipe-fitters coming down the street with pipes in their hands to get those motors back. It triggered calls to the Labor Board in Washington to solve the problem without bloodshed. Mr. Dunlap allowed the pipe-fitters to handle the pump sets. General Electric said they would no longer guarantee the pumps where the motors had been removed but in time relented. Demolition of existing work proved very difficult and revealed inconsistencies in the construction drawings.

On one occasion I was coming down from the second floor of the building at the end of the day after the workers had all gone home. I was with a friend and as we came down the main stairway leading to the exterior doors, a chap came charging up the stairs, pulled out a piece of pipe and threatened to kill me for hurting his child. I claimed not to know what he was talking about and calmed him down with a promise that I would find out about it. It turned out that his teenage son was in the process of stealing asphalt tile off the job on the prior Sunday. He was apprehended by the watchmen, who in a scuffle with the boy, struck him and knocked him down. We were losing supplies and equipment at an alarming rate, much of it clearly going into the local neighborhood. I'm not too sure of the outcome of the complaint above, which was handled by our insurance company.

There were personal accidents, fires and a variety of calamities, which meant that I was always worrying about the unexpected. The architect's drawings had shown the escalator side panels running along the glazed block wall. Fuller decided that the escalator should be installed first. We placed a protective covering over the escalator side panels. Unfortunately, when installing the sub-frame for the railing at the open above, the ironworker allowed a spark to get down and set the covering afire. The whole thing went up in smoke. The draft carried it up through the second escalator above. It was a calamity. Mr. Crandall came to the job, looked it over and placed a call to the Otis Company. He asked that they rob other jobs and rebuild our escalator in a matter of weeks. They agreed.

A week before we were to open the Service Building, I came back from lunch, walked into the main lobby and saw the acoustic ceiling tile dropping, one by one, onto the lobby floor. There was a scramble to shut off the water. Then I remembered that I had insisted that Kelly Brothers send back a mason and plug the holes that they had left in the pipe chase above the lobby. Tom Costello, Grace Kelly's brother-in-law, was the contractor. His mechanic had mistakenly walked on a water pipe in the space and broken it. Crews spent nights and weekends making repairs. All this occurred on top of my sending the construction superintendent home a few days before. There had been an argument about the installation of the rough rolled glass panels in the lobby. He had prevailed but was worn out with arguments. We put him on a train for New York City and told him not to come back. I ended up finishing the last piece of the job. I reported weekly to Crandall. When we had finished, he came out and handed Jack Heinz a bill over dessert at the Duquesne Club that I understand Heinz paid.

It was now late in the fall and after a two-year struggle, I planned to have a quiet time enjoying Christmas. Louise and I had bought a tree and the children were excited. But then the call came from New York City. Fuller was desperate for help on the Test Cell Building in Bridgeport, Connecticut. They wanted me to be the construction manager. Could I come right away? I went to Bridgeport on the

Wednesday before Christmas, which was on Monday in 1951. I met Jim Taylor, the person in charge in Bridgeport, and surveyed the scene. I promised that I would be back after Christmas. On my way home, I ran into a tie up at Pennsylvania Station. A train had been jammed in the tunnel under the East River and all the commuter rail traffic had been delayed. It was a zoo. The railroad had given up on announcements and everyone was milling about looking for a train to get them home. I adopted a young woman who was disparately attempting to get to her boyfriend in Atlanta to get married. I put her on a train that was going to Washington, DC and assumed that she could make it from there. I was to depart for Pittsburgh about 7:00 pm. I finally left about 11:00 pm and got home in the morning. I had a good Saturday, Sunday and Christmas Monday. Then, I had to go back to Bridgeport.

I found an apartment in Bridgeport shortly thereafter and Louise packed up and came with our two children. She was pregnant with our third child Pamela, who was born on March 16, 1952. Bridgeport had a Socialist mayor. We were not into political affairs but did get to see Adlai Stevenson when he came and spoke on his election tour.

The Test Cell Building was a row of square concrete boxes with open vertical sections at each end. They were for testing the radial engines that AVCO was manufacturing. The two noteworthy things at the job was one, watching a private outside contractor named Sullivan rework the 13,000 volt lines in a service manhole, and two, the revelation that Jim Taylor's secretary was a high-priced prostitute on 72nd Street in New York City and a crook. One of the salespeople pointed this out. We checked it and found it to be true. She had been a bookkeeper for a magazine in New York City and with a gentleman employee, she had run off with the petty cash. We had to let her go. She lived in the same housing complex as we did.

In the fall, I was brought to New York to work with the architect on a new Statler Hotel to be built in Hartford, Connecticut. Statler Hotel Corporation had employed a new architectural firm to design the building. The firm was headed by Bill Tabler, who had been the project architect on their Washington Hotel that which had sustained a fire during the War. Statler sought the help of the Fuller Company in keeping costs within the estimated parameters.

The Hartford Statler was a 16-story 450-bath hotel with shops on the first floor and restaurants and a grand ballroom on the second floor. With the exception of the concrete work, the exterior metal and glass cladding and the mechanical work, as the construction manager, it was my responsibility to review the sub-bids and re-advertise as necessary. I also had to prepare and award the subcontracts, watch the costs as the work proceeded, and file monthly cost reports. I had to know what was covered in each subcontract and how the contracts fit together. The architect's representative was Robert Engelbrecht. Bob grew up on a Missouri turkey farm, was dirt poor as a kid and was lucky to get a scholarship out of Notre Dame in architecture. After completing his undergraduate work, he went on to study architecture at Cornell. He joined an architectural firm in Chicago where he met Bill Tabler. He had an exemplary knowledge of all things connected with the hotel building. We became life-time friends. He was tragically killer by a drunken driver in Florida years later.

The project was fraught with problems and difficulties. The first major catastrophe was the failure of sheeting that held back the 14-foot site wall along the sidewalk. Fuller had rented the small building adjoining the site for an office. I was the last person to leave at night. I had locked the door and gone out in the direction of my car when I took a quick look in the windows of the sidewalk fence. I heard a squeaking sound and noticed the wedges holding the shoring were slipping. That was enough. I went back into the office, took out the furniture and placed it in the street. Then I called Dobson, our construction superintendent, as well as called the police and other interested parties. Within an hour, the site was busy. The electrical contractor had lit the site and men were in the hole wrestling with the shoring. Neil Horgan, Fuller's V-P in charge in New York, had been informed and he had asked Slattery in New York to send in a crew to see what had to be done. I had awarded a subcontract to an excavator contractor from Agawam, Massachusetts. His argument was that he was doing what Fuller's superintendent had directed him to do.

Well, it worked out. The shoring was reset, the sidewalk bridge was rebuilt, the excess soil was removed and the job went forward. However, the costs were substantial. I recall the call I received from Liberty Mutual a year later telling me they would accept the liability for the costs of rebuilding the sidewalk bridge. They had claimed all along that the hold harmless clause in the subcontract did not apply to them. I said no. A year later, just ahead of the statute of limitation deadline, they agreed to pay.

Fuller had back-charged the excavation contractor for the added costs. The job had run way over his estimate and he was facing bankruptcy. Fuller brought him to New York to settle at the end of the job. The conversation was circular and the lawyers could not resolve the issues. I suggested that I sit down with him and see what we could do. When we got back, I met with the contractor and we struck a deal. He did not make any money but he got to keep his business.

Roger Sherman, a descendent of the person who signed the Declaration of Independence, was the key rigger in Hartford. He bought a new rig from PH and wanted to shows it off. It was the largest in town. He decided the time to do this was when he installed the boiler stack for the hotel. Sherman brought the truck-crane to the job and positioned it in the street to lift the two- story stack sections over the concrete frame of the building and lower them down into the building. With a big crew and a crowd of onlookers standing by, his operator lifted the first section, lowered it over the building and then reported that it would not fit the opening. His foreman came in to see me with the complaint. I had checked the drawings at the time of submission and opined that the stack would clear. I had to go out and measure the opening in the concrete and then return to the office and check the drawings. I reported that it should clear. Sherman then directed his operator to lower the stack slowly. It did go in with an inch on all sides as the crowd cheered. It was just another day.

We kept the exterior wall on the second floor of the Statler Hotel open, awaiting the delivery of a large fan from Buffalo Forge. We were finally told it was on its way after prodding the manufacturer for months. The delivery driver arrived in Hartford late in the morning and decided to go to lunch. He drove his truck under an underpass and wrecked the fan. My next hours and days were spent pressing the manufacturer to repair the fan and get it back to us so as not the delay the finish of the job.

We had a labor dispute between the electricians and the telephone workers. The electricians would not install the conduit in the floor slabs until they were assured that they would pull the wires. They left the conduit out of the first floor pour before Fuller knew about it. We demanded that the union labor officials come to the job and settle the issue. White-haired Mr. Kendrick, Vice President of the International Brotherhood of Electrical Workers in Boston, showed up and insisted that their workmen would not place the conduit in the slabs unless they were told that they would pull the wires. He was a "John L. Lewis" type of person. But he did cooperate with me and helped fashion a solution. After a day of arguing, the electricians agreed to a deal in which they got the wire and the telephone workers got the installation of all the panels and switchgear.

I met and watched a number of skilled subcontractor and artisans from whom I learned a great deal. Fuller bought whole blocks of marble, had them shipped to the USA and sawed into panels. It was a fascinating process. Glazers who install large plate glass in an upper story opening of a building do not get a second chance. We built concrete stairs that cantilevered up from the floor and a lobby fireplaces in which the flue went into the floor. I enjoyed working with and accepting the challenges and excitement of construction. However, it was in many ways a combative way to make a living and particularly stressful in negotiations with subcontractors and labor unions. There were always struggles with enforcement of subcontracts, managing completion of work on the part of both companies and individual mechanics, and satisfying owners and architects who had made misjudgments and wanted someone else to pay for them. It was certainly good experience on how businesses had to run and the leadership necessary to make a success of each new building project. I always felt I was working for the best building construction company in the United States.

There was great camaraderie at the project's completion. It was nice to attend a celebration dinner which hotels put on to test the new staff. The flaming deserts brought in by the whole waiter crew were great. Engelbrecht and I were particularly pleased to have invited a number of the mechanics who had built the building attend.

The final buildings were the renovation of the Tower Building and construction of an eleven-story office building and a three-story training building for the Travelers Insurance Company. Jim Taylor was the superintendent for the first two buildings, and Lou Henze was the super on the last. The renovation had the usual trials and tribulations. The boom of the truck crane came down with a crash in the street, although no one was hurt. The top four floors of the Tower, in which the executives of the Company had offices, each had its own wood - butternut, oak, cherry and mahogany. We bought logs in Indiana and had them shipped to Wisconsin where they were sliced into fletches and then placed into sheets and mounted into plywood panels. The head of the Travelers at the time was also on the board of Chase Bank in New York City. He wanted to be sure that his $2700 desk had the latest telephone and other related office equipment.

The most significant event of that era in the lives of my family was the flood of our house in 1955. We had rented a place along the Farmington River after the owner of our first house reclaimed his home. Louise called me at the office to tell me that the Farmington River was rising and that I should come home. She also said that the owner of the house had come and taken the sewerage pump and the burner off the oil furnace and placed them on the back steps. I did come home and surveyed the scene. The property was a bungalow with a small attic situated along the river. The multiple steps down the bank led to two foot bridges that crossed an inlet that ran between the house and the bank. On the water side, there was a five-foot wall at the river's edge. The Farmington River was about a foot deep and 25 feet wide as it flowed by the house. The children had played in the water but with caution. A little boy had drowned in the river a year or so before.

When I got home about six o'clock, the river was rising but not dramatically. In time it did come up over the top of the wall but then resided about 11:00 pm. We decided to go to bed. Three or four hours later, Louise nudged me and asked what I thought the noise was. I immediately realized it was the water coming into the basement window below our bed. We got up, grabbed the kids and left the house, crossing on the foot bridge across the inlet. Water was now flowing on both sides of the house. The higher ground above the house was connected to the high school grounds. Louise and the kids stayed there while I watched the water flood the house up to the first floor ceiling. There was a small dresser which went in and then out of a window in the front by the big maple that anchored the house. The house was surrounded by threes and they held it in place. Our furniture however floated out of the bay window and went downstream. The surprising thing was the eight hundred pound piano which also went out the window and down the river. It must have become air-tight and lifted itself up to get over the window sill.

There were amazing stories about the flood. A family below us was warned but chose to diddle about getting out. They had seen summer floods before. When they eventually stepped off their front steps, they realized that the children could not walk in the moving water. They recast their plan. They then left the little girl in an up-stairs room while they took the two boys to the shore. After all the re-planning and calling their parents, they finally stepped off the porch to find that the water was now four feet deep. As they struggled to the shore, they lost control of both of their two boys. When they hit the bank, they turned and saw their house collapse, taking the daughter with it.

The people with me were calling for helicopters. The land on which we stood including the high school and adjoining neighborhoods was an island. The first to arrive was the helicopter from the Sikorsky plant in Bridgeport. We finally got to Governor Ribicoff and things started to happen. By five o'clock that evening, there were twelve helicopters on the grounds of the high school. By then the peak had been passed. The flood occurred on a Thursday evening and night, reached its peak at about noon the next day and then started to recede. The Governor called in the National Guard and we had some peace for a few weeks.

Louise and I had our second car in the shop on dry land in Farmington. We were taken out with the kids on Saturday, got into our car and took them to stay with their relatives. Louise and I returned to stay in a friend's little house on the bank above our house. The Red Cross was well organized in Farmington and we were given a new stove, refrigerator and clothing. The owner had a crew come in and shovel out the house. One forgets that a flood will snap the sewer and oil tanks free and then jostle the mix in the water going up and coming down. I had some suits that I contemplating cleaning but realized when I saw them that there were ruined. Three to four weeks later we recovered the kids and brought them home. But it was different. Everything outside was covered with sand and debris. A lot of the trees were gone and the brush was bent over. All our stuff was gone. My greatest loss was my collection of slides that were soaked and covered with sand. Without any request on our part, Fuller came through with a grant to us for $2500, the equivalent of one-quarter of my annual salary.

After 10 years with Fuller, I was thinking of moving on. I had become convinced that working for a for-profit construction company did not have the social purpose that I believed was necessary for a satisfactory career. We would build a building but ignore the neighborhood and be indifferent with the population that lived nearby. The skills, however, were helpful, and I am grateful for all the things that I learned.

I read in the Architectural Forum reports on planning work being done in India through the University of Pennsylvania's City Planning Department and was attracted to becoming a city planner. On a trip to Washington, DC I stopped at the University and spoke with Professor Robert Mitchell, head of the City Planning Department. He queried me on why one would want to leave a successful career job with a big company, who had a house and four children and move to Philadelphia and take up city planning. He did mention to me the ongoing competition for the Sears Roebuck Foundation

Fellowships and advised that I might apply for the award. When I returned home I sent in an application to the University's Planning Department, who had to select the candidate of their choice. I was told six weeks later that I had the Fellowship. After hesitating for a short time, I accepted. It turned out to be the best decision of my life. There are many ways in which one can make clear decisions about one's career, and returning to study is one of them. When one realizes there are pursuits which could be undertaken with greater happiness and fulfillment, the case is certain. This one would allow me to move to the world of nonprofit charitable corporations

We moved to a single-family house in Upper Darby, Pennsylvania. It was a city of 92,000 directly across the line from Philadelphia and its government operated as a town to avoid requirements for transparency. While we were there, the annual Girl Scout picnic was canceled because they heard that the first black child was coming.

I had developed an interest in housing and city planning over the years. When I came back from the War in 1947, I was aware of the need for modest rents for low-income workers and veterans. My brother-in-law, who was an operating engineer, managed a penicillin factory near Princeton. We discussed the lack of affordable housing for his employees. This was particularly true for minorities, a number of whom had come to Princeton to work in the University's clubs and eating halls. I had been sensitized to the minority issue on the refusal of Princeton to admit Paul Robeson. His father was a local minister. I benefited greatly through my time at the University of Pennsylvania.

I had the privilege of working with what was then a distinguished faculty in its Fine Arts and Urban Planning Departments. Bill Wheaton, Chester Rapkin, Robert Mitchell, Louis Kahn, Ian McHarg, Paul Davidoff, Edmund Bacon and others were outstanding. Steen Eiler Rasmussen, a former chief planner of Copenhagen and a visiting professor at the time, was a delight. He had worked and designed housing around the world and had a remarkable sense of how cities develop and become unique places. Wheaton as President of the National Housing Conference, was active in writing national legislation and getting it enacted by the Congress. Bob Mitchell was an expert in transportation and city planning and was leading the preparation of a plan on transportation for the City of Philadelphia. Chester Rapkin, an expert in land use economics, was active in the planning of the Westside of New York City. Bacon was the chief planner for Philadelphia. Steen Eiler worked with David Crane on the Studio Project. It was a remarkable edifying and interesting experience.

I left the University of Pennsylvania in February 1960. I had an opportunity to work with a large company that was one of the developers of the historic Society Hill Renewal Area in downtown Philadelphia. The owners were close to Lou Crandall and the Fuller Company. In considering the position, I had a concern that I would find myself serving the interests of a for-profit developer over the public goals of the renewal plan. Professor Bill Wheaton, the person who had championed my application to Penn in the first place, said he wanted to save me for the planning profession. He set up an appointment for me with Knox Banner in Washington. Banner had just been appointed the director of the National Capital Downtown Committee, a new nonprofit organization funded by the business community to create revitalization plans for downtown Washington. Banner had been a very successful urban renewal director in Little Rock, Arkansas. He had a national reputation for his successful work in implementing neighborhood renewal programs and had been President of the National Association of Housing and Redevelopment Officials (NAHRO). I joined the staff as a senior planner. The other staff members were highly qualified, experienced people and a pleasure to work with - Melvin Levine as chief planner; Bob

Morris in transportation; and later Paul Sprieregen, architect/designer. Knox called the organization DOWNTOWN PROGRESS to avoid people thinking that it was a public agency.

The Urban Renewal program, initially authorized under the Housing Act of 1949, was in full swing in 1960 when I joined DOWNTOWN PROGRESS. Cities and States across the country were receiving substantial federal funding to rebuild their downtown areas and revitalize economically distressed neighborhoods. Washington led the nation in enacting an urban renewal program before the national program commenced. It had only allowed for residential renewal. It was necessary therefore to amend the District of Columbia statute to allow for commercial renewal. As all legislation for the District has to be enacted by the Congress, a major task for DOWNTOWN PROGRESS was to get such legislation passed by the Congress. The government of the District at that time was three commissioners appointed by the President and approved by the Congress. However, the power over the District was the Congress and the DC Congressional Committee, which provided a substantial federal grant for the operation of the Capitol. The Chairman of the Committee was Congressman John McMillan from South Carolina, who during his campaigns for office stated that he would "keep the 'blank' down" in the District. The street traffic patterns are arranged so that the Congressman could get to the Capitol in their automobiles. One of the three Commissioners was an Afro-American who told us that he would undoubtedly have difficulties obtaining an apartment in Northwest Washington. This was the predominately white or affluent areas of the District with most of the fancy office buildings and institutions of the city.

DOWNTOWN PROGRESS planning area was between 5th and 15th Streets where the department stores were located. It was in financial distress and the downtown stores were losing out to the new stores and branches located in the suburbs. The area was becoming more a place for minorities and vacant buildings. By 1960 urban renewal had become a major activity in cities across the country, and cities were receiving solid funding from the national government. The task for DOWNTOWN PROGRESS was to put together an urban renewal plan and present it as a basis for seeking a legislative amendment. DOWNTOWN PROGRESS was funded by the business community and had some very active board leaders - Robert Baker of the American Security Bank, John Sweeterman of the Washington Post and Admiral Oswald Colclough of George Washington University. I and my colleagues on the staff prepared an Action Plan for Downtown after lengthy meetings with all sorts of people. The Plan projected images of how Downtown might be transformed over the next 25 years. Downtown continued though to be seen as secondary to the major government initiatives around ceremonial Pennsylvania Avenue, the White House and the National Mall.

Following completion of the Plan, Knox Banner worked diligently to sell the legislation to members of Congress. He was a great friend of Bill Fulbright, and Fulbright and others were very supportive. Congressmen McMillan and company stood in the way. McMillan and his cohorts would bring up the bill on a Monday before many members had returned to the city and have it voted down by those present. But good fortune came when John Glenn rode his spacecraft around the world. Glenn was honored on Monday at the White House and the ceremony brought back to town a majority of the House of Representatives. Knox's friends in the House introduced his renewal legislation on that morning and got it enacted. It is example of the odd ways in which legislation is passed.

This was just the beginning of renewal action. It took years to get owners to believe in the downtown's future and become interested in making firm decisions about land development. The District also suffered from the uneasiness created by a white run city with a population that was increasingly minority. The City was still rampant with discrimination of all sorts against Afro-Americans and other minorities. One of things that I was particularly aware of was the absence of minorities on our board. There were substantial relocation issues, and a numbers of minority residents who were displaced, were driven into poor quality public housing.

My family and I had moved from Fulton Street near the Cathedral into newly built Southwest renewal housing in a neighborhood which had formerly been occupied by low-income, predominantly minority families. My children went to the newly built Amadon School, which was a magnet school in the area still lacking a local school population. Residents from across the District were allowed to send their children to Amadon where they would receive a good education from quality staff. This was in contrast to a neighborhood elementary school to which the children of the nearby public housing went. River Park, where we lived, was a co-op and proposed as the moderate income housing in the area. Units were less costly than the other new units in the area but still middle rather than lower income homes. We had a number of government professionals and Congressional staff people in the development. As new buildings were built in the area, the newly arrived children, who were predominantly white, displaced the children who were being brought to the school by their parents. This became a political problem. A plan was developed to have the children circulate through Amadon and two other nearby schools but it did not last. We lived two blocks from the National Gallery and other museums. The children enjoyed the fireworks on the Mall and were witnesses to the remarkable John F. Kennedy funeral. My son and wife were able to hear the famous Martin Luther King speech.

I was a senior planner for DOWNTOWN PROGRESS and had a substantial amount of interaction with the Housing and Home Finance Agency, the National Planning Commission and the local Redevelopment Authority. It was a great learning experience on how governments work. The construction of the FBI building on Pennsylvania Avenue was contrary to good planning but the FBI could get Congress to support the project's site costs. We had hoped that the federal planning office would recognize the interaction of the Patent Office in the Commerce Building with the downtown lawyers, but alas the Patent Office was relocated to a suburban location. DOWNTOWN PROGRESS did have some real success on the location of the new subway system and its stops in the downtown area and a Visitors' Center at Union Station. It became evident to me that the crucial issues of housing were in the neighborhoods. When an opportunity came to me to come to Boston to head a community development corporation, I welcomed it.

From the time of returning from the War and through the years ending with the National Capitol Downtown Committee, my wife and I had occupied a variety of housing types. We lived first in a one-room apartment and cooked on a hot plate. We then lived in temporary row housing, which the University had created on its polo field. This was followed by a two-bedroom house, a ten-room house, three two-bedroom row houses, four detached houses, and a three- and four-bedroom row house. and finally by a three bedroom and a four bedroom row house. We then purchased a 10-room house in Waban, a suburb of Boston, and lived there for 28 years. There were issues in most of them, including an attempt to get the cooperative in Washington to make good on the deficiencies in construction of our new unit. In all it was a bit of a lesson in tenant/landlord relationships.

Chapter Three

Social Programs and Housing to 1960

America has had an unusual history in its attitude about government's role as social provider. It is a land of immigrants who survived through their own independence and self-sufficiency. They
expected little from government and wanted its powers to be both
proscribed and limited. In our early centuries, most public services
were provided locally. Towns and counties established and subsidized orphanages, reformatories, hospitals and schools. In 1737
Boston had a hospital for the care of people with smallpox and other
diseases. The poor and mentally ill were generally contracted out
by towns to the care of individuals or households. Local services to
select groups did not interfere with the culture of self- reliance that
was dominant.

Care of the sick and hungry has a long tradition. The Bible tells us
that we should take care of the needy. Feudal lords had responsibilities in connection with care of the poor. The factory and land owner,
in his/her own interests, had to provide emergency food and shelter
for their dependents and laborers. Churches and other charitable organizations have been active in the time of fires, floods, droughts
and outbreaks of disease. These calamities are hardest on those with
little resources or money to pay for assistance. Contemporary societies have now broadened these programs to benefit the entire eligible population. This requires governmental participation as administrator which runs counter to our traditions and is now a subject that
is being actively debated.

The promotion of the "general welfare" as enumerated in the Declaration of Independence was well intended. The Founders were
a very thoughtful group of property holders that sought to create

a country in which private individuals had the greatest degree of freedom to act and think as they wished Government should be both limited in its power and structured to succeed. It was a new design but was respectful of the lessons of history. While the Founders had a great deal of optimism about their new country, it was known to be an experiment. Over the ensuing years, the government has constantly negotiated with diverse interests and passed laws and regulations that pleased some parties and left other mad as hell.

Social welfare for the poor and less fortunate was not a strong point for the framers of the American Constitution. The pursuit of "happiness" ranked higher than welfare of the masses. Happiness then meant something close to progress. It was to be a country of opportunity and enterprise. The writers of the Constitution were property holders and a good percentage of them owned slaves. The issue of slavery was by-passed. An electoral process was covered in detail, but it left out half the population, namely, women.

In colonial times and well into the 19th century, the administration of welfare was local. A large percentage of businesses were owned by craftsmen and most workers were day laborers. People were required to live within walking distance of their jobs. As such, their employment was not very stable and wages were low. Many were periodically unemployed. Local assistance was extended to families through community committees, churches and private individuals. Poor farms and poorhouses or almshouses as they were called, were established and became common. They were created to warehouse the poor, as well as provide a way to discipline and rehabilitate the poor. Costs were always an issue and communities were interested in deterring applications for assistance. Some form of work was generally required except for the physically and mentally ill. "Fear of the poorhouse became the key to sustaining the work ethnic in nineteenth century America".[2] Eligibility categories for assistance were difficult to define resulting in the use of moral distinctions. There were the worthy and unworthy poor. It is surprising how jails were used to house not only the drunks and vagrants but also the poor and unemployed. The Quincy Report of 1820 suggested an increasing role for the state in order to make welfare more uniform and predictable.

As the population of towns and cities increased, the existence of families and individuals without work and the homeless became ever more prevalent and communities had to act. Outdoor relief was started in the first half of the nineteenth century. Under these programs assistance in the form of heating fuel, food, clothing and bedding was rationed out in modest quantities. There was always the concern that able-bodied household members were not working as they should. In New York State in 1840, there were 14 thousand people living in poorhouses and 11 thousand receiving outdoor relief. By 1860 there were 39 thousand in poorhouses and 174 thousand receiving outdoor relief. By 1880, there was a substantial increase to 89 thousand in poorhouses and just 70 thousand receiving outdoor relief.[4] The promise of reform of individuals in poorhouses was found to be illusionary. Poorhouses came under criticism for unsanitary conditions, mismanagement and neglect and abuse of children and the mentally ill. The assumption that poorhouses would reduce the cost of pauperism through more inexpensive care and as a deterrent against families asking for assistance proved false. Nor did poorhouses check the growth of outdoor relief.[5]

While outdoor relief became more prevalent in the middle of the century, it also came under serious criticism for being an incentive for not working and establishing a culture of dependence. Home visits and supervision by welfare agencies represented a new intrusion by government into the lives of Americans. There were new standards for child care and compulsory education and illness was a frequent cause of destitution among outdoor relief's primary beneficiaries, namely widows, the elderly and children. To its credit, outdoor relief in many cases prevented starvation.[6]

In the latter half of the century, institutional care in poorhouses became more prevalent, but their management raised many concerns. There was abuse of occupants and neglect of children. Conditions were so bad in many that there were unwarranted deaths and illnesses. In 1869, a New York State Commission of Public Charities recited the deplorable conditions of the poorhouses and blamed them on inadequate oversight and public indifference.[7] While the poorhouse had failed to be effective in reforming the ways of the poor, outdoor relief was more sharply criticized for serving the wrong people, creating dependency and refusal to work. The fact that most recipients were the sick, widows and women generally, old people and children all with little or no capacity to work were overlooked. Brooklyn and Philadelphia both abolished outdoor relief.[8]

In the second half of the nineteenth century there was an increasing concern within the church for social reform. Church members saw a better society as a way of dealing with the issues of the family, unwanted behavior and the terrible conditions in which people lived. Immigrants were swarming into American cities and the countryside, overtaxing housing supply and community infrastructure. Social inequalities between the well-to-do and lower income classes were increasing and there were problems of alcohol abuse, unlawfulness and corruption in business and local government. A new economy was proposed by writers and economists that questioned the total reliance on laissez faire and recommended public action. The economist John Commons wrote that government is "the only means whereby refractory, obstructive and selfish interested elements of society may be brought into line with social progress..". "Among such reforms he included the regulation of corporations, municipal ownership of public utilities, factory regulation, sanitary regulations and the improvement of tenement house conditions.[9] In 1891, the economist Richard T. Ely recommended that municipalities be authorized to tear down unfit tenement houses and build publicly owned housing.[10]

There were advances in social service in the period from 1890 to 1910. They were driven particularly by concerns for children, public health and unemployment. The White House Conference on Children that was called by Theodore Roosevelt in 1909 led to an increase in the role of government in the protection of women and children. A goal was to hold families together. Mother's pension legislation was enacted in Missouri and Illinois in 1911 and in more than twenty other states by 1913. This entitlement legislation was a precursor for the Aid to Families with Dependent Children title which would happen much later in the Social Security Act of 1935.

Another broad social program that evolved in the early days of the twentieth century was unemployment insurance. Stimulated by the concern of employers with liability judgments for industrial accidents, employers and insurance companies could see the benefits of a compensation regime over liability. "Compensation substituted a fixed but limited charge for a variable, potentially ruinous one."[11] State compensation legislation started in 1909 and twenty-one states had enacted laws by 1913. By the turn of the century, a majority of States had enacted laws for regulating working conditions and hours, compulsory education, boards of health, and restrictive regulations of housing. All of this was changing the role of government. Private charities increased substantially in the latter half of the 19th century. They were in many cases created under the belief that the public welfare system was ineffective and that private charity was more compassionate and thoughtful, particularly in its effort to make personal contact with families through house visits. However, there is little evidence that they softened the strained relations that prevailed between economic classes and often were in opposition to organized labor. There were many who were anxious that relief not be seen as a right. Some saw relief as a public/private activity to be coordinated wherever possible. By the end of the century, it was clear that private charity was no substitute for public programs. In New York State at the turn of the century at least three-quarters of funds used for relief of dependents came from towns and cities.

There was little uniformity in welfare administration across the country. The unemployed were often unfairly held in contempt as idlers and good-for-naught. In cases where there was an able- bodied worker at home there was a political backlash against all welfare. The national government played no role in providing a safety net under of the lives of its citizens. The notion of comprehensive solutions was not yet present. In all of this, the federal government was not involved and no one had the goal of eliminating poverty itself. The adage that "the poor will always be with us" was fitting.

The federal role in housing was slow to develop. The connection was made between bad housing and ill health of occupants. Model houses and apartments had been tried in a number of cities, but with mixed results. The Committee for the Improvement of the Poor set up a model apartment building in New York City in 1853, which was unsuccessfully managed and abandoned 10 years later. They were never able to provide the services required. There were housing commissions in cities across the country that studied local housing and called for new building regulations and sponsored the construction of model apartment building and suburban villages. There were proponents of construction of private rental housing that would utilize low interest philanthropic financing to achieve affordable rents. These efforts failed because owners found that just as we know today, poor people cannot afford the cost of maintenance, utilities and administration of a standard home let alone something for a mortgage. In July 1892, Congress authorized and funded an investigation of slums in cities and discovered that they were beset by a greater than normal number of saloons and arrests. This only added to the cries of reformers that something be done.

In 1906 President Roosevelt appointed a Home Commission to review housing needs and standards. The commission recommended that houses built for the poor should meet standards for good health and that it is the business of the municipality to see that such houses are provided. It noted that the poor should pay no more than one-fifth of their income for rent. But this amount was insufficient to pay for the costs of construction and operations. The commission further reported that in some European countries and especially in England, an attempt has been made to solve this problem by governmental action, general and municipal, and in many instances there has been co-operation between the municipality and private corporations.[12]

New political opinion saw the failures by laissez faire business to address social issues and began to consider public action and ownership in a new light. Public monopoly ownership could play a civic role, attracting more broad-minded leaders, treating workers better, avoiding strikes and lowering cost to consumers. On the other hand, the federal government was still not ready to take responsibility for social action programs. With respect to unemployment after the panic of 1893, municipal governments expanded their public works and local agencies, private and public, made extensive use of the principle of work relief for the first time in American history. However, state governments and the federal government refused to make any direct assault on the problem of unemployment.[13]

Leaders and citizens came to realize that social problems had to be addressed and that continued reliance on a laissez faire market economy for solutions was no longer tenable. When Theodore Roosevelt was Police Commissioner of New York, he toured the slums of New York City with his friend Jacob Riis, the author of the famous book on slum conditions in the City called "How the Other Half Lives." Riis showed him the unsanitary over-crowded housing and deplorable conditions in which people were living. Roosevelt was appalled and deeply influenced by what he saw. The bad housing of both cities and rural areas was an issue. Great community reformers like Jane Addams, Florence Kelly, Eleanor Roosevelt and Francis Perkins all had experiences with slum dwellers through their work in settlement houses. All came away with lasting impressions that made them reformers. When Theodore Roosevelt became President, he appointed social progressives to positions in his Administration. When he ran for re-election in 1912 he ran on a Progressive platform. It has been described as constituting a remarkable compendium of almost every social and economic reform then talked about in the United States - all bound together by one of the boldest visions in the history of mainstream American politics.[14] While Theodore Roosevelt was a progressive, he never went so far as to assign responsibility for urban problems to the federal government. Young FDR and Eleanor were active supporters of Theodore and benefited from the exposure to American politics. Eleanor Roosevelt had acquainted FDR with slum conditions by taking him to the University Settlement House in Lower East Side of New York where she worked as a volunteer.

The first federal housing construction was the housing built under the Wilson Administration's program to provide housing for wartime workers. When a shortage of housing at shipyards and industrial areas became acute, business and government leaders argued that housing for workers had to be created to maintain the war effort. In 1918 Congress authorized the creation of the United States Shipping Board pursuant to which the Emergency Fleet Corporation (EFC) and United States Housing Corporation were established. Both were supposed to work through private development corporations but it turned out to be more expeditious for the public corporations to build and own under their own name. The federal government provided funding. Qualified and respected architects were hired to design the housing which when completed were attractive well-built residential developments, many with community centers. The EFC eventually completed 9,185 dwellings and Housing Corporation 5,998 dwellings.

After the War members of Congress, fearful of a socialistic trend, demanded that the housing corporations be shut down. The properties in turn were sold and the Government went out of the business. A number of the professional people who worked on the wartime housing program went on to play important roles in the subsequent programs that were to come a decade later. One of these individual, Frederick Ackerman, Chief of Design for EFC, would propose that because of the effects of rising land values, that low-cost non-profit development be supported and remain outside of the market.[15] There had been recommendations that the wartime housing be sold to the residents or to nonprofits owners, but that occurred in only a few cases.

The 1920's were a period of transition. Suburbanization of American cities was underway bringing the issues of land use and control to the forefront. Zoning had been adopted in New York City in 1916. The Euclid decision affirming the constitutionality of zoning occurred in 1925 and the US Department of Commerce issued a model zoning ordinance in 1928. Secretary of Commerce Hoover established a Division of Building and Housing in his Department of Commerce and was pushing for improved efficiencies in home building. The construction of homes boomed in the middle of the decade with over 930,000 homes construction in 1925. The proponents of larger-scale multifamily developments were pointing to the successful new social housing being created in a number of countries in Europe. Reformers proposed that the government consider a program of government owned large-scale housing developments with related community facilities. Some of the housing could be built and operated on a not-for-profit basis. A Bureau of Labor study of housing units constructed in 31 large metropolitan cities indicated an increase in the percentage of multifamily units from 30.3% in 1921 to 58.4% in 1929.[16] The availability of home mortgage financing improved over the 20's with a large percentage of loans being short-term, low or no interest, and renewal loans which were disastrous for owners that lost their jobs during the depression. Hoover as President did introduce legislation for a system of federally-supervised home loan banks as proposed earlier by the building and loan associations. It passed in 1932 as the Federal Home Loan Bank Act, the first permanent federal housing legislation.[17]

Leaders in the Hoover Administration had seen relief as a local responsibility, public and private. Walter Gifford, President of AT&T (father's old chum at AT&T) and President of Hoover's Organization on Unemployment Relief, was clear on at least one issue. There should be no federal relief. At the same time he did not know about the ability of local communities to raise relief funds or how many people were idle. Many business leaders saw federal aid to idle men and women as the ruin of the country.[18] Even though he had established a State Emergency Relief Administration in New York when he was Governor, Roosevelt disliked the dole and as President left poor relief to local agencies.

The Depression had a dramatic impact on America. The supply of single family homes dropped to less than 150,000 in 1932 and foreclosures became rampant. President Hoover's Conference on Home Building and Home Ownership in December 1931 offered recommendations that led to the creation of the Federal Home Loan

Bank Board (FHLBB), which could provide funds secured by first mortgages to members, most of whom were savings and loan associations. The FHLBB became active in refinancing about 20% of all outstanding mortgages on owner-occupied non-farm properties.[19] The Reconstruction Finance Corporation was created in 1932 to make loans to corporations constructing housing for families of low income and in slum areas.

Business people who had had total faith in the private enterprise system to take care of all economic situations began to see the limits of laissez-faire. An example was Bill Dennison, owner and head of the Dennison Company, a large manufacture of office supplies in Framingham, Massachusetts. The business had been very prosperous since its founding in 1860. The owners had a goal of making the Dennison Company one of the best in providing benefits and good working conditions for its employees. The company instituted a generous pension plan, of which it was very proud. The program was considered immutable. However, the financial difficulties associated with the Depression of 1929 proved more than the plan could meet, and benefits had to be radically reduced. Bill Dennison had been a member of several business groups that were proponents of government unemployment insurance. He became an advisor to FDR. In 1930, he personified the new realization by the business community that government was necessary in programs such as unemployment insurance. Franklin Roosevelt, as Governor of New York, had likewise gone through a learning process about the role of government in addressing unemployment issues. He, along with Frances Perkins, had pushed for progressive legislation. Included was state-supported old age pensions, unemployment insurance, and a minimum wage for women and children. Both FDR and Perkins were aware of the Wisconsin legislation on these same issues.[20]

Roosevelt's New Deal was the first federal administration committed to the expansion of the federal role as the national administrator

88

of broad social programs. These programs would serve the poor as well as the middle and upper classes. They were to be comprehensive. During the Presidential campaign in 1932, Frances Perkins drafted a speech for FDR that included references to social security program in New York State. She used a statement that they were trying "to construct a more inclusive society." FDR revised it to be "We are going to make a country in which no one is left out."[21] 1933 was a special time with fully half of citizens surviving on some form of public assistance. Five millions elderly Americans were calling for the enactment of the Townsend Plan, under which all elderly persons would receive $200 a month. In the 1932 election Norman Thomas, the Socialist Party candidate for President, received over 2% of the votes including that of my mother.

FDR's first priority was to put people back to work. He had a prejudice against the dole. He saw it as demeaning. He had had experience with relief in New York. Two months after the President was inaugurated on March 4, 1933, Congress authorized half-billion dollars for relief. By the summer of 1933, the Civilian Conservation Corp was putting young people to work. By 1935 when it peaked, there were 500,000 serving in the CCC.[22] President Roosevelt appointed Harry Hopkins head of the Federal Emergency Relief Administration. By January 1934, four million individuals were working for the Civil Works Administration. The Emergency Relief program was not hand-outs. It consisted of public works projects, thousands of them, from schools to airports. The National Industrial Recovery Act, signed on June 16, 1933, had broad program elements but was described by the President as a means of getting people back to work. Title II Public Works and Construction Projects created the Public Works Administration. It did an array of projects. From 1933 to 1939, it built and rebuilt schools, city halls, hospitals, sewer plants, electrification of railroads, bridges and tunnels and used its allocations to pay for two aircraft carriers, cruisers, submarines, aircraft and over fifty military airports.[23]   The country was observing the federal government in action as never before.

After dealing with the banking and monetary crisis and setting in motion the National Recovery Act, economic security was next. FDR had in mind unemployment security, workmen's compensation, disability benefits and retirement benefits. Twenty-five percent of American workers were out of work, many living off relief. Of the 6.5 million over 65, many were surviving on meager public welfare stipends. The sick were going without care. Many were homeless. FDR did not believe that government was the problem as Ronald Reagan would have us believe. We are endowed with a national government that has survived and continues to function in spite of its imperfections and inefficiencies. He told Frances Perkins "that everyone should be, from cradle to grave, in the social security system."[24]   Nothing like it had ever been brought to the Congress.

President Roosevelt saw economic security as a need to remove from people's lives the threat of being out of work, being seriously ill without medical insurance and/or living their retirement years in poverty.   He sent a message to Congress on June 8, 1934, in which he outlined his ideas for a comprehensive social program. FDR raised issues about the role of the federal government, how to convince citizens to share with the less fortunate and how programs can be administered and benefits distributed. These programs were to dramatically change America.

By Executive Order under Title I of the National Industrial Recovery Act, FDR set up a Committee on Economic Security. Secretary of Labor Frances Perkins was Chair. The Committee included five cabinet officers, all of whom were sympathetic to his ideas. The Committee was charged with drafting legislation to be submitted to the Congress. Edwin Witte, a professor at the University of Wiscon-

90

sin with experience in unemployment insurance legislation, was selected to be Executive Director. An Advisory Council and Technical
Board were also created. Information and ideas were sought from
numerous persons in government and the private sector.

Unemployment insurance was a priority and already on the table.
Senator Wagner of New York and Representative Lewis of Maryland
had prepared a bill dealing with unemployment modeled on Wisconsin legislation. While the President at first supported their effort,
he began to see weaknesses in the bill. Harry Hopkins argued that
unemployment and old-age insurance be combined in the same bill.
There was an opportunity to widen the scope of the Administration's
Security Bill to cover unemployment insurance, old age and other
programs. The Committee proceeded accordingly on the basis of a
comprehensive bill.

At the first National Conference on Economic Security in Washington held by the Administration in November, 1934, President Roosevelt included in his speech a comment "I do not know whether this
is the time for any federal legislation on old age security". Perkins
was dismayed and took action with others to reassure the public that
old age insurance was still part of the Administration's bill. After
sharp criticism in the New York Times and other papers, a release
was circulated that people had over-reacted to the President's remarks, and that the Administration's program would include both
old age security and unemployment insurance.[25] Perkins spoke with
the President and received assurance from the President of his continued support.

Roosevelt insisted that the old age program be a compulsory contributory insurance system. It was not to be a hand-out from tax revenue
alone. Most of the experts agreed with the President. It would be
welfare for the middle class. In order to get social security enacted,

compromises were made that excluded certain groups - for example, persons in agriculture, domestic service and charities. FDR and his associates were, however, committed to the notion that the program should cover as many Americans as possible, both rich and poor. It was to be an insurance program to which everyone contributed. The fact that the insurance was designed to include everyone gave it political muscle and institutional stability. It was guaranteed, not so much by the government but, as J. Douglas Brown, one of the architects of the program said, "by the commitment made by the whole society."[26]

There was an intense debate within the Committee for Economic Security as to whether unemployment insurance should be a solely federal system or a plan in partnership with state governments. The Wagner-Lewis bill modeled on the existing Wisconsin Plan had been introduced and had substantial support. At the time, over three quarters of the states had enacted workmen's compensation insurance plans. Only Wisconsin had adopted unemployment insurance in 1932. The President preferred an important role for the states and the Committee finally agreed. One consideration was that if the Supreme Court found the act unconstitutional, the state plans would survive. This idea has some relevance to the recent health reform bill. The Committee submitted its final report and a draft of the legislation to the President in January, 1934. The primary driver through the whole process was Secretary Perkins. Discussion of comprehensive social programs sparked fears of socialism and communism. At one of the hearings over the bill, Senator Gore of Georgia questioned Secretary Perkins, "Isn't this Socialism?" Perkins replied emphatically "Oh, no." History has borne her out.

President Roosevelt sent a special message to both chambers recommending the legislation on January 15, 1935. There were extensive Congressional hearings and presentations to the Ways and Means

Committees in both the House and Senate, and a number of revisions were made by the committees. There was also extensive mail, mostly critical and in opposition to the bill. There were doubts about passage of the Bill. The Cabinet Committee, Administration officials, public supporters and the President's staff gathered signatures of distinguished individuals urging passage of the Act. It produced results. Congressional staff rewrote portions of the bill. In the process the name was changed from the Economic Security Act to the Social Security Act. The Social Security Act passed the House by a vote of 371 to 33 and the Senate by a vote of 77 to 6, five conservative Republicans and Democrat Moore of New Jersey. The Conference Committee report was approved by both chambers in August and the Bill was signed by the President on August 14, 1935.

The final bill provided Unemployment Compensation, Old Age Assistance, Aid to Dependent Children, Maternal and Child Health, Child Welfare Services, Public Health Services. Health insurance was one of the goals of the original security proponents. However, no provision related to health insurance was ever included in the Act. There was strong opposition from the American Medical Association against any form of health insurance. After much deliberation, there was a recommendation for compulsory health insurance by the Medical Advisory Committee that was referenced in the Committee of Economic Security Final Report but the Committee and the President did not want to support a health insurance plan until the Economic Security bill was approved. A report favoring health insurance was never publicized. Later, the President transmitted the report to the new Social Security Board for further study.

There were a number of ambiguities and imperfections in the law requiring extensive revisions by the Social Security Board. There was some current relief for organized labor through the Wagner Act of 1937 which resulted in health insurance being included among the negotiated benefits in many industrial labor contracts. Health insurance coverage for the elderly came with Medicare in 1965.

Social Security was a compulsory system of contributory payments by workers who would then have a right to retirement benefits. It was based upon the taxing powers of the government. It was challenged and held unconstitutional by a U.S. Court of Appeals First Circuit. Six weeks later, on May 24, 1937, the Supreme Court reversed that decision. In an opinion presented by Justice Cardozo, Social Security was held to be constitutional.

The sweeping social policy legislation was a first in the history of the country. It established new relationships between the national government and the lives of everyday Americans, and between it and the state governments. It was primarily federal government business, different in many respects from later social programs in which the private sector would play a greater role. Over time it has required adjustment of all sorts to expand coverage, meet new demographic demands and keep the system solvent.

The National Recovery Act of 1933 authorized the use of funds to finance low-cost housing and slum clearance projects. There was little opposition to the provision, partly because there were more representatives from northern states and there was interest in rebuilding urban slums. It was all part of a plan to create employment, particularly in the construction trades, which had been hit very hard in the Depression. Housing was carried out by the Housing Division, a semi-independent agency. Initially, the Housing Division tried to fund limited dividend developers under a program developed by the RFC. These developers for the most part were non-commercial developers with ties to local organizations. There were difficulties and only seven limited dividend projects were completed. The goal was to create high quality housing with low rents. Developers were required to put in 15% of costs as their equity. Secretary Ickes told the Congress that the limited dividend projects had failed to meet affordability goals and a decision was made that the Housing Division be the direct builder. This was pretty radical stuff - the Government building and owning housing. Some 50 low-rent public housing projects were built.

The National Housing Act enacted in 1934 included the creation of the Federal Housing Administration (FHA). The FHA was authorized to insure long-term mortgage loans made by private lenders on single family homes and to insure loans of lenders who financed home alterations and improvements. It became a central component in the American housing system around the long-term fixed-rate amortizing mortgage loan. Banks had protection and homeownership flourished.

American housing planners, architects and investors had for many years studied social housing in European countries. Some of our noteworthy developments, such as Forrest Hills in New York and Mariemont in Cincinnati, were modeled on European housing. Opinion in the US was divided between building publicly owned housing and funding development by nonprofit cooperative, labor unions or consumer groups. The Labor Housing Conference, an organization formed by a group of trade union officials, proposed in 1934 federal, state, and municipal financing of large-scale planned housing developments on a non profit basis. They would be designed, constructed and administered in direct collaboration with bona fide groups of workers and consumers.[27] Large-scale developments were favored to achieve a sense of community and economies of scale. While the Labor Housing Conference was gaining some union support for its proposal, Secretary Harold Ickes through the Public Works Administration, was trying to clear slums and build low-cost housing. Organized labor activist groups were critical of the directions the

Administration was taking in its PWA housing programs. They also complained about the FHA's emphasis on middle-income homeownership, financial success of the banks and disregard for the need for workers housing.

With slow progress by the federal government in building low rent housing, Senator Wagner of New York and his housing supporters pushed for passage in 1937 of the Wagner-Steagall Housing Act. Introduced initially in 1935, and reintroduced in 1936, the bill authorized the creation of the United States Housing Authority within the Department of the Interior. The original bill had been drafted in large part by the National Public Housing Conference, a group organized in 1931 to promote public housing. The intention was to replace the PWA's Housing Division and fund local public authorities to develop housing. This is something the Housing Division could have done anyway but Secretary Ickes never pushed it.

The U.S.Housing Authority, a public corporation, was authorized to make loans to local authorities for low-cost housing. Removed from the bill was the authorization for housing built by nonprofit and cooperative owners. It allocated new units to the lowest income level and limited the number of new units to the number of units removed. The bill put the decision to build and where to build in the hands of local governments. After its enactment in 1937, 350 public housing projects were completed or started by 1940. Congress also created the Federal National Mortgage Association (Fannie Mae) in 1938 to provide a secondary market for FHA insured mortgage loans and to greatly expanded the capacity of the home finance system. That it came to ruin in 2009 is another story.

Some interesting experiments took place in the thirties. There were a number of leaders and advocates who fought for housing for low and moderate income families and individuals. The back-to-the-land movement was alive during the Depression. President Roosevelt wrote his friend Republican Senator George Norris that he really would like to get one more bill "which would allow us to spend $25 million this year to put 25,000 families on farms, at an average cost of $1000 per family. It can be done. Also, we would get most of the money back in due time. Will you talk this over with some of our fellow dreamers on the Hill?" As author Arthur Schlesinger describes it, the fellow dreamers responded, and Senator John H. Bankhead of Alabama wrote a $25 million appropriation for Subsistence Homesteads into the National Industrial Recovery Act.[28]

The Administration built one hundred mostly rural communities under the Resettlement Administration. Three were the "Greenbelt towns" in Greenbelt Maryland; Greendale Wisconsin; and Greenhills, Ohio. They were inspired by Ebenezer Howard's Garden Cities in England. Their design was influenced by the contemporary themes in neighborhood design, of which Clarence Stein's Radburn Village was preeminent. One of the communities was Arthurdale at Reedsville, West Virginia, in which Mrs. Roosevelt played a central role. Built in a depressed area in the coal fields, Arthurdale was a planned community of homes and work opportunities. Mrs. Roosevelt heard of the self-help program that the extension service of West Virginia University and the Quakers were doing in the poverty-stricken Scots Run area near Morgantown. She drove down by herself, toured the area and spoke to a number of people. As she said later she was still so unknown that they did not recognize her as the wife of the President.

Mrs. Roosevelt was appalled by the living conditions of families, many in which the breadwinner had been out of work for three to five years and had given up hope. She was impressed that the University's and Quaker program was at least bringing some hope to the local participants. She returned to Washington and told her story to the President, who agreed that her West Virginia project might be a good initial case for the Administration's Resettlement program. From then on Mrs. Roosevelt watched over the progress at Arthurdale, supported its public funding, at times with help from the President and Louis Howe, received help from friends and in some cases invested her own money.

Unfortunately, Arthurdale turned out to be an expensive failure. Temporary houses were brought in that were inadequate in winter. Developing local industry was unsuccessful. The community school was costly. There were bureaucratic delays with program changes. As late as 1940 after her remarkable rescue of the Henry Wallace nomination for Vice-President at the Democratic Convention, she took time to go down and look at what was left of Arthurdale. Throughout, Eleanor Roosevelt did her best to make things happen, not only at Arthurdale but at housing sites around the country.

By 1937, federal housing policy was pointed in two separate directions. The first was assistance to Americans who wanted to buy a home, and the second was to provide low-cost housing for poor families. It was a two-tier policy for the well-to-do and the poor. It proved troublesome for the future.

Provisions in the U.S. Housing Act required that the cost of construction be below the then-current experience of the PWA, thereby ensuring that it would be mediocre housing (Senator Byrd of Virginia amendment). This led to overly dense developments and was an impediment to achieving the well-designed mixed-income housing that had been espoused by the Labor Housing Conference. Public housing required that contractors pay prevailing wages. In most cases, they were the usual construction wages paid by homebuilders. There were also problems with initiation of projects and site selection which was under local control. Participation in the program was limited to government agencies. Rents were to be 20% below the market. Conservatives attacked the bill as socialistic.

Meanwhile, FHA-insured home building was flourishing in the suburbs. The sale of newly built family housing was often clouded by discriminatory practices. In fact, FHA underwriting standards included discriminatory standards such as requiring cohesive white-only families. Better schools and the quality of services became controlling factors in the location of new housing production. President Roosevelt's view of economic security was very broad. It included housing as a component of family security. In his inaugural address of 1937 he spoke of the one- third who are ill-housed. Legislative action in the thirties set the stage for the launching of major housing policy advances after the Second World War.

Housing development boomed after the War. In 1940 the US population was 132 million. By 1960 the population was 179 million. There was a shortage of housing for veterans and families relocating themselves after the War. Homebuilders started larger developments, particularly in suburban areas. Highway construction had a hard time keeping up and commuter traffic jams were becoming the norm. The 1949 Housing Bill was enacted in a spirit of optimism. There was genuine support from Republicans led by Senator Taft of Ohio. The economy boomed and demand for housing increased exponentially. Rebuilding the cities was recognized as a paramount need. The passage of the landmark Housing Act of 1949, calling for "a decent home and a suitable living environment for every American family" brought new support for housing and slum clearance. The new law authorized the construction of 810,000 public housing units, along with the Urban Renewal Program.

The federal government offered incentives to allow more favorable treatment of depreciation. Through FHA, the government could insure mortgage loans at a higher percentage of house values. In fact, the Section 608 program allowed developers to obtain mortgage loans at 120% of development costs. There was a scandal and the program was shut down. In 1954, the government sought to provide lower-cost insured mortgages for rental development in renewal areas.

In 1956 Congress passed the Interstate Highway Act and commuting distances increased as jobs went to the suburbs. Travel distances to work increased exponentially. The country had limited land use controls and scattered development became the norm. The suburban development had become the home of the mainstream America and the GI veteran. By 1950, there were 23 million single-family homes and by 1960 there were 32 million. Zoning was counter-productive as it sought to protect development of new housing.

By the end of the fifties public family housing was negatively impacted by urban renewal relocations and the operation of housing authorities became financially tenuous. The residents of public housing where primarily on public welfare, which allowed rents to be well below the operating costs of standard housing. Public housing revenues fell and timely maintenance of the buildings dropped off dramatically. Public housing became the housing of last resort.

The Housing Bill of 1958 allowed HUD to insure mortgage loans on non-profit as well as for-profit mortgages. In 1959 a new program for non-profit mortgagors of elderly housing was enacted. It was the first provision for nonprofits owners only and gave them something akin to public housing financing. In 1961, the new Kennedy Administration provided for the first time Below Market Interest Rate financing for nonprofits.

Support for housing programs requires taking care of the needy while, at the same time, doing something for the average citizen. Comprehensive national programs engage the active role of central governments. A dramatic personal loss through illness or accident to an individual family or person will generate help of one sort or another. But when a whole category of families or individuals are classified as homeless, unemployed, handicapped, sufferers from a disease like AIDs or otherwise deserving, the magnitude of the problem requires a collective and coordinated response.

There are efficiencies in national programs that utilize standardized administrative procedures. There is also a need to ensure that state and local systems are meeting appropriate standards of care and services consistent with constitutional requirements. The test is for a national effort to bring sound policy and administrative order while permitting diverse local agencies to be flexible and innovative. President Theodore's Roosevelt's Housing Commission's report specified the key issue of social housing was its need to have some form of financial support if it is to serve the poor. Generating that support at an appropriate level remains the challenge.

Franklin Roosevelt, Frances Perkins, and his Administration's great contribution was their determination to achieve broad social goals through programs that were within constitutional limits on federal government activity. Roosevelt's notion of universal coverage was crucial to the success of the programs that are now enduring institutions in the life of most Americans. At times FDR found housing advocates overly insistent, but at the critical time he lent his support.

South End Community Development's first office on the 2nd Floor, 630 Tremont Street

Beatrice Karayannes at 677 Tremont Street

Lou Rota, our construction superintendent

Bracing front wall, 38 East Springfield Street

Winder stairway before reconstruction

Top floor finished apartment at 38 E Springfield

Greenwich Park Street with Prudential Building

Ms Williams enjoys her new apartment

Dwight Street in the South End

Finished apartment on Dwight Street

Interior of 535 Massachusetts Avenue before rehab

New resident of finished 535 Massachusetts Avenue

Hale Champion, BRA Director; Douglas Cochrane; and Whittlesey

Tremont Street block at Northampton Street

The closing of 544-551 Massachusetts Ave; Whittlesey, William Flynn, Regional Director for HUD, and standing, Rudy Kass, Lester Clemente, and John Hamilton

549-551 Massachusetts Avenue before construction

549-551 Massachusetts Avenue after construction

Chapter Four

South End Community Development (SECD) -
a Demonstration of What Rebab Can Achieve

In 1960 James Collins, the newly elected Mayor of Boston, convinced Edward Logue, one of the country's foremost urban renewal
administrators, to come to Boston from New Haven. Logue was
famous for his success in New Haven and had a remarkable record
of obtaining money from the feds. He was an expert in how cities
could gain by effective coordination of federal programs with local
action. He used federal highway funds to augment construction of
local community facilities.

Logue was a dynamic administrator. Within weeks of his arrival he
had preliminary plans for the renewal of several of Boston's neighborhoods as well as proposals for downtown sites. His appointment
was also controversial. He shook up the old boys' network. He
insisted upon the right to hire and fire his staff. He air-conditioned
the Authority's offices on the two top floors of City Hall and encouraged current city employees to come to work for the Boston
Redevelopment Authority under its personnel policies. Some did,
most didn't. As the BRA was largely funded with federal money,
the City Council had only limited control over its affairs. It had
an independent board, headed by Monsignor Lally of the Catholic
Archdiocese, along with the support of the Mayor and the "Vault," a
group of key bankers and business leaders. There were often verbal
battles between Logue and city council members. He was called a
tyrant. He responded by pointing out his federal funding.

Logue's ability to obtain an inordinate amount of federal money on
a per capita basis served him well. Boston in the fifties was in financial trouble. Its downtown shopping area was run down and losing

customers to suburban shopping centers. Many of its neighborhoods were financially and physically distressed. Water and sewer systems were antiquated, revenues were down and the banks would not buy the city's bonds. White people were migrating to the suburbs and industrial jobs were leaving for metropolitan locations and the South.

One of Logue's prime targets was the South End. The South End had some impressive qualities. It developed rapidly in the middle of the nineteenth century. Building lots along its lovely squares and architectural streets were laid out and sold off in the 1850's. Much of the South End was fill that followed the spit of land along Washington Street that connected the neighborhood to the rest of the city. The neck in the 18th century was subject to flooding at high tide.

Most of South End buildings were built as upper class family dwellings. They were four or five-story red brick row houses with a stately front entrance and mansard roof. The area had the largest number of nineteenth century bow front row houses in the country. With the influx of new people and a changing market, the South End became more middle-class, and new buildings became more modest in size and detail.

Boston City Hospital was built between 1861 and 1864. A number of churches were built in the fifties and sixties. The large Catholic Cathedral of the Holy Cross was started in 1867 and dedicated in 1875. The 400-room St. James Hotel facing Franklin Square was General Grant's choice when he visited Boston in 1868.

After the depression of 1873 and the opening of the Back Bay along the Charles River, the South End became a less desired area. An indicator of the South End's economic decline was the short life of the St James hotel and its sale to the New England Conservatory of Music in 1882. One of the truly handsome mansions of the South End was the Deacon mansion on Washington Street. Its architect was French and the house contained elegant French interior furnishings. The grounds were surrounded by a high brick wall with entrance gates and a porter's lodge. After a few years, the Deacons went to live in Europe and in 1871 the house and its contents were sold at auction. In 1964 the Deacon house remained vacant and boarded up near the first house rebuilt by South End Community Development (SECD).

The South End became the port of entry for immigrants that would flood into Boston. In 1910 the population of the South End was 76,000, mostly immigrants crammed into the row houses, many of which had been converted to rooming houses. They were often occupied by one family to a room. Washstands were built in the hallways and toilets added in the basements and rear yards. At the turn of the century, its 37,000 lodgers made Boston's South End the largest rooming house district in the country.[29]

An elevated train was completed over Washington Street in 1901. The two stations at the edge of the area became honky-tonk districts. The population of the South End in 1950 had declined to 55,000. In 1960 it had the highest percentage of foreign born, the highest percentage of families with income under $5,000, the second highest in elderly over 65, and the lowest percentage of sound housing in all of Boston's neighborhoods. In the previous decade, the South End had lost more than one-third of its population, and the percentage of black and Puerto Rican residents substantially increased. By 1960 many of the houses were in disrepair and vacant. Urban renewal of the South End would be challenging, but it had advantages in the special building stock that existed, as well as its proximity to the downtown and the Back Bay.[30]

South End House, a settlement house initially formed as Andover House in 1892, was one of five South End neighborhood settlement houses that were merged into United South End Settlements (USES) in 1960. South End House, under the leadership of Robert A. Woods, had been a pioneer in undertaking studies of the people in the area, the conditions of the housing and the inadequacy of social services. It had implemented a number of innovative service programs. It and several other charities had sponsored the building of model homes and apartments around the turn of the century, utilizing philanthropic funding then available.

USES's director in 1964, Charles Liddell, was one of the program designers of Boston's Poverty Program. It was funded by the Ford Foundation and the Committee of the Permanent Charity Fund, now the Boston Foundation. USES became the key organizer of the sixteen neighborhood associations in the South End participating in the urban renewal planning process. The initial renewal plan for the South End, at 606 acres was one of the largest renewal areas in the country. It proposed a greenway down the center which would have resulted in a substantial number of building acquisitions and demolitions. After some stormy meetings with representatives from the area, it was scrapped and a new planning process was initiated with USES playing a leading role.

On several occasions while I was working in Washington, Logue called me and asked if I would come to work for the BRA. David Crane, one of my professors at the University of Pennsylvania, and a number of my classmates had gone to work for Logue. I was fully occupied in Washington and did not accept his invitation. However, I did maintained contact with Ralph Taylor, a former Logue deputy, after I accepted the job with Banner. Taylor was friends with the Sheurer family, one of whom was a New York Congressman/real estate developer. Another was a major investor in the Boston Gas Company. Douglas Cochrane, a member of the board of the Gas Company and President of the United South End Settlements (USES), knew Jim Sheurer.

In March of 1963 Taylor asked me to come to Boston and speak with the people at USES. USES was the same settlement house where my uncles Henry Bruere had consulted while at Harvard Law School and Robert Bruere had visited when he was Director of the Committee for the Improvement of the Conditions of the Poor. I came to Boston and visited with Liddell. We walked about the neighborhoods and saw the dilapidated playgrounds, the vacant houses and the homeless on the streets and in the doorways. We discussed the latest version of the Urban Renewal Plan that called for demolition of 1,700 units of family housing and 1,800 units of single person apartments in clearance areas. Two-thirds of all households to be displaced would qualify for low rent public housing.

USES had consulted with several planners including James Harris, an architect/planner about solutions. Harris recommended that a nonprofit development corporation be established. The nonprofit would build new housing and rehabilitate properties for South End relocatees, particularly those with low incomes. It should be modeled on other development corporations that had been set up in conjunction with urban renewal programs around the country. Federal legislation had been enacted in 1961 to provide favorable financing for nonprofit developers. The new corporation might also serve as an advisor to others. The initial proposal indicated an annual budget of $50,000 per year. I was familiar with some of the urban renewal development corporations and saw a new South End organization as more neighborhood focused than others.

I was impressed by Liddell and the USES board that I met the next day. Charlie Liddell was a wonderful person and a great yet quiet community services administrator. He had run a settlement house in the Georgetown section of Philadelphia before coming to Boston. The President of USES was Douglas Cochrane, a partner in the prominent law firm of Ropes and Gray. I was delighted to sit next to

Melanie Cass at lunch, a remarkable leader in Boston's movement for minority rights. Her intimate knowledge of people and their concerns and her dedication to achieving change was heartening.

After lunch we went downtown to a meeting with Mr. Wilbur Bender, Director of the Committee of the Permanent Charity Fund. Bender, a former Dean at Harvard, was an outstanding individual with a renowned ability to sort out the people requesting grants from the Committee. He clearly had faith in Cochrane and Liddell and said that he was willing to support a housing effort, particularly as USES had offered to contribute to the venture. His grant letter included the following: "In making this grant the committee realizes that there is no assurance that the goal of providing decently rehabilitated housing at rents which low income families can afford to pay, will be achieved. Nevertheless it believes that the problem with which this new enterprise is concerned is of vital importance for the future of Boston and other cities and it feels justified in risking what is for it a large amount of money in an experiment under auspices in which it has confidence to see if rehabilitation can be done, successfully, in human terms. We hope that you will be able to blaze a trail for others to follow." The meeting with the Cochrane, Liddell and Bender was convincing. I agreed to help.

On my return to Washington I visited with Mr. George Nesbitt, who was Director of the Housing and Home Finance Agency's Section 207 Demonstration Program. The Demonstration Program had been authorized under Public Law 87-70 of the National Housing Act of 1961. Its purpose was to find better solutions for low income housing. Rehabilitation had recently gained prominence as a less costly method of production than building new.

Nesbitt had been an important advocate in HHFA for greater attention to race in city redevelopment. The issue of race was tearing American cities apart and the federal government in the eyes of many was not providing adequate leadership. I asked Nesbitt about models for a community development corporation. He suggested the Octavia Hill Association in Philadelphia. I found that the Octavia Hill Association, a corporation started in 1896 by a charitable group, had been modestly successful in buying and modernizing old properties for rent. They also had built a few model houses. Their goal was to use capital funds to finance the purchase of rental housing that could then operate at low rents and still pay dividends. Good management of the properties was emphasized. They were careful in the selection of tenants, attempted to minimize vacancies, and completed repairs promptly by efficient workers. Rent collectors, which were primarily women, had to be skilled in dealing with tenants.

Octavia Hill's activities had been limited since 1924. There were other citywide housing organizations with which I was not acquainted at the time such as Phipps Houses in New York City founded in 1905 and Action/Housing in Pittsburgh, founded in 1957.

Applicants for the Demonstration Program included the Marymount Program in Chicago and the Operation Breakthrough Program in New York City. The Marymount program was initiated by Mr. Marymount Plourde, who made a fortune in the automobile parts business. I visited Mr. Whitney, the Director of the program. FHA had assembled a 15 member special staff to work on the program. Several thousands of units were rehabbed. However, costs were surprisingly similar to other rehabilitation going on in Chicago and eventually the Marymount Foundation disposed of their units late in the 1970s. I investigated the Breakthrough program in New York which was predicated on the prefabrication of kitchens and baths that could be assembled off site and then lowered into the buildings as package units. I looked at some of the buildings and spoke to the Demonstration Program staff. The results did not bear out the initial estimates and the advantages of off site assembly of the kitchen and baths was more than offset by the complex tasks of making special connections in the field for the variation in floor heights and structural framing. What was demonstrated later on was the rehab program sponsored by the City of New York itself. In that case the city official became expert in the costs of rehabilitation and the program was large enough to interest a number of general contractors and subcontractors. The program was financed by the city and savings were achieved through the prompt approval of the projects.

I put together a work plan for the Demonstration and a description of the organization that might be the applicant for a Section 207 Grant. I saw long term feasibility to be significant. I proposed that a new company be formed with the purpose of using all the means possible to achieve a sustainable operation. The list included: a charitable corporation whose board included persons familiar with banking, real estate and community affairs, together with local resident leaders familiar with the area, availability of low cost properties, possibility tax foreclosed properties at no cost, a director with building experience to supervise purchase, rehabilitation and management of properties, work crews organized around key foremen experienced in rehab construction, below market rate financing through the federal government and local banks, tax relief available to a nonprofit corporation as provided under Massachusetts laws, favorable purchase of material and services; and use of the corporation's own capital for equity. Youth training programs, then being implemented by USES and other agencies, would be incorporated in SECD's program not as a cost saver but as a social program.

I returned to Boston and reviewed how the program might proceed. Cochrane and Liddell then assembled the proposal and submitted it to HHFA. USES promised a contribution of $50,000 in addition to a grant of $75,000 from the Committee of Permanent Charity Fund. We asked HHFA for $205,300. Nesbitt gave us encouraging signals about our proposal that had to be approved by June 30, the end of the federal fiscal year. On June 29 Nesbitt advised Cochrane that they could not award a grant. The reason he gave was that South End Community Development (SECD) did not have an Internal Revenue Service letter ruling it a charitable corporation. Cochrane, in his get-it-done style, told Nesbitt that he would have on his desk in three hours a rewritten submission, that substituted United South End Settlements, an IRS approved charity, for SECD as the applicant. USES could then contract the project to SECD. The rewritten proposal was hand carried to Nesbitt in Washington as promised and we did get the grant in the amount requested.

Liddell, Cochrane and others made a persuasive argument that I take on the job as Director and assured me of their commitment to the venture. I convinced Louise that a move to Boston would be a good thing. It would be a chance to deal with major issues confronting cities. I was also tremendously impressed by the quality of people I had met in Boston. I accepted the position of Executive Director at a salary of $17,000 per year.

Louise came with me on my next visit to Boston. I asked her to look at some houses in Newton, which I had identified among ads in the Boston Globe. Newton had a special education program which we wanted. The houses were to be close to transit stations and at prices below $30,000. After my meeting in the South End, I came out to look at what she had discovered. The last house on her list was 11 Irvington Street. I spoke with the owner who was asking $28,500. I offered $27,500. She accepted. I spoke to her bank which held the mortgage. I asked for a loan of $22,000 fixed at 4 1/2 per cent. The person said that they would have to take it to their loan committee. Several days later after our return to Washington, I called and they agreed to make the loan. I prided myself on buying a new home in twenty minutes. We lived at 11 Irvington Street for 28 years and sold it in fifteen minutes for $465,000. We sold it without an agent at a price somewhat below market and to the first of five buyers. Our ad said "We have enjoyed this 10 room Victorian house for twenty-eight years. Come see for yourself. $465,000." Like so many in our generation, a home was a great financial bonus.

I welcomed being recruited by a settlement house. Settlement houses had played an important role in the careers of Uncle Bob and Henry, and in Eleanor Roosevelt's life and the way in which she had acquainted FDR with the slum conditions in the City of New York. United South End Settlements was the leading social agency in the South End and a valuable neighborhood connection for the new corporation.

The politics of the South End was complicated. There were tensions between old time residents and newcomers, between whites and blacks, and between blacks and Latinos. The South End Urban Renewal Area was the largest of Logue's renewal program. The Authority was tackling issues of major displacement of existing low income residents. The area had the largest percentage of homeless people and poor elderly in the city. Renewal of the South End was a very large multi dimensional undertaking. The Demonstration Program, however, was at least focused on specific goals set in the context of current housing development built under the federal programs.

In August 19, 1964, South End Community Development held its first organizational board meeting at Ropes & Gray's office in downtown Boston. Douglas Cochrane, President of SECD, chaired the meeting. Roger Evans of Ropes and Gray was approved Clerk. The subcontract from USES to SECD was approved and I was authorized to open an office, initiate a bank account and go into business. Our first office was a room at USES's 20 Union Park building. The board of 10 members included Fred Taylor, John Stone, and Herbert Gleason, among others. At that meeting it was decided to expand the board to include a greater representation from the South End neighborhood and minorities. A month or so later, I found a small office on the second floor of a four story building on Tremont Street. From the large front windows one could see the new 50 story Prudential Building under construction about five block away.

The South End was dingy, but the neighborhood was favorably located next to the Back Bay and downtown. The office space next door to our office was the Uptown Dental Lab. We got to know its proprietor and admired the rows of false teeth lining his shelves. Our office had been a private gambling room as evidenced by the heavy steel entrance door. The first floor of the building was vacant and the upper floors where small apartments and rooms, several occupied by Catholic sisters. The Cathedral of the Holy Cross was just five blocks away. We operated out of this office for the next few months and put up with its rather modest appearance.

In consultations with Cochrane and others, we expanded the board to eighteen to include more local and minority members. We had introductory meeting with the Mayor, with Logue, with the Boston Redevelopment Authority staff, and the Building Commissioner, Colonial Cooke. Cooke was tough and his reputation was well known.

Our initial meeting with FHA Regional Administrator Jack Flynn was interesting.. We were told that FHA was not sure it could underwrite mortgages in the South End. They had never done that. I indicated some surprise and informed the Director that I not only had a grant from HHFA but also a general allocation of subsidy funds which came with the grant. A site visit was scheduled. A number of staff came down to the South End and we toured the area. The staffers suggested that we start on Presidios Union Park. I told them that we had planned to start where the vacant building owned by the

Authority were located. And so we did. FHA thereafter viewed the program as a demonstration and underwrote the projects pursuant to Experimental Section 233 of the Housing Act. Cochrane and I visited with Vice President King Upton of the First National Bank. He assured us that we would have construction funding at a below market rate.

While purchasing keys at the locksmiths several blocks away on Tremont Street, we discovered that the owner of the lodging house next door might be willing to sell. The owner, Kazoon Maloof, had recently injured her head in a fall. Her husband had died and her niece wanted her to more in with her. We negotiated the purchase of the building for $14,000, including furnishings.

I recall the board meeting at 630 Tremont at which the members questioned how we would operate the building, how we would collect the rents and take care of the place. I informed the board that we planned to go into the housing business and might just start right away. I asked Kazoon about management and she suggested that one of her lodgers, Beatrice Karayennes, might do that. I met with Beatrice. She had lived with Kazoon for 12 years and she agreed to manage the building. She did so in fact until her death in 1984. We moved our offices from 630 Tremont to 677 Tremont Street. We took the first and basement floors, Bea took the front room on the second floor and the remaining five rooms were rented to lodgers.

The significance of all this is that it put us in the rental management business. It was the beginning of our appreciation of the need for resident services. Bea had come from County Cork in Ireland during the twenties. She was one of fourteen children. They had lived in a one room house and rode a cart to school. After her arrival in America, she would take jobs as a cook, presuming that she could keep her cookbook in the kitchen draw. She married a barber named Karayennes and they settled in the South End.

Bea and her husband took on the concierge role for an absentee owner as a way of reducing their housing expense. It was a usual practice in the South End. They received an annual fee of $1,500. They had a room or two on the first floor, rented out the rooms above, and collected the rents. Bea had a regular job for many years as a product inspector at Gillette's South Boston plant. After her husband died, she had moved into Kazoon's house. She was well acquainted with the lodging business. Bea made a difference in the lives of our lodgers. She treated the house as hers, was always attentive to what was going on and made the roomers feel welcome and safe.

We inherited an interesting group of lodgers. Mr. Mendes, well over 80 years of age when we bought 677, had come from the Middle East decades before. He had no family to speak of and 677 was his home. He had lived at 677 for more than twenty years. Every morning he would go downtown to his club where he stayed all day. Beatrice would wait up for him to come in by nine o'clock in the evening after which she locked the front door. Mr. Mendes seems perfectly content with the room's modest furnishing. When we renovated his room later and put in electric wall plugs, he insisted that we keep the string from the center ceiling light to the top rail of his bed so that he could turn the light on and off. He had a small lavatory in one corner in front of which he took his sponge bath at night. He protected the floor with newspaper. His last item of the day was a shot of whiskey before getting into bed. Years later, when Mr. Mendes at 93, he came down with a bad cold. Bea made sure that he had something to eat and kept watch over him. He was visited by a doctor on occasion. These house visits were a burden to his doctor who recommended that he go to a nursing home. Mr. Mendes at first refused, but in time was persuaded he had to go where he could be attended to more conveniently. Medics came and carried him down the stairs and out to an ambulance. As he passed through the front hall, he turned to Bea and said, " Bea, they are taking me away. I do not want to leave my home and I am going to die". He lasted only a matter of weeks in the nursing home.

Roy Hughes had been a construction worker of some sort. He had come from Nova Scotia decades ago to work in Boston and had lived with Kazoon for more than ten years. He occupied the rear room on the third floor over Mr. Mendes. Roy was living on general welfare assistance. His problem was betting at the dog races. Bea was careful to make sure the old racing forms were not in sight when the social worker came. He was robbed on the street several times coming home after dark. His day journeys generally included visits to one or two institutions that gave out free meals.

Jon Santos was from Puerto Rico, a rough-cut type who had a variety of jobs. Bea watched over Jon's comings and goings. On one occasion she persuaded him to go back upstairs to put on a fresh shirt before he went out to meet his girl friend. The police came looking for Jon once and Bea played dumb as to his being in. They went upstairs, looked and then left. She went back up upstairs and Jon came out from under the bed. On another occasion, Bea discovered one morning that a young lady had stayed all night. She went in and pulled off the covers and ordered her out of the house. Sometime later there was a banging on the front door late at night. Bea could call down to people on the steps from her front window. On the top step was a gentleman with a young lady. He wanted to see Jon Santos, who his daughter said had promised to marry her. Bea refused to open the door and asked them to leave. They did after some noisy complaints. Our understanding was that Jon did marry her as promised several months later.

And there was Billy. Bea did not question applicants about their family background. Billy was a small man, bent over and sickly. After a stay of several months he became ill. Bea watched over him and brought him soup and things to eat. She tried to cheer him up which was not easy. His condition worsened and he was persuaded to go to City Hospital. He died several days later. He had no known family.

Our purchase of 677 brought a change in the people housed. Kazoon had been selective and Bea was cautious. We insisted that we should not discriminate and should allow whoever responded to the sign in the window to be accepted unless there were obvious reasons to deny them. Thereafter, the roomers were frequently minority individuals. Most people in the immediate neighborhood across Tremont Street were Puerto Ricans and so were most of our roomers. Bea had a number of regular boarders who would go home to Puerto Rico and then beg for their room when they came back. There were times when Bea had to go to the local police station and identified someone as one of her boarders or former boarders. Bea could spot trouble. She once spotted drugs in a dresser. She told me and I had to speak with the young man and tell him to leave. Beatrice made a difference in the lives of our roomers. She was always there and in charge. All of this was my initiation to rental management and my lasting opinion that resident services and engagement with consumers were the crucial ingredients in successful housing.

Our first initiation into management at the lodging house warned us about the social service needs of low income residents. I recall an early September telephone call from Gertrude Nickerson, a strong advocates of better welfare allowances. She said that she would not be making her rent payment because she had to buy a new coat for her daughter's first day at school. Another tenant, Mrs. Williams, called and asked us if we could baby-sitter her nine-year-old daughter Angela while she went to the hospital to have a bullet removed from her brain. This happened a number of years before at some festive social occasion.

As we finished rehabbing one of our buildings we discovered that while the Boston Housing Authority had difficulties renting to single-parent families, we did not. The housing authority made an issue of whether a boyfriend was legal or not, whether he was or was not on the lease, whether he would contribute or not contribute to the family income. We were, on the other hand, just accepting the mother's word. We wanted somebody in each building to take care of the trash. Frequently, one of the "significant others" living in the building would do the task. Another interesting thing we discovered was that children were bringing in the rent and we would lose track of the adults in the apartments. A sister might have moved in, was taking care of the children, and the rent was being paid on time. Management personnel must have accurate information as to who is living in a unit. There is no substitute for personal connections to every resident.

My office was on the first floor overlooking Tremont Street, which was a scene of political turmoil during the sixties. Up the street was 294 Tremont Street, a building owned by the BRA. Squatters occupied it in a protest over the lack of housing for displaced poor families and individuals. After a ruckus the police took possession of the building and the squatters landed in the police station late on a Saturday night. At that point, Dean Al Sacks of the Harvard Law School received a telephone call and had to interrupt his card game and come down to Station 4 and get Ted Parrish, a USES community organizer out of jail. Two blocks up the street was the infamous Paradise Club from which loud arguments and noise persisted into the early morning. It was a central point for the drug business. Protesters of one sort or another would march up the street in good weather and bad. Most of the stores had wire screen over their windows. I decided that we would not do so. We had a couple of small robberies but no one smashed our windows as others had been.

Our first task under the Demonstration was to identify buildings that we might rehabilitate. The BRA provided us with a list of city-owned properties and we supplemented it with additional buildings that we had uncovered. We wanted to have the properties in various locations throughout the area. We chose some specific buildings and started negotiations with the BRA on the disposition agreement under which the properties would be transferred to us.

The BRA had published a variety of reports about the costs of rehabilitation and was hoping our Demonstration would support their findings. The rents, as supported by the very low rehabilitation costs, were incorporated into the disposition agreement. I protested that we could not agree to any rents until we had actually rehabbed some buildings. On a Sunday afternoon I visited Cochrane at his office and reviewed the closing document with him. He noted the rents and asked whether I could achieve the levels indicated. I said I could not promise to do so until we knew more about rehabilitation costs. With that, he picked up a phone and called his friend Ed Logue and said that we could not accept the rents as stated. Logue knew Cochrane well enough to not put up an argument. The specific rents were eliminated.

BRA conveyed at first four vacant city-owned buildings. They including 38 Springfield Street, the one that we had decided to use as our first construction site. It was near Boston University Medical School, was on a street where most of the buildings were occupied and no buildings had been demolished.

With the approval of our board I retained James Harris as our architect for the initial four buildings. The buildings were inspected and measured, and designs were prepared. There were discussions about building costs and design standards. We had to comply with FHA and building department requirements. There were also historical preservation issues. Although code enforcement in the South End had been lacking, our publicized FHA development program brought a number of design issues to everyone's attention.

South End row houses had features that violated current codes. The famous winder stairways, the narrow rooms to the front and back of the stairways, the lack of roof parapet walls and the horizontal fire escapes between properties were key issues. Inordinate time was spent processing appeals which were finally granted. Repair and pointing of the building exteriors was required. The interiors were substantially gutted and rebuilt. Ceilings and partitions were constructed with perforated sheetrock and plaster. Mechanical systems were all new. We were required to install sprinklers in the halls and kitchens. We would become skilled in reconstructing stairways and installing special handrails that guided the person through the turns. Rebuilding burnt out stairways was possible because we salvaged handrails from buildings that were being demolished.

We encountered some criticism that our construction costs were high and built to middle class standards. This was nonsense. We installed seven foot strip kitchens, modest cabinets, standard bath fixtures, linoleum tile in kitchens and baths, asphalt tile floors and solid core wood apartment doors. Processing the FHA insurance application and obtaining the building permit took months. We filed for FHA insurance pursuant to the Below Market Interest Program (Section 221(d)(3), that provided a 3% mortgage. There were FHA processing delays attributable to delays in accepting our costs of construction, in determining feasibility of such small projects, and receiving approvals from HUD Washington after our general allocation ran out. HUD documentation was always burdensome.

Another issue that caused delay was that each little project would be treated as a separate transaction. This resulted from HUD's requirement that each insured project have its own mortgage so that HUD could separate all the risk and liability associated with non recourse lending. If there was a default, HUD could recover costs by from taking over the real estate. This requirement resulted in increased administrative and some material costs, and we argued that we should be able to do projects in the Demonstration Program under one business entity. Boston FHA's office refused to allow this, so Cochrane and I went to Washington.

We made our case to Mr. Craun, the then Director of the Demonstration Programs. As I explained to Craun the issues involved, Doug Cochran was writing away on his yellow pad. When I finished Cochrane handed his work product to Mr. Craun and told him that we would like to have his approval as he had drafted it. If we didn't get something of that sort, we would have to give him back his grant. Craun was taken aback by Cochrane's direct approach, but he agreed to look into the matter. We returned to Boston and several weeks thereafter we were advised that HUD would allow the Demonstration Program projects to be owned by one legal entity.

It was assumed that SECD would continue to operate the housing over the long term. For profit developers undertake insured projects with a promise to the government that they will maintain the properties for the low income residents for a period of years, generally 20 years. One of the major program issues that HUD has faced is the preservation of assisted projects after these twenty year commitments expire.

SECD eventually did obtain an FHA commitment and building department approval for construction. On the initial projects, FHA provided insurance pursuant to the experimental section of the Housing Act. The mortgage loans amounts were equal to 102% of development costs. It included 2% for working capital. Bank of Boston was the original construction lender at a favorable interest rate. Upon construction completion, the notes would be sold to Ginnie Mae and carry a 3% rate. In this way, the 3% mortgage financing was achieved.

We had solicited interest from contractors about the construction costs and their willingness to do the work. We were aware that we would have to pay prevailing wages to construction workers as required by FHA financing. Prevailing wages are close to the union wage and well above those being paid by conventional private contractors doing rehab work in the area. The requirement for higher wage rates was the primary reason we could not attract construction bidders. I decided that for at least the initial buildings, we would serve as our own general contractor. This allowed us to have better control over the construction work and the costs. Serving as our own contractor provided an opportunity to employ minority mechanics and subcontractors.

We advertised for a construction superintendent and were delighted to discover a very able licensed builder who had been building Class A structures in suburbia with Harvard Law School students. He had organized the projects, put in the foundations and then done the above- ground construction work during the summer with the students.

One of the components of our Demonstration was to utilize Youth Corps trainees that were provided through the local anti-poverty agency, ABCD, to perform some of our construction work. We discovered that the Youth Corps trainees generally came ill-prepared to undertake arduous construction work. There were glad to wear the construction helmets, but were upset by the dust and dirt of the building business. When they showed up initially, our superintendent had to take them around to the Army-Navy store and buy for them proper shoes and outside clothing. Frequently, they would come to work without a proper breakfast and our superintendent had to provide them lunch. They were to work a 25-hour week which was not coordinated with the usual working day, and they had appointments to go to for health checks and other training requirements. Their interest was not consistent. It often took too much of the time of our mechanics to oversee the work that they performed. Only one or two actually stayed in the construction business.

Our construction costs ranged from $11.20 per square foot to $14.30 per square foot. Total development costs were from $13,600 to

$16,600 per apartment. Prevailing wage requirement increased our labor costs by 40% and total project costs by 14%. An important problem was the requirement to send in benefits to the union. When our workers left and went to work on non-union jobs and did not reinstate their union membership, they lost the benefits we had paid.

We completed our first five-unit project at 38 East Springfield Street on May 26, 1967. We completed the last buildings a year later on May 3, 1968. By then, we had learned the FHA mortgage loan application process. We also learned how to interface the city's Board of Appeals application with the HUD processing. Our staff got to know HUD staff and they became quite helpful over the next two years as we rehabbed ten additional South End buildings. Because processing HUD insurance commitments was so erratic, we gave up doing our own construction work. Lou Rota, our construction superintendent, went off to other work and within two years was the general superintendent on the I.M.Pei designed Christian Science project.

Following the Demonstration Program, we did take on additional development projects. We were anxious to apply our skills in processing FHA financing and our knowledge of the rehabilitation of South End row houses. The BRA had several buildings in a block of houses facing on Tremont Street between Northhampton Street and Camden Street. We made overtures to the BRA that in our next phase we would like to combine rehabilitation of South End houses with new construction.

Doug Cochrane, John Box and I met with Ed Logue to present this proposal. Logue still had an opinion that SECD was a small player compared to the major developers of new units he had in mind. He suggested that we try to do something in the North End. In time he awarded a new build project in our area to the Development Corporation America, which did an inferior job and ultimately ended up in bankruptcy.

We proceeded with the rehab portion as planned. We agreed to take three buildings that BRA owned and attempt to acquire the rest. We also bought three buildings from private owners and tried to purchase a vacant corner buildings as well. We were unable to convince the trustees who controlled the corner property to sell it to us. We could not wait forever and proceeded with just six buildings. After our project was well underway, the corner building was sold to the Baptist A Church across the street. It was demolished for parking spaces. The architectural integrity of our whole block was immensely damaged.

We did all the development work on the six project, acquisition, planning, directing the architectural and engineering design by outside professional firms and processing of mortgage applications through FHA. We were by this time experts in FHA insurance and conventional bank construction financing. We knew construction costs for the South End house. We prepared all the documents and the FHA standard forms. The cost for outside legal work by Rudolph Kass, our skilled regular attorney, including the comprehensive zoning opinion and time for both the initial and final closings, was $1400. We demonstrated that, with adequate experience and cooperation from all parties including FHA, development could be done expeditiously. Sydney Construction was our General Contractor. They completed the construction on time and within budget.

My assistant and I did all the administration work preparing and processing the HUD documents. Tina was an extremely capable person. She was also the only person that I ever knew that had no clue about her family heritage.

As a young child, she was lost and picked up by a stranger in a German labor camp right after the War. The woman took care of her and at the end of the World War, she migrated to Trieste and took her along. She came to America with her adopted mother when she was about 12 years old. She went to public school and graduated from the Nyack, New York high school. She got a job, got married and supported her husband as he went through college. He then left her and she got a divorce. She got a position with the Immigration Service. In that capacity she encountered a Hungarian immigrant named Nemeth, who was trained as an electrical engineer and who had spent two years on a fellowship to the Russian space center. On his arrival to the United States the US government took possession of him as one of the few people who had worked at the Russian Center and could speak about the Russian space program. She was his handler in New York and they got to know each other and were married.

Nemeth was soon sent to Boston to attend MIT and she came with him. She got a job with the Snelling & Snelling employment agency in Boston. A lovely young woman named Betty Brown had been my assistant for five years. Betty married and left and I advertised for a new person. She was handing the case and sent over a number of applicants. When the applicants saw that the job was in the South End, they were not interested. They described their experiences to Tina. She decided she might see for herself. She rode over on her motorbike and we had an interesting meeting. She took the job. She was an immensely talented person with a great learning ability. She could write and speak several foreign languages and was not intimidated by the FHA forms. It was another example that a social enterprise such as SECD in a distressed neighborhood could attract interested and capable staff.

The next project that SECD undertook was the rehabilitation of two large mansion row houses facing Chester Park, a grand oval open space along Massachusetts Avenue. The houses were elegant mansions, famous for their use as hiding places along the "underground railroad" for slaves migrating to Canada. We were awarded one of the houses by the BRA; the other we purchased. This project was interesting in that the financing was provided by the John Hancock Insurance Company pursuant to the $1 billion commitment that the insurance companies promised to invest in distressed urban neighborhoods. I knew Robert Jordan, a senior official of the Company, who was our contact.

I was determined to work with a minority construction firm. We had involved a number of minority subcontractors, some individual proprietors, in our previous construction work but no general contractor. After establishing the costs, we awarded the construction contract to Lester Clemente, who met the FHA bonding requirement with a bond guaranteed by the Boston Gas Company, whose parent company was Eastern Gas and Fuel headed by Eli Goldston. We had worked with the gas company before and Eli was familiar with SECD. Guido Rothauth, Eli's general counsel, was on my board. It was the first time that an African-American minority contractor was the bonded contractor on an FHA-insured project in Boston. Clemente had become adept in fulfilling the prevailing wage requirements for government financed construction work. The wage rates were higher than normal but were manageable where you could man the job with adequately skilled foremen and mechanics. A number of programs in Boston had been supporting the training of minority business owners and workers.

SECD did two additional houses on East Springfield Street under the BRA's Program. The later was administered by the BRA but took considerable watching by us. The original contractor was working out of a house on Shawmut Avenue. I went to see him and concluded that he was not qualified. I then arranged that Jim McFarland be the contractor. He was fine and we fixed up 35 and 42 East Springfield and operated them. The building at 40 East Springfield was occupied by a blind couple. We had gotten to know them when we did the initial rehab on 38 East Springfield.

SECD ended up with 83 rehabbed apartments in 23 building. The income level of our residents was below that of public housing. We discovered that management of scattered site housing was costly. It was never possible to get FHA approval of rents that would cover the costs of management. This was based in part on economic feasibility but not totally. We had planned to accept residuals notes on our losses and recover the funds through later refinancing. There was also a need for residents services that was customarily not considered an essential housing expense.

SECD hired a social service person and instituted a variety of programs in which the residents might participate. We initiated efforts to have a residents association. But we found the scattered locations of our properties made that impractical. Low-income residents have a lot of problems to deal with and worrying about how your neighbor is doing is only another. The best answer was to have staff who were well acquainted with the individual residents and be able to respond promptly as resident needs and disputes arose.

SECD's development and construction costs were higher than the public agencies estimates. As the city records and documents indicated, however, they proved to be correct for subsequent housing rehabilitation programs. The BRA was annoyed because our costs were almost twice what they had advertised. At one point, BRA staff said that they would not approve our final evaluation because our costs were too high.

I fled with our report to Washington on Friday, April 5, 1968, the day of the riots in Washington, with our report. There was no one in the FHA office and I left it on Mr. Craun's desk. On leaving the building, I could see the commotion down on 14th Street near where I had worked. I walked down to Pennsylvania Avenue and noticed the few agitated government workers hurrying home before hitting the subway for the airport.

The Demonstration Program contract made no note about property management. Yet we found management to be crucial. We knew most of our residents. I was known to a number of them and understood the difficulties many faced. There were abusive relationships in which the woman of the household would end up with a blackened eyes and bruises. In one account, the woman struck a kitchen knife into her husband's arm during a brawl. We would rent an apartment to the mother knowing that the boyfriend would probably show up. In many cases this was central for her livelihood and stability. In one of our newly renovated apartments a woman with four young children, had several who clearly needed medical attention. The apartment was in disarray. She had not paid the rent, and she had refused our offers to bring in a service. She moved out one night. and I discovered her a month later living in a dingy dark apartment where the children could mark up the walls without causing her to worry about the landlord. The new light painted walls and cabinets of our apartment had been an unmitigated burden for this poor woman.

I remember a second mother who would leave her four children in the apartment with the front door locked as she went across the street to work in the local bar. I had to knock on the door and get to know the children to make sure they were all right. At times, she shut her boyfriend in to hide him from the police. I helped her relocate to a newly refurbished apartment in public housing but the social worker called me and condemned my moving her into a situation where she might incur discrimination because the development was predominant black. She was persuaded to reject the newly rehabbed apartment in public housing and accept a unit in a dilapidated building which was scheduled to be demolished by the BRA. Years later I received a copy of a notice about the same woman who was the subject of a drug bust in which she was named.

FHA always allowed mortgage loans adequate to cover construction and development costs, but the financing was never adequate to pay for operating expenses. The loans got the projects built and left the problems of the operating period for others. Operating costs of scattered low income housing is more costly than those for larger new developments. It is not surprising that operating losses could for a time be converted into tax shelters. We accepted the FHA approved rents, but in our report stated that the projects were not economically feasible. In time we did recover the losses that were included in residual receipts. They were recovered years later when the buildings were refinanced.

Creating a community development corporation does not come easily. SECD started with $330,000 in the bank, wonderful officers, and board and a program for action that took four years. We did gather skills and smarts and became relatively self-sufficient. But we were also blessed by proceeds earned in tax syndications and other forms of development fees that came along to help us.

Oliver Ames presides at GBCD board meeting

South End Tenants news coverage

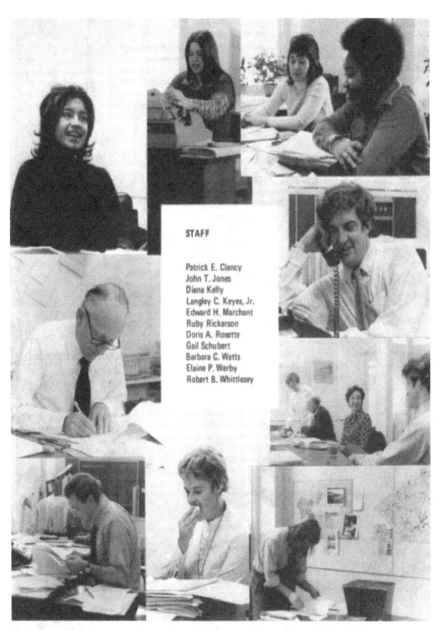

STAFF

Patrick E. Clancy
John T. Jones
Diana Kelly
Langley C. Keyes, Jr.
Edward H. Marchant
Ruby Rickerson
Doris A. Rosette
Gail Schubert
Barbara C. Watts
Elaine P. Werby
Robert B. Whittlesey

GBCD staff in 1972

138

Whittlesey meets with South End Tenants group

Dawson make a point with Don Stull

Dawson signing documents at FHA closing

Danial Soltern, Ann Kerrey, Kevin Earls, FHA Deputy Director, and Whittlesey

140

IBA celebrates completion of Tower Building

Viviendas La Victoria under construction

IBA's Viviendas and Tower Building

Central Grammer School Building in Gloucester

142

Whittlesey with Mary Bates and Joseph Poirier of The Community Builders staff at Central Grammer Building

St. Stephens Elderly Tower in Lynn, Massachusetts

*Lincoln Foundation closing: William Haynesworth, Whittlesey, Joseph Bower, William White,
Director of Massachusetts Housing Finance Agency, Huson Jackson, Roger Evans*

Lincoln Woods development

144

King's Layne development

Children at Warren Gardens

Judge Paul Garrity and Whittlesey

Bradley Biggs tours BHA developments with Dan Sullivan and others

146

Joseph Corcoran, Christopher Norris, Gary Jennison, Mary-Anne Morrison, Massachusetts Department of Communities Development, Whittlesey, Sandra Henriquez, Assistant Secretary at HUD, Richard Lowell

Chapter Five

Greater Boston Community Development -
developments with community partners

In the mid-sixties, the civil rights movement was gaining momen-
tum, and the federal housing system was caught in the cross-fires.
The Department of Housing and Urban Development was enacted
in 1965 as Johnson's Great Society was underway. There were questions emerging locally about who should control policies and the
flow of public funds in urban areas.

The urban renewal program was facilitating projects in downtown
but it was also continuing to force families from their homes. They
were often compelled to accept public housing. In Boston the Government Center project in the old West End was moving forward. In
the South End and Roxbury sections of the city, displaced families
were still struggling to obtain affordable housing.

The National Commission documented in 1968 the frustration of
neighborhood institutions and groups that did not receive satisfactory responses to their protests for attention. I and many others became acutely aware that groups in the South End and Roxbury were
demanding recognition and representation in social changes that
they believed were due and in which they were demanding a part.
The Housing Act of 1968 represented a new push for social housing,
incorporating the goal of 1.3 new units per year.

From the beginning SECD's role as a community development corporation was under study. Over time, the board was modified to include
a majority of South End residents and business owners. There was extensive strife in the South End between residents and landlords, as well
as protests against the BRA's displacement and relocation of families.

Modest gentrification was occurring in certain sections and speculation in South End properties abounded.

I knew of one young person, a recent graduate of Harvard University, in Botany, who acquired within a period of about a year, forty different houses and sold them to new owners. By 1970, one could buy a property for six thousand dollars and several months later sell it for ten. A number of the churches in the neighborhoods became involved with housing issues and were willing to sponsor new housing ventures. However, these institutions lacked people with development skills. There was frustration and some resentment around these efforts. SECD with demonstrated skills had offered assistance but many groups wanted to do their own thing.

SECD realized that on completion of the Demonstration that its future operations needed scale. Robert Tracy, a young assistant to Eli Goldston, the head of Eastern Gas and Fuel, had investigated the ownership of South End houses. It turned out that there was a surprising number of substantial owners, included Israel and Joseph Mindick and Joseph Aranella. Most properties were in the hands of absentee investors who were doing a poor job of managing their housing. We assembled a list of these owners with whom we might purchase multiple buildings. We then submitted a proposal to FHA for the purchase and rehab of 100 buildings containing 425 units. This was an ambitious request and there were doubts about whether this scale of funding could be obtained.

About the same time, there was agitation by the tenants in properties owned by Mr. Israel Mindick. The tenants had protested the conditions of the properties, and his failure to make building code repairs. With the assistance of several churches and legal firms, the tenants organized and then sought relief. They protested to the city and demonstrated at Mindick's home in Canton, Massachusetts. He was not there at the time and they said that they would be back, possibly to his temple in which he was a cantor. This alarmed Rabbi Judea Miller, who was social action chairman of the Massachusetts Board of Rabbis. After he had attended the demonstrations to make sure that the protest was not an episode of black anti-Semitism, Rabbi Miller recommended that the parties take their complaint to the Boston Rabbinical Court.

A Rabbinical Court usually handles disputes among Jews and between Jews and non-Jews. The Rabbi saw the court as a means of resolving the dispute even though it would not bind Mindick. Mindick agreed and the Associated Synagogues of Massachusetts heard the evidence and made rulings. An agreement was proposed and approved by Mindick that he would make the repairs and the South End Tenants Council would serve as the representative of their residents.

Within months, the agreement was in trouble. The repairs were not completed, and SETC initiated a rent strike. The BRA was concerned and was considering what steps they might take. I had previously attended a meeting with officials of the temple and had discussed with them possible paths of resolution. At a second meeting with Hale Champion, Director of the BRA, and members of Jewish Combined Charities, who were in touch with the Rabbinical Court, we fashioned ways in which the SETC group of buildings might serve as the first submission of a new rehab program.

My good friend Walter Smart, then Deputy Director and the top ranking minority person on the BRA staff, became a central figure in what to do next. Smart had been recruited by Charlie Liddell from the same organization in Philadelphia where he had served. Smart was a wonderful, optimistic and energetic person. He was assigned the task of putting together a three-way partnership among the BRA, the SETC and SECD. The BRA would supply the buildings, SETC would be the owner and SECD would be the consultant/developer. I recall the meeting with FHA and its Deputy Director Kevin Earls at which I explained that Mary Longley and her group would own the properties and I would be the consultant. Their jaws dropped. But they were pacified when I told them that I would be in on everything. The project would initially involve 20 buildings with a total of 100 units.

SECD had increased its board of directors to 33 individuals, about half of whom were residents of the South End and most represented minority groups. They were starting to tell SECD that the minority groups wanted to be their own owners and to control what got fixed and when. SECD had reached a point where BRA and FHA recognized it as a highly competent owner/developer, but this did not address their political needs. I concluded that even though SECD had important South End officials and citizens on its board, competing as an owner against other neighborhood groups for project funding was unwise. An alternative was to act as a consultant. We could still play a significant part serving as a technical partner.

Groups were stirring in the South End and Roxbury, and we had been approached by some of them, as well as suburban groups like St. Stephen's Church in Lynn and the Lincoln Foundation, asking for assistance. I discussed the modified role of SECD with Doug Cochrane, John Bok, Bernard Rothwell, and other board members. This led to my decision that SECD should modify its role, and avoid ownership. Instead we would be the best nonprofit regional provider of technical assistance to neighborhood groups.

Citizens Planning & Housing Association (CHAPA) was trying to launch a housing development fund to support affordable housing. I discussed with Bob McKay, the Executive Director of CHAPA,

SECD intention to modify its role. He agreed that the two proposals be joined and that a funding request be filed by SECD with the Ford Foundation. With supported from the Permanent Charity Fund (Boston Foundation) and the Hyams Trust, we applied for a three-year grant with the Ford Foundation. It was approved.

I then visited with a number of SECD's board members and discussed with them our new role. We decided that we should change our name to Greater Boston Community Development. A new board would be appointed with technical skills drawn from the metropolitan area. Douglas Cochrane would provide continuity, and John Bok was on CHAPA's Board. The neighborhood residents on the SECD board were on the boards of the organizations they represented. The only opposition came from George Farrar, a city employee and resident of the South End. He saw it as a loss for the local groups. However, I and others argued that the new role for the corporation put the organization in a supportive position to the neighborhood groups when dealing with specific developments. We would continue to perform in a consultant capacity if requested. All board members were then asked to resign, with the exception of Cochrane and Bok, and a new board was appointed. The GBCD board was made up of representatives from CHAPA, the banks, the business community, related professions and representatives from the neighborhoods. We moved into our new offices at 177 State Street in downtown Boston in September, 1970.

By this time the Tenants Development Corporation had organized and selected Marion Dawson and Mary Longley to head their development efforts. The TDC board had a number of members who could and did volunteer. For the next 15 months I met with Ms. Dawson, Ms.Longley, and their associates on Fridays at 4:00 pm to work out details of the design and specifications, the building department filings, and the zoning appeals with the city of Boston. We worked with TDC on retaining architects, Don Stull, David Lee and Louis Hater. Hater was the Principal who did most of the work. We had background on all the buildings selected and the relocation plan was prepared by the TDC.

TDC decided early on to do the first project as a nonprofit development. While TDC retained their own attorney, SECD had to back them up. Working out the details on each building took time and fitting in the subsidies was important. The FHA-insured mortgage loan was for 100% of the project's costs. The project held the initial closing and the rehab construction by CW & Company was completed. An interesting event occurred when Pat Clancy, our attorney, had to leave the initial closing, go over to the Federal Court and obtain the federal decision that cleared the way for the Initial closing to continue. Protesters had argued in court that the "lifestyle of the poor" was an "adverse environmental affect" and that the project would harm the neighborhood. Clancy came back with the announcement that the federal judge had held for the residents.

Clancy had joined GBCD full-time in October 1969 following his summer as a work-study student. The possibility of doing a second phase of the TDC rehab project and the first phase of IBA rehab block as syndicated projects was enticing. We could help groups to organize the owning corporations to do the projections with the help of Robert Kuehn, an architect and housing economist, perform the legal and syndicate work in conjunction with Roger Evans of Ropes & Grey for TDC, and to manage the construction, rent-up and continuing ownership participation.

On completion of their first project of twenty buildings, TDC took on a second project in 1974 of 36 more buildings with 185 apartments. The architectural firm of Stull and Associates was again engaged and most of the development and legal work was done by GBCD, particularly in the person of Pat Clancy. Clancy was a progressive from Green Bay, Wisconsin. He had a beard and long hair down his back. He was determined to complete the project and fought hard to keep it moving. A for-profit housing developer that was active in the South End contacted Ms. Dawson and framed an outcome for the second phase. They proposed to Ms. Dawson some training and a role in management for TDC. When I caught up to what was happening, I sat down with Pat and we put together a plan that gave TDC the control of the project's syndicated net proceeds and a fee for being the owner.

The project had a 1% mortgage loan insured by FHA. A tri-party agreement was fashioned among TDC, Greater Boston Community Development (GBCD), and the BRA under which the properties would be developed. It was clear that HUD wanted GBCD involved to ensure that the owners had the necessary development skills. The BRA supported our participation in issues dealing with the city and HUD. The architects made a significant contribution in the design of the buildings.

The FHA loan was closed and construction was completed close to schedule. The contractor was CW Company again, of which Ben Polishook was the head. Ben, a friend and skilled rehabilitation contractor, always gave me credit for establishing the rehabilitation costs of South End houses. He was by this time well acquainted with prevailing wages. The project was syndicated and fees were paid to the owners and to GBCD. Clancy and I represented the owner's interests through the ups and downs of the development process.

The National Housing Partnership (NHP) had been created under the Housing Act of 1968 to facilitate subsidized housing developments under the Act. While GBCD was just the second agency among their national group of associates, we found that the NHP was not competitive on the distribution of proceeds it offered associates. GBCD could do better, particularly on rehab projects, on its own, although NHP did manage to win some projects with other developers.

There was a junkyard on West Dedham Street and several abandoned industrial buildings. They posed a hazard to children living in the immediate area. The residents, who were primarily Puerto Rican immigrants, organized a group called Inquilinos Boricuas en Accion (IBA) to protest their issues to the BRA. The BRA asked what they wanted and that led to the idea of their being the developer of the parcel. The group retained John Sharratt, a local architect, to prepare a redevelopment plan. IBA's leader, Israel Feliciano, and John Sharratt, who had visited Puerto Rico, grafted a number of ideas about the buildings, gardens and spaces. They made presentations to the group and to the BRA.

The redevelopment plan gained support from William Dryer of St. Stephen's Episcopal Church on Shawmut Avenue, where they held their meetings. Others in the neighborhood such as Helen Morton, Harry Dowd, Jorge Hernandez, were also active supporters. Israel Feliciano, who was an energetic and personable leader, hired staff and raised some funds, primarily from churches. Their offices were at 672 Tremont Street across the street from SECD/GBCD. Shortly thereafter, the group retained David Rideout of Palmer and Dodge as their attorney, largely on a pro-bono basis, and GBCD as the Consultant. We worked on a contingent basis on syndicated deals.

Palmer Dodge proceeded to establish the legal and corporate structure for IBA and for its affiliated development entity. I was busy with Israel in pursuit of seed money from the churches and foundations. The BRA was initially doubtful of IBA's ability to take on redevelopment work but they had respect for Feliciano's leadership and saw the benefit of selecting a Hispanic development group.

The BRA saw IBA with GBCD as their consultant as the potential developer of Parcel 19. After some months of discussions and presentations, IBA was formerly recognized as the developer by BRA. The first project was the rehabilitation of 13 buildings with 71 apartment and four commercial stores on Tremont Street between West Dedham and West Brookline Streets. The stores included a drugstore on the corner of Dedham Street and SECD's old office on the second floor of 30 Tremont Street at the other end.

IBA held community meetings to establish the preliminary design. Architect John Sharratt, a local architect, then prepared the designs while GBCD prepared the paperwork for the approval of the BRA, the city departments, and the FHA. The development, which was originally a non-profit project, was turned by GBCD into a syndicated limited partnerships. IBA's for-profit arm would have a 4.5% interest. Additionally, there was a 0.5% interest for Stanley Sidney; a 27.5 % interest for Sidney Construction as the Builder; and 67.5% interest for the equity investors, who made contributions in order to obtain tax benefits.

The partnership also needed a general partner satisfactory to FHA that possessed the financial means to backstop the project if additional funds were needed during the construction phase. I had gotten to know Stan Sidney on our project on Tremont Street. I convinced Sydney to take the role of "net worth general partner" on his understanding that GBCD would be there throughout. David Rideout and his firm would provide the necessary legal work. The project was financed by a FHA-insured mortgage loan at 1% interest rate for 90% of the costs. IBA's share of syndication proceeds purchased amenities for the apartments: parquet wood flooring, oak spiral staircases, and landscaped yards.

The success of the initial project gave the BRA confidence that IBA and John Sharratt could handle the design for the entire Partial 19.

The plan would include several high-rise structures, as well as construction of new buildings and community facilities. The first new construction project was a 201-unit apartment building for the elderly to the rear of the buildings first rehabbed by IBA.

At first, the BRA plan showed two 12-story buildings as design elements for the overall South End Renewal Plan. Sharratt showed these buildings in his plan and the proposed builder for the project reviewed it. A turnkey program had been assumed by the parties under which the completed building would be sold to the Boston Housing Authority on completion.

Feliciano called me and asked that I join him and his group on a visit to the HUD's New York City Department of Public Housing. They were the office that approved turnkey project designs. We met with the officials of the Department and reviewed the plan. As it turned out, the estimated cost for the two buildings was too high. IBA's people agreed to do further work on them.

On our return to Boston, the builder advised IBA that the only scheme he thought would be feasible was a single 19-story building, and IBA was in charge of getting it approved. They took it on and had Sharratt revise his drawings. The BRA accepted the taller building with reservations. There was concern about the foundations. Low-rise housing had rested upon a clay laver about 12 to 15 feet below the surface. After the borings were completed, the decision was made to use deep 95 foot piling down to hardpan.

There were also questions about services and where to locate the washing and drying rooms. All of this delayed the processing. The builder got tired and resigned. IBA, with GBCD's help, looked around and came up with a successor builder, the Carley Corporation out of Wisconsin. Carley had heard of the impasse and volunteered their participation. They did not have a project in the Boston area and being connected to a Hispanic developer would be helpful.

IBA's need was to locate a serious player who could front for the construction risk exposure. Carley brought in Turner Construction, who had jobs in the area at that time. They put together a tentative proposal which IBA reviewed. I recall the subsequent meeting at which Carley presented their plan and laid out their fee demands. They were clearly burdensome and left little room for paying for extras that IBA was anticipating. The result was that Carley and his associates withdrew from further consideration.

My next move was to meet with Bill White, the Director of the Massachusetts Housing Finance Agency. We had planned to request construction financing from MHFA. With each new proposed partner, IBA had advanced the drawings. By the time Carley departed, the designs were well along and approvals by the required agencies were largely in place. It occurred to me that IBA could proceed as a sole nonprofit developer, utilizing its fee to underwrite the construction risk. What we needed was a bid from a solid contractor. If it was satisfactory, then construction financing through MHFA would be possible.

White took it all under advisement. After several weeks he said MHFA would do it. We had agreed to work with known builders. We interviewed Thomas Gilbane in Providence and Peabody Construction in Boston and the construction contract was awarded to Peabody. We then filed with MHFA for construction financing.

BHA had approved the plans and specifications, as had HUD. The building would face a small community park. Sharratt designed the building but left the park out. IBA saw the park as part of the renewal plan's site work. Torre Unidad, the name of the elderly building, was successfully completed, and IBA invested some of their fee in upgrades of the finishes in the building. It was a demonstration of a community development corporation creating public housing as attractive as apartments on the private market.

At one point there was an instance of a misuse of funds by the Executive Director. Israel Feliciano had drawn funds from a discretionary account and had used them for a well-intentioned but unauthorized activity—support of a baseball league. It caused a scandal and led to his resignation and move out of the city. Several IBA directors left as well, and Helen Morton and I had to quiet the foundations and other supporters. A good part of the missing funds were recovered from the banks.

IBA's next project was Viviendas la Victoria I. This was a 181-apartment development. It framed the Plaza Betances, the large plaza with benches and extensive plantings in front of the elderly building. GBCD again demonstrated its ability to maximize the mortgage proceeds. Sharratt put an arcade along the plaza, but HUD would not allow the cost. I worked with Howard Humphreys, the FHA cost official, and got the costs included as non-attributable special items.

The project then encountered problems when the net worth general partner kicked up his heels and wanted a bigger fee. IBA sought to remove him. He counted with the threat of a suit. GBCD and Palmer and Dodge were instrumental in bringing the parties back together. The project was completed with the general partner's affiliate being the contractor. Community spaces were created along the plaza, plus a day care facility and an employment office. IBA was by now functioning as an important social agency.

The dynamics of the revitalization of economically distressed areas were becoming more dramatic as the 60s and 70s proceeded.

African-American and Latino groups were becoming stronger and more effective in dealing with government and private institutions. Resident groups were blocking highway projects, such as the Southwest Freeway through Roxbury, and residents were demanding jobs and employment on reconstruction projects. Hispanics were in greater numbers and were forming institutions and protest groups in their neighborhoods.

With urban renewal in difficulty, the federal government was looking for change. A program to provide funding at a low 1% rate was an important subsidy. The Nixon Administration attempted to gain support for its family allowance program, but it was defeated by the Congress. Nixon declared a moratorium on new federally supported housing in 1973. In 1974, the federal government started to provide community development block grants as a possible source of subsidiaries to developers and Section 8 rental assistance for low-income families. The idea of low-income families receiving a stipend to help them pay for rent goes back to the 1930s.

When the first housing certificates were proposed under FDR, there was a fear that payments to residents would be lost as profits to landlords. The idea had resurfaced in 1970 under the private leased housing program. The government decided to launch the largest social program to determine the trade-offs with respect to rental assistance. Were people moving into new areas to receive the subsidy? Would it help stimulate housing renovation? The results were that when families are displaced, they predominantly move in the same neighborhood with or without a certificate.

GBCD was a model of how a partnership between a community group and a technical developer might work. GBCD was contacted by the Community Action Program (CAP) in Gloucester. The CAP agency, which was doing a series of things including running a successful bus line, was looking to do something with the abandoned school in their downtown area. One of our staff had been a star football player at the Gloucester public high school and facilitated our way through the local political scene. St. Stephens Church in Lynn, Massachusetts, came to see us about the construction of a high rise building for the elderly. Another request came from a group of citizens who lived near America Park, a troubled, partially empty public housing development in Lynn. I had also been engaged with representatives from Lincoln who sought help in getting affordable housing in their town.

Our role in housing development and operation was largely set by the program and its funding. But the actors and the situations were different in each case. In Gloucester the housing sponsor was a community action agency. It was energetic and looking for things to do. The old high school was sitting there in the central area of town, vacant and in disrepair. The school building had opened in 1889. In 1924, an addition doubled its size, and in 1940, it was converted to a grammar school when the new high school was built. In 1971 the school department closed down the building because of inadequate mechanical systems. The building then passed into the hands of the Gloucester City Council, which began to consider alternative reuse proposals.

After rejecting a proposal from the Council for Aging, and after an advertisement for proposals nationwide in the New York Times, the City of Gloucester agreed to sell it to the local nonprofit community agency. Action Inc. would convert it into housing for the elderly. Action Inc. asked GBCD to become development consultant to assist it in organizing and financing the proposed recycling of the school. GBCD met with Action's principal staff members to discuss their housing objectives.

Since Action's goal of producing quality subsidized housing was consistent with GBCD's corporate objectives, GBCD agreed to participate. Our examination of the site and building revealed that it was structurally sound, that it had the potential to be successfully converted, and was well located for housing for the elderly. GBCD then prepared preliminary development and operating budgets, and submitted an initial application to MFHA on behalf of Action, Inc. In April 1973, MHFA approved the Central Grammar Apartments project.

In August 1973, GBCD prepared Action's detailed application to MHFA for a proposed $1.6 million project for 73 apartments. The project would be feasible if three conditions were met: (1) market rate rents for one-bedroom apartments were $169 and rents for two bedroom apartments were $199; (2) MHFA committed Chapter 13A interest reduction subsidies for a $1.6 million mortgage; and (3) the City of Gloucester agreed to charge Central Grammar Apartments 16% of its collected rents under a Section 121A tax agreement. MHFA approved the application, and in January 1974 the state interest subsidies were earmarked. Gloucester agreed to limit real estate taxes to 16% of rents in March.

Unfortunately, these financial arrangements did not last. Due to design changes, revised construction cost estimates and inflation, the proposed renovation costs grew by $175,000 during the next six months. A new financing scheme would be needed. First, the design of the building was altered to increase the number of apartments from 73 to 80 in order to reduce the average per unit construction and operating costs. Then GBCD approached both MHFA and the City of Gloucester with new financial alternatives to generate the additional $175,000 needed for construction. Both responded positively. MHFA agreed, based upon a market study prepared by Action, Inc. and GBCD, to increase the rents to $185 for one-bedroom apartments and $215 for two bedrooms. MHFA also increased the interest reduction subsidy from $72,400 to $95,800 per year. Together, these two changes would support only a $130,000 increase in rehabilitation costs. Finally, Gloucester agreed to reduce the real estate taxes from 16% to 14% of the collected rents. This meant an additional 2% of the rents, or $3,600 per year, would be available to cover debt service instead of taxes – enough to carry the debt on $45,000 of additional construction costs. Based on the City's new tax agreement, MHFA in October 1974 approved the required mortgage increase.

High ceilings were preserved. Oak wainscoting, oak strip flooring, wide corridors, exposed interior brick, oversized windows and generous community rooms were provided. By completing unfinished attic and basement areas, the gross building area suitable for apartments was increased from 54,000 to 72,500 square feet. By lowering window sills to create doorways, ground floor apartments were given direct access to private yards. In part of the building, the roof line was cut back to create large private balconies for apartments on the top floor. In other sections of the structure, duplexes were built into the attic space with living room and kitchen on one floor and bedrooms on the floor above. In fact, no two apartments are alike, a feature which helps make the project an exciting, non-institutional place to live. The Gloucester project was one to the first successful rehabs of a former school building in the state.

Our staff on the project included Clancy and Edward Marchant, a young Harvard Business School graduate. We had advertised for a position of project manager and Ed showed up. We reviewed his resume and conducted an interview late in the day, but had not made a decision. The next morning I received a call from Ed in which he told me he had read my book on the South End, had decided he wanted the job, and had obtained a Community Employment Training Allowance (CETA) to cover a large portion of his salary. My reply was to congratulate him and tell him that he had the job.

The same staff group was involved in the development of a ten-story apartment building for the elderly. Ron Garmey, President of the St. Stephens Congregation, had spoken with me and we had looked over the site in Lynn. St. Stephen's Church was three blocks away. We worked with Garmey and his group to gain approval by the city. Architect Stull & Associates were chosen and a ten-story structure with 130 units was designed. Financing of a 1% FHA-insured mortgage for forty years was obtained, and rent supplements and Section 8 units for portions of the occupants were received. Barkin Construction, the contractor, completed the project in 11 months. GBCD became the manager of the property.

One issue was that the mechanical room was located on the roof. This yielded an empty basement floor which in time was converted partially into community space. The project was syndicated successfully. One of the issues in any development is obtaining necessary funds for the preliminary design, legal and development work that is done up-front before the financing is closed and available. Boston had a number of sources for such money. One was the Episcopal Church, to which we applied and received a grant.

GBCD became involved in another important project in Lynn. Housing Opportunities, Inc., a civic housing group, became concerned with a distressed and partially vacant public housing development named America Park. They contacted GBCD and asked whether we could do a cost and benefit analysis of a major restructuring of America Park. GBCD saw the request as an opportunity to look at the complex series if issues involved in converting troubled state public housing into a more viable living situation. GBCD took the lead in gathering information to serve as the basis for a detailed study. Langely Keyes was the GBCD point-person on the report.

164

America Park was a 408-unit state-aided family public housing development in Lynn. It had one of the highest vacancy rates in the state. Seventy-seven empty apartments were in need of major rehabilitation before they could be re-rented, even though America Park was only twenty-two years old. A large proportion of families in America Park were dependent on welfare. The turnover rate was 26% to 30% percent.

Because of the high turnover rate, America Park had been pressed into service as a "regional housing resource." Tenant eligibility and screening had been relaxed. It was operating at a financial deficit. The 1970's was a time when the frustrations and anxieties of resident groups all over the country were boiling over. The residents of America Parks were tired of their isolation and the lack of attention to the obvious need for services.

A Fact Finding Committee was organized. It included three tenants from the development including Eleanor Atkins, Chair of the America Park Tenants' Association. Langley Keyes met with the Committee on June 20, 1972, and consensus was reached on the following matters: (1) the modernization program that was planned would be phased out and replaced by a new mixed-income development plan with supporting facilities; (2) there would be a guarantee to re-house residents; (3) the report on America Park would be the basis for analyzing alternative development approaches; and (4) the GBCD scope of services would focus on relocation, demolition, site design, character of construction, income mix, supporting private and public services, the development mechanism, land write-down, and the overall development mechanism and process. The path should be geared toward producing a development plan which could be implemented given the necessary funding and legal mandate.

With the report filed with the department, the work turned to the legislation that was needed. Speaker Tom McGee of Lynn was sympathetic. Keyes, with the help of Roger Evans of Ropes & Gray, worked with Speaker McGee on Chapter 884, the law amending the state public housing laws, to provide a mechanism for the sale of blighted state-aided public housing to a private developer for subsequent redevelopment into mixed-income housing. It authorized funding of relocation and re-housing expenses, paying off residual debt, and other miscellaneous expenses associated with the conversion of the housing.

Drafting the bill was not easy. A balance had to be struck between having the new law allow for the sale and demolition of existing housing that had been found to be substandard and deteriorated beyond repair and to replace it with a private mixed-income development. It must avoid being a mechanism for cities to dump their distressed public housing. The bill called for the conversion of state ownership to a private development which would be a joint venture between the tenant task force and a private developer. The project would contain one-third low-income, one-third moderate-income, and one-third market-rate families. Keyes went back and forth among the parties to make sure Eleanor Atkins, Don Wessell, and the task force members were all satisfied and still aboard. The bill was the cornerstone of the future community.

The next challenge was the financing. It was assumed that MHFA would provide the mortgage loan. Created in 1971, MHFA could provide a 7.5% loan to a private developer. There would also be available federal rental assistance subsidies that would pay the difference between the low-income and market rents. MHFA negotiated a role for the proposed developer who would manage the development with the residents after completion of construction. MHFA prepared a request for proposals under which a developer was chosen. In August 1974, the development firm of Corcoran, Mullins, Jennison, Inc. was selected by the American Park Associates, Department of

Community Affairs, Lynn Housing Authority, and MHFA to rebuild America Park. GBCD was active throughout the bidding period.

Negotiations on design solutions took patience and the ownership arrangements were difficult. The original architects were Sasaki & Associates. The residents differed with their approach. A new local architectural firm, Claude Miquelle, which had designed Corcoran's project at Queen Anne's Gate, was hired. There was also a zoning battle with the City of Lynn. It resulted in the developers reducing the number of units to 441 and eliminating all the five-, six-, and seven-bedroom units.

The City took umbrage at the tenant task force being a co-partner in the project. Action on the project, however, did not stop, and MHFA resolved the impasse between the developer and the tenant group as it took on the role of arbitrator. MHFA opened an office at the site to allows its designers to work out details with the residents. Eleanor Atkins was the first President of the residents' corporation. Langley Keyes, and later Ed Marchant, worked with them through the design process and construction period and into ownership.

The joint ownership and control of King's Lynne was an education for everyone, including Joe Corcoran and his associates, MHFA, the City of Lynn, and other developers. It led to the future work by the firm of restructuring the Columbia Point development in Boston, as well as other projects nationally.

On another occasion I received a call from Saundra Graham requesting that I accompany her to her meeting with the Harvard University Overseers. Saundra Graham was famous for her interrupting a Harvard University commencement several years earlier. She had grabbed a microphone and addressed the attendees, complaining about Harvard's site acquisition policies and lack of dealing with the residents from her neighborhood. It disturbed those present and put the University on notice that they would have to be careful in the future. She went on to become a city counselor and led the planning effort for the construction of housing in her neighborhood.

I agreed to go with her. I had never met Saundra Graham before but was aware of her present activities. I went over to her office, discussed the situation, and then we went over to a small two-story building in Harvard Square. The meeting was held in the second floor meeting room. Hugh Calkins, a Harvard Overseerer from Cleveland, met with us. Calkins was very cordial as he listened to Saundry's story. He then assured Saundra that he would relay her story to those in charge.

Several days later, Charles Daly called Saundra and invited her and her group to a dinner at the students' union. I was asked to attend, as was Sy Mintz of the law firm Mintz Levin, and the architects who had done some schematic work for the group. At the dinner Saundra and her associates made a presentation. Daly assured the group that he had heard the issues. I was appalled to learn later that he had called in Mintz the next day and berated him for encouraging the neighborhood representatives.

Harvard did respond in time and turned over a site to the residents for housing. We worked as a consultant on the project called the River Howard Townhouses. The initial management was handled by the local group, but problems arose and the management was turned over to the Cambridge Housing Authority, who were the actual owners of the project.

Finally, there was an interesting project in Lincoln, MA. Huson Jackson, architect and planner, and his wife Polly, were active players in housing efforts. Huson called me and asked that I come to a meeting in Cambridge. I went and learned of the effort people had been making in getting some affordable housing going in Lincoln. The Lincoln Foundation plan was to purchase part of the land from the Codman Estate and build a mixed-income development. From the beginning, the ownership of the development would be a cooperative, providing a way of giving the new people a stake in the town.

The cost of the land was not cheap. The Rural Land Foundation was an organization in which investors would put up $10,000 each and the aggregate fund was used for town projects. The price of the land for the cooperative was $309,000. It was the lower section of the land. The upper land was to be dedicated to saving the existing Codman Barn, the community gardens, and a commercial area. The plan called for citing the housing on the land near the street and using the balance for the septic system and open space.

Working with the Lincoln Foundation and its counsel, GBCD organized the cooperative's ownership and financial structure. Jackson prepared preliminary drawings which were presented to the town for a zoning approval. The design called for flat roofs that were controversial. After an hour or so of discussion, Cabot Lodge, who was a legend in Lincoln, made a plea for reconsideration. Senator Jimmie DeNomade, a person who had not been that helpful before, rose to the occasion and suggested the project proceed. At that point, representatives of the Lincoln Foundation hurriedly offered the agreement that the project go ahead but on the understanding that the design would have to be approved again when it was brought back for a building permit and final documents. The zoning vote was two to one in favor.

The project proceeded but with delays for design and construction revisions, in particular the design of the sewer treatment plant. The project was reviewed again and a final building permit was issued.

A mortgage loan application was approved by the MHFA and construction commenced.

We had an inspector who looked over the foundation work. There were questions about the design of the above-ground building structures and the contractor's performance. There were also issues that led to revisions in the sewer treatment plant. A change order was negotiated with the MHFA. The Lincoln Foundation decided to retain an independent construction manager to supervise the balance of the building construction work.

The sponsoring group determined that the owner be a nonprofit cooperative. Clancy and I, with the help of Roger Evans, wrote the cooperative book. The issues were to maintain equity between the residents even though there would be three levels of monthly charges. GBCD was to act as a housing authority since the town did not have one. The second tier was units which were to have state subsidies. The last group would be market-rate units for moderate-income residents. At the start of the project, the Charlesbank Foundation gave the project $100,000 toward the cost of the land. However, as I knew that the mortgage would cover the total land cost, I assigned the gift to a fund that could help some of the new members meet their equity requirements. This fund was later used for rent subsidies. This structure now has been incorporated in the deal under which The Community Builders (formerly GBCD) has taken back the development and converted it into a rental project.

Charlesbank made another grant to GBCD of $275,000 for seed money for a number of other projects. The original amount was to be invested in projects on an as-needed basis and then returned to GBCD. However, when Mr. Charles Waite, Director of the Charlesbank Foundation, saw the first report he realized that he was not in a position to make judgments about how the funds were being spent.

He called and told me to treat the fund as a grant to GBCD. It became a Charitable Trust Fund which exists today.

Throughout these years, GBCD demonstrated its ability to develop and manage a variety of housing in conjunction with local nonprofit organizations. Some provided a consultant fee and in others a share of syndication. proceeds. GBCD designed its contribution to range from carrying out specific development and management tasks to merely augmenting the sponsor's capacity. Its services might include:

- Assisting community sponsors in defining local housing needs and objectives
- Identifying suitable sites and negotiating for the acquisition of land and buildings
- Evaluating the reuse potential of existing buildings
- Identifying potential sources of seed money, construction loans, subsidies, and permanent mortgage and equity financing
- Project and asset management and resident services.

In time the local community development corporations that GBCD worked with either grew and developed their own skills to acquire and develop more units or they remained small and concentrated on resident services, limited asset management, and community planning. TDC and IBA were of the former category. TDC went on to own over three hundred and fifty units of housing. IBA currently has over four hundred units. Projects in Lynn and Gloucester remained local operations. The cooperative in Lincoln ran as a one-off development but in time the requirements with regard to the three income levels of the residents, the continuation of the state subsidies for a portion of the families, and the use of the reserves became too burdensome for a volunteer board of directors. By a vote of the members, the coop was terminated and the project sold back to The Community Builders to be operated as rental housing. Each member recovered the equity that they had accumulated.

My experience with cooperatives ended later when I served as the GBCD's consultant in the acquisition of their developments by the residents of Warren Gardens and St Marks. Both were developments that HUD had taken back because of the original owners failed financially. Residents of both developments had been interested in purchasing the properties as resident owned cooperatives.

In the case of Warren Gardens (WGRA), Paul Chan, the site manager for L E Smith Management Company, had made some repairs and was recommending that the residents be trained and allowed to acquire the property. I was employed under GBCD's contract to provide assistance to WGRA in all aspects of the conversion process including legal and organizational matters, sales and subscription programs, and an in-depth ownership/management training program upon acquisition. I spent the next three years meeting with WGRA, negotiating the terms of the sale, and how the sale and conversion would be achieved. The HUD processing was performed in HUD's Boston office, and a sales price of $746,000 was determined. We agreed and the package was sent to Washington for approval.

The first change that HUD-Washington made was for technical reasons, to adjust the amount of the mortgage to $872,300. To our surprise, the second change was to adjust the sales price to $2,447,100. This was a time when HUD was attempting to recover as much money on these deals as possible. They accomplished the increased amount by introducing a second mortgage in the amount of $1,483,100, with payments deferred for ten years, to recover potential appreciation. This was required by Mr. Roy Demon, a Special Assistant to the Assistant Secretary for Housing-Federal Housing Commissioner. Mr. Roy Demon had been on Nancy Reagan's campaign staff.

I was furious about the added mortgage. I took Betty Royston, President, and Sherry Smith, Vice President of WGRA, to Washington to argue our case. They turned down Mr. Demon's suggestion that they could make money on a $5,000 down-payment. They explained that their purpose was only to get good housing for their members. Later the Boston office advised the WGRA that the down-payments were reduced to the original amounts, but the second note remained. I complained but was told that the deal was the best we could get.

About a year after purchasing and occupying Warren Gardens, I wrote a ten-page letter to Maurice Barksdale, Assistant Secretary/ FHA Commissioner, challenging the second note. I pointed out the irregularities in the processing and the non-compliance with HUD regulations. I received a call from one of HUD's Assistant General Counsels, acknowledging their receipt of the letter and saying that they were working on a response. Shortly thereafter HUD ruled that the second note was improper and ordered that it be discharged.

In my years working with HUD officials, I have had good luck. I have never been turned down on a mortgage increase or failed to complete a project. Warren Gardens was close, but I did win in the end.

Chapter Six

Boston Housing Authority

Judge Paul Garrity, Chief Justice of the Housing Court of the City of Boston, had for a number of years heard cases involving complains by Boston Housing Authority tenants about their apartments. Finally, on February 7, 1975, Greater Boston Legal Services (GBLS) filed a class action complaint against the BHA in the name of Armando Perez and eight other residents. After hearings and inspection of apartments, the Judge, on March 28, 1975, issued his Findings, Rulings, Opinions and Orders in the Perez case. It stated:

"The facts as found above indicate beyond any doubt that the countless violations of the State Sanitary code exist in developments owned and operated by BHA... That the physical conditions existing in some, perhaps many, of BHA's apartments are so intolerable that relocation is immediately required, that unoccupied apartments filled with rubbish and garbage and uncovered incinerators constitute a present danger of fire and disease, and that serious crimes and the fear of it make the developments intolerably unsafe."

This was the start of Judge Garrity's nine-year ordeal to address with the help of an appointed Master and Receiver the ills of the Boston Housing Authority. It was an endeavor made more difficult by an indifferent mayor and a misguided Board of Commissioners. The responsible federal and state agencies were generally watching from the sidelines.

Shortly thereafter I received a call from Felix Vasquez, a friend from the South End, who worked at the Court. He told me that Judge Garrity was looking for a master or a receiver in the Perez case and had scheduled a hearing in the case. I attended the hearing. In his March 28, 1975 <u>Order,</u> Judge Garrity required that the BHA submit plans with respect to immediate actions that might be taken by the authority on an interim basis. The Court found BHA's responses to be entirely inadequate. The appointment of a receiver or a master was raised. GBLS asked me to meet with them, and after our meeting, they gave their approval should the Judge appointment me.

I met with the Judge and he told me that he did not want an organization such as GBCD but rather an individual. I agreed to give at least one day a week for a year with help from GBCD staff. Following consultations with the parties, the Judge by Order of Reference dated May 22, 1975 appointed me as Master, with the purpose of preparing an interim and a comprehensive long-range plan for the BHA and monitoring of same.

Judge Garrity's decision held the State of Massachusetts partially responsible for BHA's troubles, ordering it to provide funds. It was a gutsy move and characteristic of Judge Garrity. He was an activist judge. He saw the courts as a vehicle to address long-standing issues which were detrimental to the public welfare, particularly in cases where there was political indifference.

Garrity had worked at Harvard's Community Assistance Office and taught trial practice at Boston College and Northeastern Law Schools. He was active in establishing the Housing Court and became its first Chief Justice. The Housing Court, he thought, had an obligation to seek a remedy for the BHA's tenants. His decision led to the presumption that additional funds might be forthcoming. BHA saw the case as nothing more than a way to obtain more funding. Garrity's decision was not even mentioned in the minutes of the BHA board meeting following the decision. They saw no liability for poor management in the Judge's decision.

My legal friends suggested that serving as Master was a thankless task. But it appeared to me to befit the role of GBCD and I would have help from the staff as required. There was a complaint to the Judge that he should have appointed a person of color as a large percentage of people on the Authority's waiting list were minorities. The Judge responded with a firm letter of support for my appointment. With the help of Julius Bernstein, a former Chair of the Authority and a social legend in Boston, I retained Joanne Barbosa Ross as a consultant at the same day rate as myself. Joanne had been a remarkable resident leader at the famous Columbia Point development, BHA's largest. I spent the following weekend visiting every one of BHA 62 developments.

The Governor, Treasurer and State Department of Community Affairs (DCA) appealed Judge Garrity's decision and liability with respect to the State and DCA. The appeal was dismissed by the Supreme Court on July 19, 1975. The case was remanded to the Housing Court. The Supreme Court noted that:

> Nevertheless, further proceedings, despite the lack of availability of State funds as decided in this case, may result in appropriate orders against BHA related to the sanitary code. See G.L.C. 111. pg 127 H. Moreover, additional proceedings may well offer guidance and precedent for future cases involving not only mandatory action by BHA, but also discretionary action by the legislative and executive branches.

Discussions among the Judge, GBLS and myself led to continuing the case in order to responds to the legitimate complaints of the residents and in view of BHA's mismanagement which had been a matter of controversy for years.

I was a board member of Citizens Housing and Planning Association of Metropolitan Boston. CHAPA had been active in attempts for reform of the BRA. In August 1967, a coalition of public interest organizations led by CHPA sponsored a study of BHA which concluded, among other things, that:

> Many of Boston's housing projects (particularly those for the non-elderly) are in need of major or minor repairs, and in some instances wholesale remodeling. The quality of maintenance in most projects is far below acceptable standards.

> Hiring policies at the BHA remain essentially 'closed'... there is virtually no open recruitment, no attempt to seek out the best possible men and women for key administrative posts. Most Housing Authority's positions are regarded as being in the patronage category, to be filled by directive from City Hall... a spirit of professionalism is notably lacking.

> The "life tenure" system for Housing Authority employees, enacted in 1962, has led to severe personnel problems at the BHA. The system leads to poor work performance and inadequate supervisory mechanisms...

> The Housing Authority's present five-man board has failed to exercise imaginative and forceful leadership in introducing new forms of publicly assisted housing and adapting the program for changing conditions. It has also failed to make the necessary distinction between policy making and administration. Per diem compensation of the board members encourages excessive participation in the Authority's day-to-day business.

The first recommendation in the report was, in fact, to "improve the quality of appointments to the BHA board." Six years later another report published by CHAPA reached similar conclusions, including that:

All employees, except the administrator, qualify for tenure after five years of service... Political sponsorship provides an (sic) additional layer of security for many BHA employees. The reporting and accounting system should provide for better control of vacancies and rent rolls, accounts receivable and arrearages. Maintenance is one of the most critical problems of the Boston Housing Authority... The maintenance services of the Authority are inefficient, unevenly distributed among the developments and incomplete.

It was a classic story of a large housing authorities poorly managed, serving as the housing of last resort, flooded with urban renewal relocatees, the vast majority minorities and poor. The Brooke Amendment, named for the Senator of Massachusetts, was enacted in federal legislation in 1969. The amendment limited rent payments by families to a percentage of income, thereby drastically reducing rent receipts. The federal government failed to compensate with increased funding. Conditions in the developments across the country deteriorated and the "political" management of many authorities made the situation a national disgrace.

In 1972, HUD made a comprehensive consolidated management review of the BHA operations. This 200-page report, in which 70-staff members participated, made hundreds of recommendations. HUD determined and found among other things that the board did not restrict itself to establishing policy but rather became involved with the daily routine business of the BHA. Furthermore, supervision and disciplinarian action had been negatively affected in varying degrees by political and quasi-political considerations, and there were no annual performance evaluations of personnel.

With respect to the BHA's management of its fiscal affairs, HUD found that a lack of financial data had resulted in an almost complete breakdown of planning, controls and reporting. There was no procedure for the preparation of budgets, which were consistently late and of no value for budget control purposes. HUD found that housing managers were not responsible to maintain viable projects and did not know what they were expected to do. With respect to maintenance, HUD determined that because of low productivity, maintenance at the BHA "must presently still be adjudged poor in most major respects." HUD found that there will were excessive delays in the rehabilitation of vacant apartments which led to increased loss of rentals and vandalism and that BHA's security programs were fragmented. The review found that BHA's legal department was not providing a full range of legal services.

HUD made a second management review in 1976. It was even more critical of BHA's management and operation. It found, among other things, that the BHA lacked coherent processes for problem identification, planning, service delivery and control. The review determined that no change in personnel administration could occur as a result of "political" processes related to personnel selection, discipline and evaluation. It found that continuous, effective financial management in its broadest sense was non-existent. As in the 1972 review, several specific and organizational recommendations were made to the BHA by HUD.

The BHA, the fourth largest housing authority in the U.S., had built by 1954 fifteen federal projects for families with a total of 10,156 apartments. There were also 10 state-assisted projects for families with a total of 3, 681 apartments. By 1975, BHA also had twenty-six federally assisted and two state assisted project for the elderly with a total of 3,077 apartments and a leased housing program of about 3,500 apartments.

The BHA had approximate 700 permanent employees and an operating budget of more than $55 million per year. Less than one-quarter of its operating funds came from tenants rents; all the remainder being made up of subsidies provided by HUD and DCA. Over the years BHA had large waiting lists. Nineteen percent of the apartments in the family developments were vacant in 1975. Squatting was common. BHA had also been affected by the social trends of the 60's and 70's. In BHA's family developments, single-parent households had gone from 44% in 1969 to 72% in 1975. Households with no wage-earner increased from 65% to 79%.

For years the BHA had argued that the deplorable conditions in its developments and lack of services to the tenants was the fault of HUD and DCA because they did not provide adequate funds. The City chose not to take a position of responsibility even though four of the five BHA Commissioners are appointed by the Mayor. Mayor White, first elected in 1967, had his chosen administrator fired by the board over the a plan to hire a number of city employees for senior positions. The Mayor, in turn, brought misconduct charges against one, then another Commissioner who was removed by the City Council, only to be reinstated by the Supreme Judicial Court. After several years of tension, the Mayor selected and had appointed Samuel Thompson, Administrator. A former deputy director of Boston's Model Cities Program, Thompson was seen by some as ineffective. All of this reflected Mayor White's lack of interest in the Authority.

HUD and DCA both said that BHA's difficulties were a local matter, which is obviously inconsistent with the supervisory controls set out in their Annual Contributions Contracts with BHA and their myriad regulations.

The Authority had faced litigation on a number of fronts. Several cases preceded the Perez case in which tenants sought a remedy to the deplorable conditions. In 1970, several tenants in one of BHA's large state developments filed suit in the Superior Court seeking to have BHA and DCA maintain their development in compliance with the state sanitary code, which prescribes minimum standards of fitness for human habitation. The tenants argued that conditions in most apartments and common areas were below the standards. In affirming the Superior Court's dismissal of the Case, the Court ruled in part that:

> The case, as alleged......resembles those more commonplace situations in which courts have regularly resisted the temptation to substitute their initiative or judgment for that of agencies charge, as did defending agencies are here charged, with primarily responsibility for discretionary choices. West Broadway Task Force, Inc. et al. The. Commissioner of the Department of Community Affairs, et al, 363 Mass. 745. 751 – 2 (1973).

Another suit was brought by tenants in the U.S. District Court of Massachusetts. In an order dated October 20, 1974, dismissing the suit, the District Court Judge, while noting that "it is uncontroversial that the 15 low-cost housing projects are in a deplorable state of repairs," ruled that:

> One can only sympathize with the plight of the tenants residing in Boston's low income housing projects. The projects are mismanaged and in a poor state of repair. Yet the federal court cannot pretend to be the cure-all for America's housing ills. Federal courts lacked expertise, the staff, and the Congressional mandate to do the job. On the other hand, the housing court for the city of Boston has been established by state legislation, which is better suited to solve the enormous housing problems encountered by the tenants of Boston.
>
> Boston Public Housing Tenant's Council, Inc. v. Lynn, 388 F. Supp. 493, 498 (D. Mass 1974).

Over the years DCA had also been critical of BHA's operations, but had not been effective in dealing with the BHA's problems as it perceived them. In fact, there had developed an almost antagonistic relationship between DCA and the Authority, partly as a result of BHA's efforts to obtain more funding and modifications in DCA's regulations. The failure of the supervising agencies to fully acknowledge BHA's difficulties, some of which were related to their own regulations, and to follow-up in an effective and significant way on their own determinations, was a major factor in the eventual intervention by the Court.

My assignment to make plans with the Authority met a mixed response by the BHA staff. Some departments were cooperative and others not so. There were issues about access to information and the extent of our inquiries. GBLS also brought complaints to the Court about BHA's operations.

Prior to the issuance of my Masters report, the Court had issued some 24 orders. Primarily, they required limited but essential repairs in several BHA's developments. Secondarily, the reports responded to rises which occurred with regularity in BHA's operations. Performance by the BHA under these interim orders was in many cases unsatisfactory and the Court made a number of findings in this regard. At one point, the Court, in response to an appointment of an unqualified individual selected by City Hall to be Director on Management, issued an order that senior management position could only be filled with appointees approved by the Court.

One of the issues that plagued the BHA was its labor negotiations with its unions. There were jurisdictional arguments among the classes of workers. Also, union wage disputes would sometimes last for years and clearly interfere with labor relations.

BHA would make wage commitments which were subject to funding from HUD and DCA. Disputes were inevitable. On one occasion, BHA decided to make retroactive payments to the white collar staff which had not been authorized by HUD and DCA. I advised Administrator Thompson not to issue the payments until I had spoken with DCA. The Teamster Union protested the delay. In fact, Ralph Gilman, Secretary-Treasurer of the Teamster Union called my office and on my not being available, asked if I had any kids and if so, then threatened that "he is not going to have them."[31] After meeting the next morning with Secretary Flynn of the Department of Community Affairs and receiving some assurance about funding, I advised Thompson he could release the checks.

My five volume Masters report was submitted on July 1, 1976. It documented numerous findings including board and staff failures to provide leadership and direction, that BHA was in a perilous financial condition. The report gave specific, detailed recommendations for changing that many of BHA's administrative and maintenance procedures. For virtually every one of BHA's departments the report documented serious, long-standing problems which the board and Administrator had failed to resolve and described the staffing and organizational changes which would be needed to improve effectiveness and to better serve tenants.

Unfortunately, the board's response to the Master's report was to authorize its outside counsel to file various motions to seek a termination of the Court's decree and the Master's involvement in the BHA's operations. The tenants, represented by GBLS, who had initially requested the appointment of a receiver following Judge Garrity's initial decision in March 1975, countered BHA's motion by filing a motion for the appointment of a receiver. A hearing on the receivership motion was scheduled for the following September.

In the meantime, I had private discussions with Thompson who indicated that he supported reform and that he agreed with most of the recommendations that we had made in our report. After further meetings with BHA staff and attorneys and GBLS, it was agreed to allow BHA to draw up plans for approval by myself and the Court under which they would implement the report's recommendations.

I had extended conversations on a Saturday with Gary Ratner of GBLS. We discussed my refusal to support receivership at the time. He was not happy. I was of the opinion that with the Administrator by agreeing to institute reforms and in light of the history of under-funding by HUD and DCA, arguing for receivership at this juncture would be premature and hard to defend in court. I thought that we had to explore administrative remedies short of receivership. It may have been a misjudgment on my part in view of what happened later.

The receivership hearing was postponed and the parties, with the Court participating, then commenced negotiations on the terms of a consent decree. The negotiations, initially thought to take a month or six weeks, were protracted and difficult. BHA's counsel insisted upon negotiating each phrase and term of the 250-page document. Negotiations lasted six months. They required several hundred hours of the Judge's time, most of which he spent after working hours. The presumption of the Consent Decree was that if the BHA filled positions with highly qualified persons and made extensive revisions in its management and operating procedures as recommended, there would be improvements in BHA's management that eventually would pay off in improved conditions at the developments. The Consent Decree agreement was approved finally by the BHA board and signed on June 1, 1977.

The Consent Decree consisted of three principal sections. The first was the order and/or decree to recertify the tenants as a class, reap-

184

pointed the master, and provide certain periodic reports to the Court by the BHA and by the Master. The second section established procedural rules governing the rights and responsibilities of the Master, the BHA, the tenants, and the citywide tenants' council which had been allowed into the case in September 1975 as a plaintiff. The third section consisted of 13 plans which set out specific goals for various departmental activities. The plans required that the BHA develop in detail and then implement specific changes in BHA's organization, procedures and programs.

Under the terms of the agreement, the Master was to monitor, be informed and participate in the selection and hiring of senior staff. The agreement provided procedures under which disputes arising during the implementation of the Consent Decree were to be resolved by the parties and where necessary by the Court. However, adequate resolution of disputes proved to be elusive when determinations of the Master and Rulings of the Court were legally challenged by the BHA. The preamble in the agreement stated "it is understood that for this agreement to function successfully, there must be mutual cooperation of all parties hereto and the Master," and that differences were to be resolved in a cooperative fashion.

For many reasons, BHA's performance under the Consent Decree was mixed. Despite efforts to carry out the reforms called for in the Consent Decree, there were significant shortcomings. A number of positions were filled with qualified individuals both before and after the signing of the Consent Decree. Within the first year, new personnel procedures for hiring and promotions, a reorganized supervisory staff for field management, and new procedures for award of modernization contracts were developed and implemented. There were cases where BHA staff cooperated with my office and things got done. For example, John Murphy, Director of the Tenant Selection Department, worked with my staff, developed a new Tenant

Selection Plan, had it approved and implemented it. A new Budget Officer came in and initiated reform in the way BHA prepared its budget.

We had sought project-based budgeting and steps were underway to initiate it. Procedures for modernization work at the projects were reorganized and made more effective. One of the new people hired was Paul Merrill as Director of Management. I was instrumental in recruiting Paul. He was an experienced and skilled person who had had interesting housing management experience with University of Minnesota housing and in West Virginia. He came to work and soon had plans to restructure the management department. He set up district management teams and instituted a training program for district managers. His plans required modifications in the Consent Decree requirements which were approved.

Some of the existing senior staff were helpful. I consulted frequently with Deputy Director Neil Connors, who had been with the Authority for decades and knew existing personnel and practices. Leo Donovan, a patronage appointment of years ago and Director of Management, was a caring and admired person. I recall walking through the Columbia Point development with Leo and having residents on the third and fourth floors calling down to say hello to Leo, who had been the project manage years before.

The Consent Decree was explained to the staff but many did not fully understand its provisions. Lack of effective leadership and coordination from the top hurt staff performance. A lot of the staff were hardworking individuals who found themselves without direction and adequate supervision under difficult circumstances.

Four months after the Consent Decree was signed, Administrator Thompson resigned. This presented a real opportunity to bring in a new highly skilled administrator, much like the receiver that GBLS sought. One of GBLS's prime goals was to have a capable leader in charge. It was their contention that a highly skilled chief operating officer could make real improvements in BHA's operations if left alone by the board. Unfortunately, BHA responded to Thompson's leaving by taking the position that hiring a new administrator was not covered under the Consent Decree. The Court ruled otherwise, requiring that the procedures in the Consent Decree be followed. The process of hiring senior staff was that BHA would interview candidates, then select candidates they believed to be qualified, submit the names to the Master, who in turn would have to select at least two that he thought were "most qualified". BHA would then make their final selection from those selected by the Master.

The Administrator position was advertised and twelve candidates were interviewed. I was present at the interviews. BHA selected and submitted five names to the Master's office. I had made efforts to attract strong candidates. In an effort to attract strong candidates, I had made calls to people around the country, visited possible candidates and had encouraged some to apply. The latter included Harry Spence, formerly Administrator of the Somerville and the Cambridge housing authorities, and Robert Rigby, Administrator of the Jersey City Authority. Both were experienced and highly regarded in and out of the public housing sector. BHA's list submitted to me included Rigby but not Spence.

Not choosing Spence was shocking. I inquired of Commissioner Barbara Carpenter why and she said that the Globe had written an editorial suggesting that Spence was a great candidate and that the board did not want to be told what to do by the Globe. Also, their list did not include John Vitagliano, a well-respected individual politically active in East Boston, who was later to be City Hall's desperate final candidate for Administrator two months after the proceedings for receivership had begun. The BHA list included the Mayor's candidate who was a department head with no public housing experience.

The list included Robert Carey, a deputy administrator in San Francisco. He was supported by Commissioner John Connelly, who had been helpful and who I had consulted on a number of occasions. I made it my business to visit the Miami and San Francisco authorities where Carey had been or was employed and checked on Carey's references, and spoke to his former associates. I decided not to select Carey on the basis of what I discovered. My judgment was affirmed later by difficulties Carey had in San Francisco.

Another person on BHA's list was Bradley Biggs. Biggs was a remarkable individual. He was the first black US Army Officer in a Parachute Unit. He had been a professional football player before entering the Army. His Mother lived in Newark public housing. He was an acquaintance of John Eisenhower and a protégé of General James Gavin, the renowned Lt General of the 82 Airborne Division and Missile warfare. He had managed thousands of European housing units for the Services. He had the rank of Lt Colonel. He was for ten years the Administrative Dean of Middlesex Community College in Connecticut and later Deputy Commission of Public Works Department in Governor Thomas Meskill's Administration. Meskill had been appointed to the federal bench. I spoke to him at length, described my role and asked that he give me a frank appraisal. He gave Biggs high marks. Biggs was well liked by all his references as a very able and kind individual. In view of what I heard, I had no basis to disqualify him. I advised BHA that Biggs and Robert Rigby were my two selections.

At one point in the process BHA Board Chairman Pascuicco called me from Florida and offered to make a deal in which we could select the Administrator if they could have Kevin Feeley as Deputy Administrator. It was totally out of order. Feeley, a longtime associate of the Mayor, was appointed BHA Counsel in 1975. The Legal Department of BHA had a poor record, famous for mishandling tenant eviction cases.

After weeks of delay, in March 1978, the Judge lost patience, called a hearing, asked BHA for their decision. They said that they had selected Biggs. I had spoken to Biggs' references and all said they had not been contacted by BHA. Biggs had not heard of their decision. They did not choose Rigby, in part no doubt because I had interested Rigby in applying.

BHA invited Biggs to a 4:00 o'clock meeting that afternoon. As he described the meeting, no sooner had introductions been made than he was told that they had selected Kevin Feeley to be Deputy Administrator.[32] Biggs realized that this would be disputed by the parties. It was an ominous start and the beginning of his struggles with the board. A Feeley appointment as Deputy Administrator was disputed and this led to a protracted delay in filling the position as well as others.

Senior staff looked to Biggs for guidance but his plate was full with issues about his role. The disjointed relationship between Biggs and the board interfered with his ability to act decisively and that was troubling for the staff, particularly the new hires. Board members questioned his decisions and he had difficulties resolving personnel issues. For example, Merrill was proceeding with substantive personnel changes in the maintenance department to which a Board member objected. Merrill was annoyed and Biggs gave mixed support. At this point our monitoring role was an additional burden for Merrill. Biggs did his best but his directions became erratic as he attempted to please everyone.

Staff admired Biggs but saw his leadership as confused. Biggs was not a political operator and he had trouble sorting out the layers of patronage that existed within the staff. We were his primary supporters but that was considered by the board, Feeley and others was letting the Masters' office run the Authority. The tension between the board and Biggs made his job impossible and after six months on the job he decided to resign. This was in late September 1978. Over the ensuing months the agency suffered without effective leadership. Feeley served as acting Administrator but his authority was in dispute. Performance under the Consent Decree became lackluster and conditions at the developments deteriorated. Vacancies rose.

In my Report of July 5, 1978, I had cited "a growing concern that the Board of Commissioners of the Authority is not fully committed to carrying out the purposes and requirements of the Consent Decree and is not providing the necessary support to the new Administrator." With Bigg's resignation and an absence of effective leadership, there were substantial non-compliances with many of the requirements of the Consent Decree. On January 9, 1979 I reported the failures in progress under the Decree and noted that the tenants, as represented by Greater Boston Legal Services, had filed papers asking the Court to place BHA into general receivership.

The absence of an administrator became a critical matter. There were efforts on the part of the board, led by Barbara Carpenter and myself, to see if we could arrange for the filling the administrator position. I suggested Rigby and the board said they would not consider him. Several names were proposed but nothing materialized. After negotiations failed, the board agreed that a new search should occur. The position was advertised and BHA stated that they had some qualified candidates.

Interviews were scheduled for February 18 by the Board but did not happen. I protested the delay. A meeting then occurred at City

Hall attended by three board members at which a representative of
the Mayor's office proposed the name of John Vitagliano for Administrator. 32 On March 21, 1979, the board submitted Vitagliano
name as a single candidate. I met with Vitigliano. whom I regarded
as a competent individual, and we had a pleasant conversation. I
presumed that he had the Mayor's approval to apply. I pointed out
that the board had not followed procedures called for in the Decree
and that irregularities would not be allowed by GBLS or the Judge.
GBLS was looking for a Court-appointed, eminently qualified person found through a national search. The Judge saw all of this as
reckless behavior and in bad faith on the part of the board.

The Mayor made an additional effort in January 1979 to avoid receivership and have an administrator of his choosing. He appointed
a commission to review the BHA litigation. Its report was released
prematurely just three days before the hearing on receivership. The
commission opposed the hearings on receivership and stated that
they would have "disastrous results" on the BHA.

While indicating support for the Consent Decree and decrying the
absence of a permanent administrator, the report overlooked the
stated procedures in the Consent Decree to recruit and hire an administrator, procedures that BHA had disputed and then affirmed by
the Court. The commission did not meet with GBLS and the report
did not reflect their interest in having a "court-appointed" Receiver.
Later, when the Mayor was advised of Garrity's Receivership Order,
he said, "That's all right. He's got it. He can have it."

By the spring of 1979 my staff and I came to the conclusion that the
Consent Decree would not achieve the purposes set forth and it had
become unworkable. Preliminary meeting of the parties started in
January. This meeting was followed by Judge Garrity scheduling for
late-March the start of the proceedings on GBLS's motion to vacate
the Consent Decree as unworkable and appoint a Receiver.

Over the course of my four years as Master, I had come to appreciate the work of GBLS, their concern for their clients and their legal skills. Gary Ratner and Bruce Mohl at times were my legal advisors and defenders. Even so, I was unhappy to hear that they planned to present their case through my testimony.

The hearings commenced on March 26, 1979. I was on the stand for 16 days which is a long time for any witness. BHA's lawyers were argumentative but we all survived. BHA's counsel called just one witness. After a hearing lasting 34 days, Judge Garrity issued a 152-page opinion vacating the Consent Decree and ordering the appointment of a Receiver.

Judge Garrity found that the BHA had failed to meet many of the requirements of the Consent Decree. In particular, they had failed to meet its obligation to cooperate with the Master's office and that the Board of Commissioners had failed to provide leadership for the Authority. For example, the Consent Decree required that BHA prepared three-year financial plans to provide guidance in the preparation of its annual budgets. This was not done as specified. BHA also failed to implement an approved plan for project-based budgets and complete the reorganization giving managers responsibility for maintenance at their developments. The Authority was to revise its work-order procedures for security and prompt re-rental of vacant apartments. The plans that the Authority submitted to the Master and the parties were inadequate.

Judge Garrity found evidence that revealed the board's unwillingness to carry out compliance responsibilities. Incompetence and indifference to those obligations had directly and substantially contributed not only to BHA's failure to implement important provisions of the Consent Decree, but also to the unprecedented deterioration of the developments and the widespread violations of the sanitary code. "Throughout the four-year history of this case, the board has shown itself to be capable of nothing more than gross mismanagement. The unabated miss and nonfeasance of the board necessitates the extraordinary action of appointing a receiver in this case."

The Judge found that the board had failed to make policy, been ineffective in providing general direction for the administrator and staff, and failed to ensure that the Authority was meeting its legal obligations. Two board members who testified at the hearing indicated that they had not made any serious attempts to supervise such plans. One did not know what a fiscal year was, when it began, or how deficits were indicated on the balance sheet. Board members had little understanding or comprehension of BHA's budget and could not recall without difficulty a discussion of policy matters at board meetings.

Over the written objections of both HUD and DCA, the BHA board appealed Judge Garrity's decision, which was affirmed by unanimous opinions of the Supreme Judicial Court in February 1980. The Court's decision rested on its equitable powers to correct violations of law where they are committed by public officials or private individuals. Appointment of a receiver was seen as a last resort to provide the tenants with a remedy to which they were legally entitled.

From the summer of 1976 through the summer of 1979, the BHA, in addition to the costs of its legal staff involved in the case and the cost of the Master's office, spent over $500,000 in fees to its outside counsel. Throughout this period the supervising agencies found themselves funding BHA's defense against the Court's intervention and its attempt to reform the agency, as sought by the Master and as generally recommended by HUD itself. The regional office of HUD did not support receivership even though officials in Washington did. Throughout my time as Master, I had support and encouragement from Steven Coyle, Special Assistant to HUD Secretary Harris and Senator Edward Brooke. Washington staff indicated that when there was a resolution in the case, HUD would provide some additional funding. They had apprehensions about liabilities that might be inferred from a State Court's proceedings. After the receiver was appointed, HUD responded with special funding.

After the Receivership Orders of the Judge, I advertised the position, recruited applicants, processed applications and conducted interviews. After an exhaustive search with my staff's help, I made a selection and reviewed applicants with the Judge. He selected the individuals he wanted to interview. The final choice was Harry Spence. By Order on February 5, 1980, Harry was made the Receiver.

Harry Spence was an articulate, thoughtful, skilled person who had a very good run as the Receiver. Spence moved rapidly in taking charge. There was no board to interfere. The Judge had ordered that the board or any of its individual members, shall not "assume or exercise any authority" over BHA funds, matters, etc.; "shall not meet..."; and shall move out of their offices. They were not to direct any employee or receive any compensation. Spence hired an entirely new set of senior officers and put in place new personnel procedures.

Accomplishments under the Receivership were many: getting control over vacancies; major redevelopment of projects; improved delivery of maintenance services; improved management and implementation of modernization programs; better fiscal management and planning; instituting an effective tenant selection plan; and with the help of foundation funds, improved relations with residents and increased participation of residents through their own organizations. He was well received and admired.

Spence received little help from the Mayor at first, but things improved over time. He addressed security and got some help from the city and from HUD. He served four years. Raymond Flynn became Mayor in 1983, and Garrity terminated the Receivership. On November 13, 1984, the Mayor had full authority over the BHA.

One of the contributions of the Perez case was to put Harry Spence in the role of a national spokesman for public housing. Harry was the key in CHAPA's sponsoring the incorporation of the Council of Large Public Housing Authorities (CLPHA). The larger urban authorities were operating in a very different world than the more numerous small authorities. CLPHA became a force in assisting the Congress and HUD in fashioning programs for the large authorities. Gordon Cavanaugh, CLPHA's counsel, with a long experience in government assisted housing, was remarkably successful in making the case for well managed public housing. The Reagan Administration had proposed slashing operating funds, and CLPHA saved the day. There were times when a Congressional staffer wanted to know something about public housing. If asked, HUD would want money for a multi-year study. With a call to CLPHA, they would have information in a day or two.

One of the by-products of Spence's successful receivership was that it produced a number of skilled officials, like David Gilmore and Jeff Lines. Upon finishing at BHA, each went on to be appointed receivers for HUD in other cities. While the Perez case reflects on generic problems with public housing, it should not be seen as an indictment of whole the system. The case was an effort to save critically needed housing in which almost 10% of the people Boston lived. Inadequate funding was a factor, but leadership and sound public management were key issues following years of political abuse. BHA failed because of a lack of effective leadership. There was also political neglect at the local, state and federal levels.

Judge Benjamin Kaplan, who wrote the opinion for the Supreme Judicial Court affirming Judge Garrity, noted the difficulty posed by inadequate resources. He expressed the hope "that the government sources which furnish funding, as well as those which provide services, will be sensitive to these consequences and give all feasible help to the receivership." US District Court had said early in its 1974 decision on the tenants' action for more funding, "In the last analysis, a long-range answer can best be provided by political branches of government." It is they who have the resources, the duty, and the power to make significant changes in the field of housing." Notwithstanding the issue of money, Judge Kaplan also noted, "A receivership ought to be able to do a better job with the funds that become available than has been done by BHA in the past."

The Perez case was a milestone and constituted a message to any local public agency operating contrary to law, and any that repeatedly fail to serve its customers because of an absence of leadership, ineptitude, or political stalemate. While continued short funding had a corrosive effect on the BHA, there were other housing authorities in the US, such as Cambridge, Massachusetts, and Saint Paul, Minnesota, that performed well even under limited funding. Continued strong and effective leadership was crucial. There can be little doubt but that my experience in the Perez case confirmed my apprehensions about public enterprise that is prone to abuse in an indifferent political environment.

I also had the satisfaction of working again with a great group of younger people. Dan Sullivan, our counsel and a brilliant lawyer, accepted my friend Rudy Kass's practice on his elevation to the Court of Appeals; Louise Elving, my key staff person from beginning to end, and Mat Thall went on to successful careers in housing and community development; and Joel Kershner in employment services. Sandra Henriquez, a wonderfully capable and personable individual, whom I hired when the BHA didn't, served with Spence for a few years and later returned for a successful 16-year run as the Administrator at BHA. She was appointed HUD Assistant Secretary for Public and Indian Housing in the Obama Administration.

My work with the Court did bias my view as to whether government owned and developed housing was the most beneficial way to meet housing needs. The regulatory restraints in government programs impede initiative and high performance. Leadership turnover and absences occur, and they harm the enterprise in so many ways. Some European countries have made a decision to convert much of their public or municipal housing to private nonprofit ownership. That is a relevant choice today for the US. I was glad to return to nonprofit settings when I took a job with the Boston Housing Partnership three years later.

Whittlesey and William Edgerly

Mayor Raymond Flynn, Whittlesey, Joan Divers of the Hyams Trust

198

Beth Smith, Hyams Trust, Whittlesey, Anna Faith Jones of the BHP.

*Master's staff including Astrid Calderone, Ann Kerrey, James Luckett, Ana Boyd,
Reggie Nunnally and Whittlesey*

Whittlesey and Edgerly visit Park Street residents

Chapter Seven

Boston Housing Partnership –
with the banks and corporations as partners

At a chance meeting, Pat Clancy told me that Mr. Edgerly of the State Street Bank was looking for a Director for the Boston Housing Partnership (BHP). I called him to set up an appointment and went to see him.

We discussed his goals for the BHP, and I briefly outlined my experience, both working in the neighborhoods with CDCs and as a developer of federally subsidized housing. I had not read the ad for the position nor submitted a resume, but it became clear that Mr. Edgerly saw my experience as fitting the job. I was tremendously impressed with Mr. Edgerly's clear commitment to the success of the Partnership and the special role he would play. At the close of the meeting Mr. Edgerly said that he was scheduled to make a speech at Boston University the next day and invited me to attend. I did show up. He met me at the steps of the building and introduced me to his acquaintances as his friend. I can say that from that moment on we had a wonderful working partnership.

Bill Edgerly was an immensely successful business executive. He had joined the board of the State Street Bank and Trust Company as an outside director from the Cabot Corporation. He was selected to be the Chief Executive Officer in 1977. Between the time of his appointment and his starting the Partnership, the Bank had made remarkable progress.

He also had a real commitment to corporate citizenship and the role that corporations play in the community in which they were located. He invited several hundred business and civic individuals to take part in the first meeting of the Goals for Boston. It was a diverse gathering, including city officials, neighborhood activists, corporate executives, ministers, college professors and citizens. The meeting was designed to stimulate a joint attack on the city's problems.

Goals for Boston had four target areas: education, employment, housing and race. The impression was growing that Boston was on an upswing. The city was emerging from a decade of doubt and conflict, with new jobs and new aspirations. Model partnerships were being created to deal with such basic urban issues such as education and job training. Mr. Edgerly had for several years been associated with the Community for Economic Development (CED) and its experience with public/private partnerships in which the corporate community provided leadership.

The 1970s were a decade in which corporate America turned its attention to rebuilding cities and neighborhoods. In 1972 the Congress enacted legislation to create the Neighborhood Reinvestment Corporation; its purpose was to rebuild neighborhoods one at a time with the help of local financial institutions. The Carter Administration set up a Neighborhoods Division within HUD and provided funds. In 1978 Congress passed the Community Reinvestment Act which called on financial institutions to reinvest in urban areas where they had been active and had received deposits.

CED and other research institutions were identifying areas in which public/private corporations might be effective. Urban renewal had contemplated land clearance and new construction, but the program had not been very effective in economically declining areas of cities, particularly near downtown areas. The settlement houses and other nongovernmental organizations, the universities and urban institutions such as hospitals and churches, were each considering their role in revitalizing distressed areas. There were active business executives working in the fields of education and employment. An outstanding example of the latter was Boston's jobs program. There were leaders who had worked for years on the issues of race and diversity.

Affordable housing in Boston had a great variety of advocates from the Archdiocese of Boston and other religious organizations, from the universities, and from the professions. There was, however, little coordination from the business community. Mr. Edgerly decided to take a leading role for himself if he could get the participation of the other leading commercial banks. He asked them to participate and they agreed. The board of the Boston Housing Partnership had representatives not only from the banks but also the insurance companies, universities, professions, social agencies, real estate and otherwise. It was a strong group which would clearly have the respect of the Boston community

At that first meeting of the business group, Goals for Boston, there was a common concern about deteriorating housing in Boston. There was an interest in defining achievable goals for the BHP as targets for the next five years. Participants saw that in strong market areas of the city, lower-cost rental housing was being lost to higher priced condominium conversions, while in weak market areas lower-cost rental was being lost to abandonment.

There was widespread concern that the number of buildings being abandoned each year was rising. However, there was no effective program to address the issue given the complex economic pressures involved. During the previous decade some 20,000 housing units were abandoned. Public funds were used to demolish over 10,000 of these. With the elimination of deep subsidy housing programs by the Reagan Administration, the largest public catalyst to intervene was gone. There was no way economically to reverse the process without a coordinated public and private effort.

My first task as Director was to visit with the chief executives of the other three major commercial banks that had joined Mr. Edgerly. I found them all to be enthusiastic participants who were ready to offer the help of their staffs and resources to make the Partnership successful. The BHP was incorporated as a 501(c)(3) early in 1983.

Our goals of the Partnership were to:
(1) Promote, organize and manage programs that can salvage declining and abandoned housing and convert it into decent, affordable housing for low and moderate income families;
(2) Mobilize funding and other resources from the business community, government agencies and neighborhood-based organizations so that the public and private sectors attack housing problems jointly
(3) Identify and implement effective methods of interrupting the cycle of decay and abandonment so that Boston's housing stock is preserved.

From my point of view, I added four additional goals that reflected Mr. Edgerly wishes. The first was to demonstrate that even under adverse circumstances, BHP partnership had the capability of successfully completing programs; second, we would enhance the capability and financial strength of the neighborhood organizations with whom we were engaged; third, BHP would undertake programs of scale which are clearly above what individual neighborhood organizations could accomplish singly; and fourth, we would operate a public/private partnership that could serve as a model for a national program.

The initial discussions about the BHP called for linking together the city government, Boston-based financial institutions, state agencies, and a variety of community organizations. It was felt that this new collaborative organization could then harness the resources and experience of all parties involved to develop strategies and programs to combat disinvestment and decay. The Boston Housing Partnership was conceived as an action organization that would figure out how to intervene in local housing markets in order to retain or, where needed, re-create affordable housing for low-income people since they are the households most likely to be displaced.

Initial funding for the Partnership included a $200,000 grant from the Permanent Charity Fund of Boston (now the Boston Foundation), a commitment of $1 million of Community Development Block Grant funds from the city, as well as grants from the Heinz trusts, the Ruddy Foundation, the Public Welfare Foundation of Washington DC, and Local Initiatives Support Corporation. The grant of CDBG funds was especially fortuitous. The NAACP had a suit pending against the city in which it argued that federal block grants funds had been administered improperly. Mayor White saw the grant to the Partnership as being widely dispersed among the neighborhoods and supportive of local organizations.

When I came aboard, the BHP had retained Greater Boston Community Development to assist it in designing a development program and obtaining mortgage and equity financing. I welcomed the opportunity to work with my former colleagues whom I enjoyed and in whom I had great confidence. After some discussions among the members and consultants, it we decided that the initial program would be a renovation program carried out by the nonprofit community development corporations (CDCs).

A Request for Proposals was prepared by the consultants and distributed to the CDCs with a request that they submit proposals for the renovation of buildings in their neighborhoods. One of my first jobs was to select the proposals that were feasible and met our specifications. Among these requirements were that the buildings have clear titles and be available for purchase, that the renovations were necessary, that they could be feasibility rehabbed, and that there was a successful operating plan for the buildings.

There were questions about the capacity of the neighborhood organizations. I employed Robert Kuehn, a consultant, with a wide experience with rehabilitation and a knowledge of the CDCs and their background to help with the evaluations. We set up a committee, viewed the buildings, examined the proposals and made a selection. All of the various available funding sources were employed in the proposals, and we had to make determinations as to whether the funding agents would approve each project.

To everyone's surprise 14 solid proposals were submitted from neighborhood organizations throughout the city. After interviews with each of the 14 community development group, ten projects with 700 per unit were chosen. The total costs of the program exceeded $39 million. Funding for development of these 700 units came from 20 different financing sources, including: $4.5 million from city in CDBG funds; $700,000 from foundation grants and corporate contributions; $23 million in first mortgage loans financing from the Massachusetts Housing Finance Agency; and $10 million of equity financing.

BHP I, as it was called, had a special MHFA bond issue. Some of the units were financed with the SHARP program, which had recently been enacted by the Massachusetts legislature and administered by MHFA. SHARP provided rental subsidies to qualified developments. The state had committed 200 such subsidies to BHP I, and 250 units of federal Section 8 Moderate Rehabilitation subsidies were applied for and received after a visit to HUD in Washington.

Board meetings of BHP were both productive and informative. Mr. Edgerly ensured that the agendas would be well organized. and that meetings would start on time at 8:30 am and finished at 10:00 am. All the members of the board were committed individuals. For the most part they had to familiarize themselves and understand the complexities of housing finance and work in the neighborhoods.

I had included in the board meeting agendas presentations by the individual CDC directors so that the members could better understand the difficulties the CDCs were encountering in negotiating the purchase and then managing distressed, sometimes occupied buildings. The buildings were rife with burglaries and drugs. I recall the day when Jim Luckett of Dorchester Bay Community Development described how a gang had occupied one of his buildings, bypassed the gas meters with garden hoses, and made the place comfortable with heat from the stoves. In some cases it was better to have some squatters in occupancy rather than have the building be totally vacant.

Buying property in distressed neighborhoods is not easy when one has to convince a rational seller or a rascal landlord to finally give up on a property. One needs to make a quick purchase. I was able as Director to facilitate some of these acquisitions with my lines of credit with the banks. In one case I put up $440,000 to purchase several buildings on a 24-hour notice. After spending years gathering resources for single, federally-assisted housing projects, it was a distinct pleasure working with aggregated resources. It was also comforting when we had received syndication proceeds sufficient to repay the $4.5 million bridge loan from the city.

There were difficulties with tax syndications. The general partner in the BHP-1 failed, and the Partnership had to negotiate with the Limited Partners on how to proceed. There is no guarantee that the tax laws enabling syndication are permanent. In 1986, for example, there were substantial changes made to federal taxes laws and the introduction of the Low Income Housing Tax Credit was created.

BHP allocated funds to make each project financially feasible. These funds included the federal block grant awarded to the city. The BHP allocations were made in a transparent manner and encountered a minimum of dispute and controversy. This feature of our financing led me to look at the funding of the nonprofit housing associations in the UK. Each CDC in our programs looked to one source for funding. It became a model for the country.

BHP and the banks and investors associated with it were the funders for the program. While we had difficulty assembling the necessary funds, the program did serve as a single source of financing for the CDCs. It was an attempt to consolidate funding in the hands of a major financial institution and thereby relieve the undercapitalized CDC of the task.

There were questions at the time about the complexity of the transaction. Fitting a variety of loans and grants together was both time-consuming and costly. It stood in contrast to the much simpler federal funding of public housing for families and elderly housing. Public housing has had single-source financing from the federal government from the beginning and there was a HUD program for the elderly under which a nonprofit developer received a capital grant. BHP's programs were more complicated than most as we put ten CDC-owned developments within one financing structure.

FHA insurance meant non-recourse loans. The owners of the project were not personally liable. If the property defaulted on the loan. FHA could go after title to the property, and not the assets of the owner. In many cases, by the time FHA took the property, it had serious issues in both management and physical condition.

In 1987 BHP II was undertaken. It called for the renovation of over 900 apartments in the HUD-foreclosed Granite properties in Roxbury and North Dorchester neighborhoods. With Bill Edgerly as the salesperson, twelve Boston companies invested a total of $16 million of equity. The city committed $1.7 million of interim financing and $3.3 million of linkage funds as a reserve for the program.

MHFA sold $55 million of bonds to provide mortgage loans. After their experience with BHP II, MFHA later undertook a demonstration program involving another 2000 units of similar housing several years later.

The last program that Bill Edgerly and I had a hand in was a group of cooperative apartment projects undertaken by five community development corporations. The processing was lengthy but ultimately successful.

BHP became aware that as construction of individual projects was completed, the job of management and residents services had to begin. We provided funds for the CDCs to organize and train residents in management and services that the resident families needed.

BHP was a model public/private partnership in its demonstration of a business community working with government and neighborhood organizations. It took on the task of being an intermediary. BHP never did any development in its own name, in part because the Boston area was blessed to have experienced and active private and public developers. Led by Bill Edgerly, we introduced tax credit equity to the banks of Boston. For example, David Spina, Vice President of the State Street Bank, had made a presentation to the board and been helpful in selling equity interests to the individual banks. He could take a complex financial transaction, break it down into parts and explain how it went together. He used these skills when he became the first Chairman of the Massachusetts Housing Investment Corporation (MHIC). MHIC had been formed in 1990 by a consortium of banks to address the equity needs of affordable housing developers. Its purposes were to finance quality affordable housing, to supplement financing available from other sources and to aggregate and coordinate the use of public and private resources. MHIC had taken over a role that had previously been played by BHP. In 1991 BHP and the Massachusetts Housing Incorporation (MHI) merged to form the Metropolitan Boston Housing Partnership (MBHP). It was the Boston piece of the network of regional nonprofit housing agencies. The merger occurred when BHP was adjusting to the fact that some of its central functions were being performed in separate agencies. It had over 5,000 scattered Section 8 units in the 34 towns around Boston. MBHP focused on leased housing. Christopher Morris is now President and CEO of the organization and doing a wonderful job. He is dealing with many landlords and working with the state trying to solve the problem of homelessness.

The State Street Bank along with a number of other corporations and institutions remain key supporters and funders of MBHP. It has played an important role in a variety of housing issues from foreclosure prevention to homelessness.

Whittlesey with Mark Willis, Kirsten Moy, Michael Lappan and others

Jon Zimmer, former Executive Director of Action/Housing, with Dennis Yablonski, Secretary of Community and Economic Development, Pennsylvania State government, and Regional Director Ellen Knight

Larry Swamson and staff at Pittsburgh Green House Opening

Joseph Errigo at Advantage Center planting

212

Rick Kupchella, Shirley Land, Joseph Errigo, Paul Fate

Father Michael Groden

St. Aidan in Brookline, a 59 unit mixed-income and mixed-tenure development

Tina Brooks, Tom Gleason (MFHA), Cardinal O'Malley, Congressman Barney Frank, Lisa Alberghini, Bob Allen, Bob Gallen, President of Mass Bank of America, and Michael Jesse, President & CEO, Federal Home Loan Bank of Boston.

Carol Lamberg, Settlement Fund in New York City

New Settlement Community Center in New York City

Patricia Garrett, formerly President & CEO, Charlotte Housing Partnership

Donald Terner, initial CEO of BRIDGE , and Alan Stein, Chairman of the Board

216

BRIDGE's Pickleweed Housing

*Cynthia Parker, President & CEO, BRIDGE with staff at Ribbon Cutting of AL TA Torre,
56 unit development*

Carol Galante, former head of BRIDGE and now FHA Commissioner and Assistance Secretary of HUD, Jeffery Hayward, Vice President Fannie Mae, Lamar Seats, CEO, Bellwether Enterprise, and Hunter Johnson, President & CEO, LINC Housing

Congressman Kurt Schrader; Dee Walsh, REACH's former CEO and now a Vice President with HPN; Nick Fish City of Portland Commissioner; and Margaret Van Vliet, Director of the Portland Housing Bureau, all at the groundbreaking of the 209 unit Gray's Landing development.

218

Janaka Casper, President of Community Partners, and Elisabeth Willis,Housing and Community Development Project Manager, Town of Blacksburg, Virginia

William Perkins, formerly Head of the Wisconsin Housing Partnership and former Chairman of the Housing Partnership Network.

Amy Anthony, President and CEO of POAH, speaking at RibbonCutting with Chicago Mayor Rahm Emanuel, HUD Secretary Shaun Donovan, Alderman Willie Cochran, Congressman Bobby Rush, and U.S. Senator Richard Durbin.

Graduation at The Community Builders' facility at Plumley Village Apartments

Chapter Eight

Public/Private Partnerships – of all kinds

My busy years as Director of the Boston Housing Partnership allowed me only limited opportunities to learn about what other public/private housing partnerships in other regions of the country were doing. I did have speaking engagements in a few cities but these were generally in and out occasions.

I received a call one day from my friend Jan Jaffe of the Ford Foundation. She asked me if I would like to join a small group on a cross-country trip to look at public/private housing partnerships. She said Kirsten Moy of the Equitable Corporation was arranging the trip. I agreed, and we went in February 1988 to visit BRIDGE in San Francisco, McCormack Baron in St. Louis, and BHP in Boston. The group included, addition to Kirsten, Michael Lappan of Community Preservation Corporation in New York City, Mark Willis, then with the City of New York and Diane Suchman of the Urban Land Institute.

It was a successful learning experience and Lappan and Willis were interesting companions. We reconvened several months later at the Ford Foundation's office in New York. Questions came up as to how many and what sort of organizations like the Boston Housing Partnership and BRIDGE actually existed in the country. I agreed that with a small grant I could survey a number of cities and see about convening interested parties at a conference in Boston.

In the following year I visited some 25 cities. In each city I met representatives from any public/private housing partnership that existed as well as representatives from the banking and foundation communities, local government and neighborhood organizations. On the basis of these contacts, I sent out 175 invitations and got 135 individuals to attend a meeting in Boston in February 1990.

Participants welcomed the opportunity to discuss matters of common interest. They expressed enthusiasm for further meetings. This led to annual meetings in different cities that I organized with the help of the local partnership and a paid conference coordinator. I incorporated the National Association of Housing Partnerships in 1992 with pro-bono assistance from John Bok and his Associate Paul Feinberg at Foley, Hoag & Eliot.

There was a misunderstanding by the Internal Revenue Service that initially awarded NAHP determination as a 501©(6) trade association. On a resubmission with a more complete explanation of what the local partnerships were, we obtained a ruling that NAHP was in fact a charitable organization pursuant to Section 501©3 of the IRS code.

I managed the affairs of the National Association of Housing Partnerships over the next six years, holding annual meetings, collecting membership dues and publishing a catalogue of members with information on each organization. This allowed me to identify the members without formal criteria. NAHP grew over the first five years from twenty-six to more than fifty members. The Ford Foundation provided a second year grant and Fannie Mae provided modest grants to HPN and some of its members. I received particular help from the officers like Bill Perkins, head of the Wisconsin Partnership for Housing Development and Tom Bledsoe, Treasurer, who had become head of the Metropolitan Boston Housing Partnership (MBHP). Legal assistance from David Feinberg, staff work from Manuel Muelle on a counseling award, and bookkeeping assistance from the MBHP were helpful. The members of NAHP were all locally initiated nonprofit organizations, each of which was distinctly different depending on how it was established and programmed. Americans have the genius to invents things and create organizations for any and all sort of reasons. Public/private housing partnerships were created by a variety of people and initiated under a variety of circumstances. Some banks and financial institutions reacted to incentives under the Community Reinvestment Act, and others were motivated to be good corporate citizens. Support from corporations and foundations were crucial.

There were agencies started by the Neighborhood Reinvestment Corporation, Local Initiative Support Corporation (LISC) and the Enterprise Foundation. By the nineteen eighties, it was apparent that many banks and other financial institutions were ready to join efforts to address the redevelopment of cities, and they were looking for a vehicle in which they could participate. A public/ private partnership was a good answer. Some of the partnerships were the work of one or several individuals who managed to attract the necessary help and funds to launch an on-going sustainable organization.

The NAHP changed its name in 2002 to the Housing Partnership Network (HPN). Its members are high performing, mission driven organizations well established in their communities and regarded as credit worthy by local financial institutions. Each is unique. Some of these organizations are described below to indicate the range of differences in originators, missions and accomplishments.

Phipps Houses

Phipps Houses, is New York City's largest non-profit affordable housing developer, and the oldest member of HPN. It was formed in 1905 with a $1 million investment from Henry Phipps. Phipps, born in 1839, came to Philadelphia from England as a shoemaker. As a child, he came to know Andrew Carnegie and in time became Carnegie's business partner. He made major investments and philanthropic grants to institutions in both Pittsburgh and New York. Phipps Houses is a multi-faceted real estate organization. It is involved in the construction of new housing, rehabilitation of existing apartment buildings, and management of both residential and commercial property management in and around New York City. It has a non-profit subsidiary that provides human services for residents and a for-profit management Throughout its history, Phipps has developed nearly 6,000 affordable apartments, and currently has over 13,000 units under management.

Phipps Houses has a strong and well-connected board of directors. Ronay Menschel, has been President and CEO and is now chair of the board. She was formerly a Deputy Mayor and Executive Administrator of New York City. She has served on numerous prominent boards and commissions, including the Metropolitan Transportation Authority and the Federal Reserve Bank of New York. She has served as a Trustee of Cornell University for twelve years. Adam Weinstein, who joined Phipps House in 1989, has been President and CEO since 2001. He oversees more than 50 corporate entities and a staff of 1,000 employees.

Phipps Community Development Corporation, Phipps's human services subsidiary, serves 8000 children, teens and adults in more than 40 programs, on-site and neighborhood based. They include Head Start, youth programs, literacy and college preparation, work training and family support programs. Phipps opened in 2008 New York's first Financial Empowerment Center offering free financial counseling, a partnership that was funded initially by the insurance industry. Phipps sees its social and educational services as primary components in fulfilling its mission.

ACTION-Housing

ACTION-Housing in Pittsburgh is another early public/private housing partnership. It was not a member of the network in the initial years, but I knew them and kept them involved in our annual conferences. ACTION-Housing's history starts a few years earlier than SECD. Its creation was led by banking and city officials. A predecessor agency, the Pittsburgh Housing Association, had been trying to address housing issues since 1928 with little to show for its efforts. The new organization with its more substantial business and political backing was expected to make a real difference in producing needed housing and improving neighborhoods.

The history of ACTION-Housing stem from World War II when Pittsburgh served as America's workhorse, producing most of the steel needed for construction of the planes, battleships, tanks, artillery, rifles and other armaments that were used to defeat the Axis powers. When the war ended in 1945, Pittsburgh was in terrible shape environmently. The skies were black from soot and smoke, and the rivers were filled with industrial pollution. Economically, downtown property values were collapsing, major business leaders were making plans to move their companies to other cities, and housing conditions were among the worst in the nation.

In response to this crisis, two enlightened leaders, Mayor David L. Lawrence, a Democrat, and Richard King Mellon, the City's most prominent businessman, a Republican, joined forces to launch the renowned Pittsburgh Renaissance. Through their highly-effective public/private partnership, guided by the newly formed Allegheny Conference on Community Development, the city's skies were eventually cleared of smoke, the rivers were cleaned and a new lock and dam system was built to prevent future flooding in the downtown area. Most important of all, the nation's first major urban renewal project was implemented in Pittsburgh's central business district. It led to the development of Point State Park at the convergence of the Three Rivers and the construction of Gateway Center, a modern office and commercial complex.

As the physical redevelopment of the city proceeded, it became increasingly apparent that Pittsburgh's Renaissance needed a new vehicle to address the community's critical housing problems and neighborhood needs. On May 22, 1957, Mayor Lawrence announced the formation of ACTION-Housing. In describing the private, non-profit organization, he noted, "we are now getting the renaissance out of the glamour stage and into a down-to earth problems". At ACTION-Housing's second annual meeting in 1958, Richard King Mellon said: "I believe an urban center, such as Pittsburgh, does not achieve true greatness until its people are well housed – regardless of how many new office towers, expressways and industrial plants are built."

ACTION-Housing has always had strong relationships with the City of Pittsburgh and its business community. Richard King Mellon was a Director and the Assistant to the President of the Mellon Bank, Stanley Purnell, was the initial Chairman of the board. ACTION-Housing was fortunate to have had an active and effective board representing leadership from many segments of the community. The members consistently demonstrated a willingness to become involved in the nitty-gritty of programs and policy.

In addition to maintaining a strong board of directors over the years, ACTION-Housing has benefited from outstanding executive leadership starting with Bernard Loshbough (1957 -1972) and more recently with Jonathan Zimmer (1977 - 2006) and Larry Swanson (2006 - present). Equally important, the skills of the agency staff have ranged from housing development management, to weatherization, homeless assistance, asset building, supportive services, youth development, and education and employment. Nearly a third of the staff members have been with the agency for more than ten years. This longevity is unusual in non-profit housing organizations and represents one of the ACTION-Housing's principal strengths. ACTION-Housing has developed more than 6,000 housing units. They have also improved over 20,000 units and implemented an array of residential service programs affecting the lives of thousands of families and individual in the Pittsburgh region.

ACTION-Housing has had great support from the citizens of Pittsburgh and Allegheny County. It has received financial support from the United Way since 1958. Additional contributions have been provided by the community's foundations, business corporations, and numerous local, state and federal agencies. This support has been essential to everything ACTION-Housing has accomplished over the past 52 years and will continue to be of crucial importance for the agency's future initiatives.

The staff has been encouraged to respect all those with which it is involved. Treating everyone with respect has fostered a more positive and creative work environment throughout the organization. It is also one of the principal reasons why so many individuals have made a career working at ACTION-Housing, investing 20 or more years of their lives helping the agency to pursue its mission on behalf of the community's most vulnerable populations.

Program managers at ACTION-Housing are given a high degree of latitude in operating their programs and building them into something bigger and better than when they started. The managers are also encouraged to provide similar work environments for their staff members so that they will also have the opportunity to grow and develop. The agency's new leaders focused on transforming the agency into a strong development entity serving Pittsburgh and Allegheny.

ACTION-Housing has made diversity a central theme in all of its activities, not only because it is morally right, but also, because it increases the agency's effectiveness in pursuing its mission. All staff members are constantly encouraged to pursue excellence in everything they do, whether it is building a high-rise for the elderly, helping an unemployed family to save their home from foreclosure or preparing the agency's annual report. ACTION-Housing's dedication to this principle was validated on October 28, 2003, when the agency received the prestigious Alfred W. Wishart, Jr. Award for Excellence in Non-Profit Management.

ACTION-Housing initially utilized new community planning tools to address two critical housing problems that impacted some of the low-income families that were being displaced from their homes as a result of a massive urban renewal project being implemented in 95 acres of the Lower Hill District, a severely deteriorated residential community adjacent to downtown. This project involved the dislocation of more than 1,500 families, two-thirds of whom were African-American. ACTION-Housing's initial response was to develop the 209-unit Spring Hill Gardens Apartment on Pittsburgh's Northside in 1959.

During this same period, the agency's board of directors formulated an ambitious long-term agenda consisting of six primary goals:

- Increase the supply of moderate cost housing
- Rehabilitate old housing and to revitalize old neighborhoods
- Assist neighborhood citizen participation in urban
  renewal participation
- Encourage county-wide planning
- Promote building innovations, and
- Educate the public on housing problems and on methods of
  improvement

The first step in enlarging capacity to develop housing was to make funds available for initiating projects. A $1.6 million Pittsburgh Development Fund was established in 1959. It enabled ACTION-Housing to turn talk into action. Supported by grants and loans from 30 foundations and corporations, this revolving fund financed some of the front-end costs and activities essential to the development process. Between 1959 and 1976, the Development Fund was utilized to support the construction of 2,833 new and rehabilitated affordable housing units throughout Pittsburgh and Allegheny County. Permanent financing was then provided by private lenders utilizing various FHA mortgage insurance programs. The total development costs exceeded $57 million.

East Hills Park, a planned community of nearly 1,000 single family homes, townhouses and apartments, was ACTION-Housing's most ambitious undertaking. Developed in five separate phases on 130 acres at the eastern edge of the city, East Hills received national recognition for major innovations in design, construction techniques and financing strategies for low and moderate-income housing.

In 1966, ACTION-Housing took on the challenge of rehabilitating 22 severely deteriorated row-house structures in the Homewood-Brushton area of Pittsburgh. This highly successful project became recognized as a national model for the production of moderately priced housing through the rehabilitation process. On the basis of this success, the board decided that the rehabilitation of Pittsburgh's aging and deteriorating housing stock should be pursued on a much larger scale, and the profit-oriented Allegheny Housing Rehabilitation Corporation (AHRCO) was created. Forty Pittsburgh-based corporations purchased more than $2 million worth of stock to finance the new entity. Between 1967 and 1972, AHRCO rehabilitated more than 1,600 units of housing for low and moderate income families throughout Pittsburgh and Allegheny County.

One of ACTION-Housing's most important early accomplishments was to demonstrate that urban renewal did not have to involve major clearance activities and the dislocation of low-income families. Bernard Loshbough believed strongly that the proper way to renew Pittsburgh's older neighborhoods was to seek improvements in every aspect of neighborhood life, including the housing stock, schools, local businesses, city services, recreational facilities, health-care programs and social services. Most important of all, local residents had to be directly involved in the planning process.

This more comprehensive approach to neighborhood renewal was actively pursued by ACTION-Housing through the Neighborhood Urban Extension Program (NUE) established in 1960. Initially supported by grants from the Ford Foundation and a number of Pittsburgh-based foundations, the NUE was implemented in four economically depressed neighborhoods. In each areas outreach workers from ACTION-Housing worked with citizen groups to identify the most critical problems and needs and to develop appropriate responses. Through this process, ACTION-Housing and locally-based organizations became full partners in the broad physical and social revitalization of these four neighborhoods.

Hundreds of new and rehabilitated housing units were developed in conjunction with the NUE, but the agency also became involved in reading programs, training projects, recreational activities and citizen action committees. The Neighborhood Urban Extension Program subsequently became a model for many of the new neighborhood-based services that were implemented nationally during the 1960's through the federal anti-poverty program.

Most of the multi-family housing developments built by ACTION-Housing during the 1960's were financed under HUD programs that subsidized the interest rates on mortgages. Unfortunately the subsidies were not adequate to support both the operating and debt service costs. This led to major financial problems. ACTION-Housing eventually restructured the developments with new partners and new operating subsidies available under the federal rental assistance program. Two projects were saved by converting them to housing cooperatives.

After this very difficult experience, ACTION-Housing temporarily ceased its direct development role for several years and sought new ways to attach the community's housing problems and neighborhood needs. After researching the factors that contributed to the cycles of neighborhood decline and revitalization, the agency helped to create and operate the Allegheny County Neighborhood Preservation Program. This program was utilized to revitalize 19 declining neighborhoods and renovate more than 1,000 homes in economically depressed areas throughout the County.

In 1977, the board engaged in a strategic planning process which resulted in some important changes in the general orientation of the agency and how it pursued its mission. It moved away from a traditional focus on concentrated neighborhood development and by addressing the community's housing problems and supportive service needs in a more comprehensive manner, it directed resources to a large number of economically depressed communities in Pittsburgh and Allegheny County, it utilized development activities and supportive service programs to assist families and individuals with the most severe problems and the greatest needs by concentrating on high volume programs in an effort to reach larger numbers of people in need. It also provided technical and financial assistance to other non-profit organizations and neighborhood groups in an effort to further expand the supply of decent, affordable housing and essential supportive services for the most vulnerable populations.

A new mission statement was also approved at this time to guide

ACTION-Housing's programs and activities in future years. This statement changed the focus of the agency's activities from simply developing affordable housing to utilizing this housing and various supportive service programs to empower the people being served to build more secure and self-sufficient lives.

ACTION-Housing's new emphasis on assisting families and individuals with the greatest needs led to increased involvement with special needs populations, including elderly individuals, persons with mental and physical disabilities, women and children in crisis and very low-income families. The projects that were undertaken to assist these populations required a range of skills and resources and a base of knowledge that went far beyond what was normally required for more traditional housing development activities. They also required the direct involvement of other organizations and service systems from the public, private and non-profit sectors of the community. Action-Housing developed practical methods and techniques for mobilizing and coordinating these important community resources.

Pittsburgh's mortgage foreclosure problems of the early 1980s were caused primarily by a precipitous decline on the steel industry. Thousands became unemployed with little hope of ever returning to their jobs. In response to this crisis, ACTION-Housing formed a Mortgage Delinquency Task Force comprised of leaders from major lending institutions, city and county government, the United Way, a private mortgage insurance company, the Federal Housing Administration and the Veterans Administration, several social service agencies and the Mon Valley Unemployed Committee, a non-profit organization representing unemployed steelworkers. Free financial and legal counseling was available to the unemployed who were in default on their mortgages, partial payment plans were offered by participating lenders, and direct financial assistance could be found from ACTION-Housing's newly created Mortgage Foreclosure Prevention Fund.

Over a three-year period, the mortgage assistance program helped more than 2,500 unemployed homeowners in Pittsburgh and Allegheny County to save their homes from foreclosure. It also laid the groundwork for establishment of the Pennsylvania Homeowners Emergency Mortgage Assistance Program (HEMAP) that has since saved the homes of more than 50,000 unemployed person throughout the state.

ACTION-Housing utilized a similar approach in addressing the problem of homelessness. A major plan of action was developed in 1985 by the agency's staff with the assistance of an advisory committee appointed by the Mayor and the Chairperson of the County Commissioners. Over the next few years, this plan led to the development of 16 emergency shelters, 22 transitional housing facilities, and a wide range of health education and supportive service programs that collectively served more than 2,400 homeless men, women and children each year.

Since 1986, ACTION-Housing responded to the increasing need for housing with supportive service by developing, or assisting others to develop state-of-the-art special needs and permanent housing facilities throughout Pittsburgh and Allegheny County. Supportive Housing Management Services was established in 1990 as a subsidiary of ACTION-Housing to manage these facilities. All of the agency's special needs housing facilities include supportive services component to help the residents achieve higher levels of independence and self-sufficiency.

The agency also serves its low-income and special needs clients through a broad range of other programs in the areas of weatherization and energy efficiency, accessibility modifications, asset building, youth development, and scholarships to support educational pursuits.

ACTION-Housing now serves more than 12,000 highly vulnerable people each year in Pittsburgh, Allegheny County and other portions of Southwestern Pennsylvania through its housing initiatives, supportive services, asset building programs and educational and employment opportunities. The cumulative accomplishments of ACTION-Housing over the past 54 years have placed it in a prominent position among the nation's leading non-profit housing organizations. The following factors have played key roles in the successes that have been achieved to date and will remain as important elements in the agency's strategy for the future. First is a willingness to take risks. Almost every major initiative undertaken by ACTION-Housing over the past 54 years has involved a significant degree of risk. The willingness of the Board of Directors to accept these risks has enabled the agency to pursue new approaches to emerging problems and to maintain a leadership position in the field. Second is a willingness to create partnerships with others. ACTION-Housing has recognized for many years that major impacts in the fields of housing, neighborhood improvement and human development can best be achieved through effective partnerships with other public, non-profit and private sector organizations. The agency has achieved some of its most significant successes in recent years by forging such partnerships to address the shelter and supportive service needs of homeless families and individuals and other highly vulnerable populations.

CommonBond Communities

CommonBond in Saint Paul, Minnesota, the Planning Office in Boston and Mercy Housing in Denver are fine examples of housing organization sponsored by the Catholic Church in America. They have all gained prominence and are leading members in the Housing Partnership Network. The success of these organizations was in large measure the work of three extraordinary individuals - Joseph Errigo in Saint Paul, Father Michael Groden in Boston and Sister

Lillian Murphy in Denver.

I made trips to Minneapolis-St Paul in 1988 and 1990. Among other things, I learned about the impact of CommonBond in and around the Twin Cities. My host was Charles Krusell, President of the Greater Minneapolis Metropolitan Housing Corporation that was formed in 1971, the same year that CommonBond Communities started. Chuck Krusell was a delightful individual and totally generous of his time. GMMHC's mission was to improve the availability and quality of housing for low and moderate income individuals and families in the Minneapolis area. They provided non-interest bearing seed money loans for financing and technical assistance for nonprofit groups.

In addition to founding GMMHC, Krusell was famous for his work with the Minneapolis Urban Renewal Authority leading the effort to build the Hubert H Humphrey Metrodome. He knew everybody in both the business community and the neighborhoods He invited me to his board meeting and I was impressed by its membership of leading citizens from the Twin Cities area. He took me around and introduced me to staff at several CDCs. Later I had an opportunity to visit with city officials. One of the organizations that was spoken of and praised was the Westminster Corporation, one of the many names adopted by CommonBond since its founding in 1971.

On the final day I went over to Saint Paul and visited with Joseph Errigo, President of the Westminster Corporation. His office was in the basement of one of the Archdiocese buildings. While the office was not impressive, Joe Errigo was. He was dedicated to the mission of his organization and what they had to do to achieve it. In my travels I discovered a number of remarkable people working in the housing partnership field. Joe Errigo was certainly one of the best. I made it my business to keep Errigo involved and CommonBond joined the Network a few years later.

Joe Errigo grew up in Wilmington, Delaware. All of his grandparents were first generation Americans born in Italy. The family tradition was to succeed in America. His father attended the University of Pennsylvania and its Law School and became the first Italian-Americans admitted to the Delaware State Bar in 1929. A lot of his cases involved social issues and had an influence on Joe, who worked in his father's office during his high school years. Joe attended Catholic University in Washington, DC, completing a five-year architectural program in 1966. He did graduate work at the University of North Carolina, earning a Master's in City and Regional Planning in 1968. These were days of civil rights and Vietnam War protests. Several of his friends in Washington and North Carolina were killed in the war. Joe, like many others of his generation, was moved to seek employment where there was an opportunity to address social injustices.

A job opening to work for the Saint Paul Housing and Redevelopment Authority was announced. Joe was interviewed by Ed Helfeld, one of the best urban renewal directors in the country. He was impressed by Helfeld and accepted a job as a planner with the authority. Joe says he earned a "post – post graduate education" working for Helfeld in several Saint Paul inner-city neighborhoods. Three years later, he accepted a job with Ed Flahavan, a priest who was running the Urban Affairs Commission of the Archdiocese in Saint Paul and Minneapolis.

The Catholic Church in the Twin Cities was dealing at the time with some tough issues, the traditional Catholic concerns of birth control and abortion, along with increasingly visible and challenging social justice issues such as poverty and neighborhood redevelopment. The Commission had been set up on a recommendation from a group of inner-city priests to be the official Archdiocesan social justice agency to address these concerns. One of its goals was sponsoring low and moderate income housing.

Shortly after Errigo was hired, the Commission accepted his recommendation to establish a separate legal entity called Urban Affairs Community Development Corporation. The first project it took on was housing for the elderly in two small rural communities. Joe Errigo considered this to be a hands-on-learning exercise on how to plan and operate affordable housing in collaboration with representatives of the community, government agencies and financial institutions. Lessons learned would serve them well in the future decades.

The first housing development in the Twin Cities was a rental project developed with a community partner in Saint Paul's West Side Latino community in 1972. Errigo received tremendous help from several members on the corporation's board, in particular Frank Mullaney, who was one of the founders of both Control Data Corporation and Cray Research and had great leadership and management skills. He considers Frank Mullaney to be one of his most important mentors during those early years.

During the 1970's nonprofit community development corporations learned to utilize partnerships with private investors as a source of additional funding for HUD-financed housing. Errigo and his staff learned how to do this with the assistance of outside professionals and guidance from board members. It required that the ownership of the development be a limited partnership in which a for-profit subsidiary of the nonprofit sponsor could be a general partner. For Errigo's organization, the name of that subsidiary was Westminster Corporation, because the development was located on Westminster Street on the East Side of Saint Paul.

Eventually, Westminster became the property management company for all of their housing after they made a decision in 1974 to do property management with their own staff. Westminster became a very skilled and well regarded property manager. It also developed skills in providing resident services in cooperation with human services professionals, health care providers, community organizers and teachers. The Westminster name was adopted by the parent organization and was seen as a highly competent group that would take on the most difficult challenges. It took over Torre de San Miguel Homes on Saint Paul's West Side to save it from foreclosure. Torre was a socially and economically troubled development and Westminster turned it into model housing with a strong supportive service program. In Minneapolis, Westminster was named court-appointed receiver for a large, troubled Native American sponsored housing development where HUD was dealing with a foreclosure situation. That receivership lasted for over ten years until HUD finally agreed to a settlement when Henry Cisneros was HUD Secretary.

The Westminster name was changed to CommonBond in 1993. Preservation of HUD housing became even more important as projects built in the seventies required renovation, and the original owner commitments to provide low and moderate income housing had expired. A crucial role was played by CommonBond in partnership with Greater Metropolitan Minneapolis Housing Corporation (GMMHC) and a local community organization to rescue Seward Towers, a 640 unit affordable rental development. A large portion of the financing came from the City of Minneapolis. Redevelopment included creating Advantage Centers that would provide needed support services for residents. The success of the project strengthened Commonbond's image as a highly competent housing developer, manager and social service provider. In 2000, Commonbond successfully completed the $31 million acquisition and renovation of the 504 unit Skyline Tower in Saint Paul. It was another model preservation project that eventually received a HUD award for excellence. Construction at Skyline Towers included a new 17,000 square foot state-of-the-art Advantage Center and many partnerships with local service providers and the Saint Paul School District.

The Corporation's largest and most complex project was the 2004 refinancing and renovation of 17 of their elderly housing developments containing 767 apartments with $60 million tax-exempt bond financing from the U.S. Bancorp. New kitchens, new baths, new flooring, energy efficient boilers and hot water heaters made the properties long term assets. Success was symbolic of the housing management, financial expertise and credit worthiness of Common-Bond today. It was well received by the community and recognized by HUD and others as a national model for preserving HUD-financed senior housing.

In addition to its leadership in housing preservation, CommonBond has continued to develop and operate new housing in inner cities, suburban communities and smaller rural cities. It has mastered the art of effectively combining the physical, financial, social and political elements that assure the success of affordable housing.

The corporation demonstrated its concern and success in providing special resident services. They were smart and successful in giving their services a brand name, Advantage Centers. They created what they called Advantage Centers at each housing development with carefully designed service programs that included job training, youth programs and services to help seniors stay in the community. They also established advisory boards that serve to connect the residents to Commonbond's operations. It was a centerpiece in their successful fund raising campaigns.

About one half of the existing portfolio is new housing built by CommonBond. CommonBond now owns and manages over 5000 rental apartments and townhouses in 50 cities in Minnesota, Wisconsin and Iowa. It serves over 8000 residents and has innumerable supporters and partners for both the real estate and the Advantage Centers. CommonBond continues to have a strong balance sheet and first rate leadership.

Joe Errigo was appointed Director of the organization in 1971 and later was given the title of President and CEO. His 35 years of leadership made CommonBond what it is today. At the end of 2006, his retirement story was featured in major articles in both the Saint Paul Pioneer Press and the Minneapolis Star Tribune. One of Joe's comments at the time was that, "no one seemed to be paying much attention to this work during the past 35 years, but it was sure a big deal when I stopped doing it." The key to his success was the long-term leadership that Joseph Errigo provided his board and to the organization. Errigo was able to attract very capable staff and board members who believed in the mission of the company and worked hard to get results. The organization is now the largest nonprofit provider of affordable housing in the Minneapolis-Saint Paul area and the five-state region of the Upper Midwest.

CommonBond Communities new president is Paul Fate, formerly a Vice President of Local Initiative Support Corporation (LISC) in Saint Paul. Fate is an extremely able successor. He believes in the organization's mission and continues to expand its reach and impact. Over the last five years they have built or preserved over 1,800 units, expanding their portfolio by 43% during challenging economic times. They are currently doing their first ever housing for homeless vets at two sites, They will total about 100 units. They are doing more and more acquisition rehab and preservation of expiring use properties and see this as a growth area. They are now active in Minnesota, Wisconsin and Iowa They have become more recognized nationally and are now included in the top 50 affordable housing producers in Affordable Housing Finance.

They have completed successfully a $21 million dollar capital campaign. CommonBond will have attracted national funders for the first time including the MacArthur Foundations (Windows of Opportunity), The Kresge Foundation, and NeighborWorks America with which they are now affiliated. CommonBond has worked with Enterprise and LISC/NEF for many years for equity in housing. More recently they have received new funding for operating support and LISC Social Innovation Funding for new Financial Opportunity Centers at their sites.

CommonBond hired their first Director of Asset Management and have been building out that critical capacity. They have strengthened their property management function and are currently achieving 98% physical occupancy and 97% economic occupancy across the portfolio. They have strengthened their Advantage Center services and achieved new heights with metrics and evidence based approaches.

CommonBond is now a national model for regional social housing developers. It's trademark or brand is "more than housing." It is about creating fine housing and communities where people choose to live and have an opportunity to improve their lives. Common-Bond over the years established itself as a high performer worthy of support from public agencies and private supporters. The fact that CommonBond received over five million dollars of private grants and contributions in 2010 is evidence of their position as a worthy and admired organization. It is a model social enterprise in every respect and an important player in the Housing Partnership Network.

Planning Office for Urban Affairs (Boston)

The Planning Office for Urban Affairs of the Archdiocese of Boston was opened in 1969. In the late-sixties and early-seventies, the Planning Office was the primary voice in getting an OEO Grant for the East Boston CDC. They were the guiding light in establishing St. Joseph's Cooperative in Roxbury. Northridge in Beverly, a 98-unit cooperative, was the first housing in the Commonwealth to be built under Chapter 40B. It was also the first cooperative to be financed by the Massachusetts Housing Finance Agency, and the first to offer a three-level income structure for families, including Low-Income, Moderate Income and Market Income.

The Planning Office's initial director, Father Michael Groden, was for a time on GBCD's Board. Lincoln Homes Cooperative, also with a three-level income structure, was being developed by the Lincoln Foundation at the same time. In both developments, all families received the tax benefits of homeownership and built equity in their homes, guaranteeing for some future low-income families access to affordable shares in the cooperative. Recently, the cooperative in Lincoln has been reacquired by the Community Builders and converted to rental housing.

The Planning Office has demonstrated its ability to undertake very complex projects, particularly mixed income projects, in which they complement national, state and local funding with the proceeds of the sale of market-rate units. They now hold 30 developments with 2500 homes. The Planning Office is also famous for its pursuit of a 64-unit development in Scituate, Massachusetts, that went through 10 years of litigation objections to the proposed housing. It all culminated in a decision by the Supreme Judicial Court of Massachusetts permitting the right of the Archdiocese to construct the development.

The Planning Office and its current Director, Lisa Alberghini's ability to bring diversity to their projects is illustrated by their Rollins Square development on a two-acre urban renewal site in Boston's South End. The 184-unit mixed-income development has 20% low-income rental apartments, 40% moderate income first-time homebuyers units, and finally, 40% are market-rate condominiums.

242

It is high quality housing for people with a broad range of incomes, reflecting the neighborhood in which it is located. The grounds include a landscaped park, 6,000 square feet of retail space and an underground parking garage.

There were a number of challenges in financing the project. The Planning Office had to place some of the moderate-income first-time homebuyer units in escrow awaiting the sale of market-rate units. It is a pattern that has been copied by other developers. The site design, placing the six-story buildings on the main street front and four-story townhouse on the interior streets with a park, reflected the existing style of architecture in the South End.

Settlement Housing Fund

Helen Harris, the head of the United Neighborhood House in New York City, hired Clara Fox, an energetic and passionate advocate for early childhood education and better housing, to head their housing department 1969. Clara wrote a grant proposal to create a housing corporation called Settlement Housing Fund.

The corporation's goals were to form cooperatives and provide technical assistance and seed money for settlement houses to develop low and middle income housing in their neighborhoods. The proposal was successful and they were funded for two years. Clara then hired Roger Schafer, a housing expert. Carol Lamberg was working for Schafer and was assigned to work as Clara's assistant. Carol is still there in 2013 after 40 years, serving as Executive Director.

Carol Lamberg worked originally on legislative issues, lobbying Congress and the State of New York for changes in laws and regulations that they needed for their projects. The organization supported the changes for which Senator Robert Kennedy was a leading advocate, like the accelerated depreciation of the capital cost of construction. Because the organization was and remains a nonprofit, it was necessary to form partnerships with for-profit developers and use the tax benefits. One of her victories was an amendment to the law that allowed federal support of mixed-income housing.

Settlement Housing Fund completed a variety of housing developments, acting as consultant or sponsor of 8,700 apartments, and rental agent of 12,000 apartments. In 2003, Settlement Housing Fund acquired ten buildings from the city that had been in receivership for years, needed major repairs and owed millions of dollars in taxes. The buildings were structurally sound with good sized apartments and excellent room layouts. But extensive repairs were required for the roofs, plumbing, heating systems and hook-ups for washers and dryers. Eighty-percent of the current residents were low-income families.

The Settlement Housing Fund formed a partnership with the Urban Homesteading Assistance Board and New York City to rehabilitate the buildings, converting most of them to cooperatives. With municipal funds from the city's Third Party Transfer Program, the Department of Housing Preservation and Development provided low-cost loans to cover the costs of acquisition and repairs. Several of the buildings are now limited-equity cooperatives, making homeownership a reality for the lower-income tenants and new residents alike.

The Fund's latest project is the New Settlement Community Campus. It is located a block and a half from New Settlement Apartments and consists of 17 buildings with 1.022 apartments. The complex began as the largest site in the former (and now late) Mayor Ed Koch's ten-year housing program. The first fourteen buildings were occupied in 1990, with three additional buildings added over the years. The Campus, which opened in September 2012, includes two public schools, pre-kindergarten through 12th grade, a school for children with special needs, and a community center with a 75-foot swimming pool, a dance studio, a cooking classroom, and a green learning roof terrace. Programs are up and running with over a thousand members at the center.

The Settlement Housing Fund now owns, through its affiliates, 32 buildings with 1,750 units. In addition to housing, Settlement Housing Fund creates and operates community programs, commercial facilities and whatever it takes to create viable neighborhoods.

The Housing Partnership (Charlotte)

The creation of the Housing Partnership in Charlotte, North Carolina, was the work of civic leaders and the banks with support from the city and the county. By 1986 the reputation of the Boston Housing Partnership was attracting visitors to see what we had accomplished. Betty Chafin Rash (former Charlotte City Council Mayor Pro Tem and Co-Chair of 1987 Housing Task Force) and Kathryn Heath (former Director of Training and Development, First Union National Bank, and the other Co-Chair of 1987 Housing Task Force), came and visited with me in 1987. Betty Rash later described her impressions of BHP, "I think when we went to Boston we were captivated by what a partnership could accomplish. Their program had strong public sector involvement, strong involvement from the financial community, the social service component and even strong involvement by the religious community." Kathryn Heath noted, " All of the forces lined up. Everybody wanted to make it happen, and it seemed as if there was a tide moving us forward."

The task force's charge was to raise awareness of community housing issues amidst a climate of rising costs and diminishing federal resources. Their efforts culminated in a pivotal, city-sponsored symposium which challenged Charlotte to eliminate substandard housing and expand affordable options. Out of this came the concept of creating a community wide organization to coordinate public and private resources to address the city's housing needs. John Boatwright (retired Executive Vice-President of NCNB and first Board Chair), said, "Studying those other cities convinced us that a partnership was the way to go, being able to pull people together and get them to work together more than anything else. We already had the advocacy so we went to work on the partnerships and started with single-family housing."[33]

The result in 1988 was the Housing Partnership, which was initially the Charlotte/Mecklenberg Housing Partnership). It was described by Boatwright as, "a broad-based, private, non-profit housing development and finance corporation organized to expand affordable and well maintained housing within stable neighborhoods for low and moderate income families in Charlotte and Mecklenburg County with a continuing interest in the ability of occupants to more fully enter the economic mainstream." The original board was diverse. It included neighborhood activists, former city council members, a mayor pro-tem, a lawyer and advocate for the poor, a social services coordinator, a real estate developer and bankers. A number of these were leaders of the Housing Partnership.

At the time, people were aware that Charlotte was losing a lot of housing units due to urban renewal and stricter code enforcement and that there was a need for more resources for low and moderate-income housing. The formation of the Partnership had stimulated concern in many quarters. Officers from North Carolina Nations Bank and a Senior Vice-President from First Union got involved. Duke Power was helpful. In 1987 the City of Charlotte appropriated by unanimous vote $2.5 million for the Innovative Housing Programs. Betty Rash noted, "I remember sitting down with Pam

Syfert, who was Assistant City Manager at that time, and she actually agreed to come on the board. City staff members don't often do that." Syfert was a big supporter of home ownership. In October 1989 the Banks collectively committed $17.5 million for a first mortgage loan pool for the Partnership. The city and the banks wanted to do the right thing.

In March 1989, the Partnership hired it's first President, Patricia G. Garrett. Pat Garrett had been Executive Director of Macon Program for Progress in Macon County, North Carolina, a Community Action Agency. She had been a leader in a number of fields including Head Start, day care, and employment and training. She had also initiated the North Carolina Low-Income Housing Coalition and the State's Housing Trust Fund. She was an innovator with an entrepreneurial spirit, skilled at building relationships and alliances and a wonderful manager. She could marshal resources and bring disparate individuals and organizations together to get things done. There was unanimous agreement that she was the right person for the job.

Patricia Garrett and her Board Chairman, John Boatwright, came to the initial 1990 Network meeting in Boston. They heard a lot of talk of multi family development and had to remind those attending that her partnership was new and that she was focused on single-family ownership. As one of her Board describes it, they had been able to get a good group of volunteer lawyers to do all of their closings for first-time homebuyers. They created a whole loan closing system that worked very effectively. The loan pool was crucial. It was to be only the first of many successful programs and projects.

The Partnership's homeownership program was well run and successful. As Mike Rizer, former Board chair put it "The innovation that has become the trademark of this successful partnership continues as more neighborhoods are transformed and lives touched.

Homeownership changes one's perspective, gives a family a sense of permanence and responsibility that carries over into all aspects for their lives. Although structures and improved neighborhoods are the outward sign of the progress of The Housing Partnership (the so called 'product') – the underlying purpose of it all is to change lives by reaching out with a helping hand."

They built consensus among the rich and poor, developers and city staff, Democrats and Republicans, black and white. These leaders took professional and political risks to forge this unity because they were passionate about affordable housing and determined to create a solution. Their vision resulted in the creation of a community-wide non-profit housing developer that designs, develops and manages both multi-family and single-family housing.

Today, The Housing Partnership's success continues to stem from its ability to create bridges between sectors and communities, bridges that cross political, regional and organizational divides. By leading and remaining focused on our community's desire to increase affordable housing, The Housing Partnership is able, again and again, to truly live up to its name.

The success of The Housing Partnership lies not only in the strength of the early leaders and other pioneers, but in the partnerships that they cultivated across sectors. The public, private, corporate and neighborhood ties remain strong today. It has created over 1,700 rental properties. More than 11,000 people have participated in its homeownership education and counseling programs. More than 1,100 homebuyers have been created. The Housing Partnership has led the way in revitalizing five inner city neighborhoods, has a pivotal role as master developer in the HOPE VI redevelopment of The Park at Oaklawn and has embarked on a plan for the market driven redevelopment of Double Oaks.

Since 1989 the Partnership has been responsible for the production of over 3700 units of affordable housing, both single family and multifamily, and has another 186 units in development. Early on the Partnership financed several apartment units but in the past several years, the organization has invested primarily in its own developments. The agency works to involve the private sector, particularly partner banks and governmental agencies, and the community in solving affordable housing problems. The Partnership has also been active in national organizations, such as the Housing Partnership Network and the Neighborhood Reinvestment Corporation and is designated as a Community Development Financial Institution by the US Treasury Department.

The Partnership has been particularly active and successful in leading the revitalization of several inner city neighborhoods. Genesis Park was a neighborhood alongside the expressway and a source of trouble and drug trafficking. There were a number of vacancies. The Partnership bought over half the houses including the vacant units and organized the neighborhood. They rebuilt the deteriorated buildings, helped homeowners fix their own houses and put in new streets and sidewalks. In time they turned the area completely around. Pat took Hugh McColl, President of the Bank of America through the area. He noted a building that lacked a front porch. When told that the budget would not allow the cost of a porch, he said, "put one on and I will pay for it." Pat did just that.

The Partnership was the master developer in a $34.7 million HOPE VI redevelopment, which includes 178 family tax credit units financed by the Partnership, building the first HUD 202 project and contracting for the construction of 71 single-family for-sale units. The Partnership's largest undertaking to date and the culmination of all they have learned over the last twenty years is the master planned

Double Oaks development. They purchased a large tract of land for revitalization in 2007 securing unprecedented support for a mixed use, mixed income, market driven redevelopment. Guided by a ten-year master plan, the Double Oaks community will feature affordable multi-family and senior rental units as well as market rate rental and single-family homeownership opportunities.

In 1992 Governor James Martin awarded Pat Garrett the Order of the Long Leaf Pine. She has also received awards from the North Carolina Community Development Association and the North Carolina Head Start Association. She has served in several statewide and regional positions. She is the past chair of the North Carolina Housing Partnership, which administers the North Carolina Housing Trust Fund, a founding member and officer of the North Carolina Low Income Housing Coalition, a member of the North Carolina Housing Finance Board of Directors, a board member of the Housing Partnership Network, and a former member of the Atlanta Federal Home Loan Bank Advisory Board.

Pat is a superb manager and decision-maker who knows where she wants to be. She has handled her board thoughtfully and has recruited staff well. Her organization recently went through Neighbor-Works and the city's performance reviews and once again achieved the highest possible ratings from both entities.

In March 2013, Pat resigned. Her successor is Julie Porter.

Foundation Communities (Austin, Texas)

The origins of Foundation Communities (FC) of Austin, Texas, demonstrate what can occur when a single individual is the prime mover in the startup of a new social enterprise. Francie Ferguson was involved in student cooperatives during her undergraduate days at Oberlin College. She became acquainted with Stewart Kohl who had graduated two years ahead of her. He was running a small organization in Ann Arbor, Michigan, called North American Students of Cooperation (NASC). She accepted a position on Kohl's staff as Director of Member Relationships at five dollars an hour.

Francie spent three years with NASC. The job involved a lot of travel about the country during which she did a variety of tasks including reviews of organizations from student housing to food coops, training of boards of directors, investigating HUD programs in Washington, and attending conferences. It was a great learning experience. She became acquainted with numerous officials and staff members of organizations across the Country. The job took her frequently to Austin, Texas, which she decided was an attractive place to live. She left NASC and moved to Austin.

Francie became involved with the University of Texas cooperatives organization. Members' monthly contributions provided a small surplus, and a few of her co-members got permission to create the Austin Community Neighborhood Trust, a housing program for low-income families. It had a five-person board, most of whom had cooperative housing experience.

The operations of the Trust started with the purchase of a single house that they rented out to a group of people. They arranged for some part time help from a staff person in the University's housing office who had been a City Counselor. Francie then decided that she had to have more real estate skills. She enrolled at the University of Texas and received a Master's Degree in Business Administration in 1986.

Francie attracted new people with real estate and banking experience for the board, which was now called Austin Mutual Housing

(AMH). One was a banker who served as her Chairperson. At this point she resigned from the board and started with a small stipend as the Executive Director. The real estate market was then in disarray with the failures of savings and loan associations and other market problems. Properties were sitting vacant but not yet foreclosed. As they did not have the money to purchase properties, Austin Mutual Housing started to do property management of projects that they might be able to buy in the future. Two of the properties were owned by the city's Housing Authority. Their desire to involve residents in management led them to a decision to manage their own developments. Management fees provided some income for their operations.

They made a contact with Neighborhood Reinvestment Corporation (NRC) headed by Bill Whiteside and Deputy Director George Knight, that resulted in NRC inviting a group from Austin, politicians, supporters, staff and others, to a Neighborhood Reinvestment Conference in Baltimore. It was a positive meeting. The group met with NRC officials and others in the industry. It was a time when NRC was not so much supporting new groups but starting organizations. They had a particular interest in mutual housing. They had two day workshop meetings for new groups and awarded Ferguson's group $10,000 for such a workshop.

The Baltimore visit and the workshop in Austin energized the Austin housing community. NRC provided small annual grants and Austin Mutual Housing started to look for properties. In 1989 they bought 122 units in 61 duplex buildings located in a desirable middle class residential neighborhood. The purchase was financed by a loan of $150,000 from NRC. NRC wrote off the loan in three years and provided additional capital over the next few years.

Between 1989 and 1995, Austin Mutual Housing acquired 1,250

units at favorable prices. The largest property was a 403 unit complex in Arlington, Texas. It had three community centers and two pools. Their first tax credit development was a 200 unit new development completed in 2000. AMH was renamed Central Texas Mutual Housing Association in 1990, and it became Foundation Communities in 2001.

The driving force behind all this was Francie Ferguson. She had the energy, skills and persistence to build the organization. Contributions from the Reinvestment Corporation were crucial, and Ferguson believes she succeeded because at each stage she had a sound business plan. She never intended to be a neighborhood based organization. She hired an able deputy director named Walter Moreau in 1995. He succeeded her as Director in 1997. Francie left, she says, because her interest was in "starting things." She was looking for new challenges. She negotiated a position with the Reinvestment Corporation that allowed her to continue to live in Austin.

Foundations Communities has had a history of delivering superior residential services. Its mission is to create housing where families succeed. It does so by developing, owning, and managing quality affordable housing communities and equipping low-income families with programs that educate, support, and improve their financial standing. Foundation Communities works in four areas – housing for working families, supportive housing for homeless families and individuals, children's learning and adult literacy, and financial stability.

One program, Children's Home Initiative (CHI), provides stable homes with reduced rent, creates opportunities to achieve goals for self sufficiency, increases financial literacy to make money go further, and improves employment and/or job skills to increase income. CHI contributes to overall mission by empowering families to break the cycle of poverty through housing stability and tools to increase their financial stability. The three-year strategic plan sets the CHI goal of 100 apartments/families. CHI provides a, "hand up", for working poor families with children who face homelessness and have no means to increase their income, moving them from crisis and instability toward long term self sustainability. Foundation Communities is uniquely qualified to address this need because of our established mixed income model of housing—no more than 20% of residents at our communities are CHI participants. Surrounded by working families, those overcoming challenges that led to homelessness can observe models of success. This approach also provides financial stability for the organization (affordable housing residents pay up to twice as much rent as CHI families).

Since 2000, the poverty rate in the community has grown 35%. Families with children, especially single mothers, are most affected. With the highest housing costs in Texas and 30% of most popular jobs paying less than $10/hour, Austin is a challenging place to live for low wage workers. High rents mean that 54,000 Austin families pay more than they can afford for rent—leaving less for food and healthcare. As a result, families get behind on rent, move frequently, and often face eviction. During the 2006-2007 school year, 1,800 Austin ISD students were homeless. On average, homeless children attend three or more schools per year and show a marked increase in academic and behavioral challenges. With 20,000 of Travis County children living in poverty, many more are at risk of homelessness.

Foundation Communities receives about 80 calls weekly from families in need of shelter, with half qualifying for CHI. Yet, currently they only have rental subsidy and case management for 38 families. To help meet this overwhelming need, FC seeks to expand this proven program. A grant from Impact Austin, awarded at this crucial time, will help leverage City of Austin Affordable Housing Bonds to permanently subsidize rents on 18 apartments, while directly pro-

viding the first two years of case management.
Childrens Home Initiative utilizes the best practices identified by the
Corporation for Supportive Housing, including:

• Case Management Assistance
  Each family works closely with an on site case manager who
  supports them in achieving self-sufficiency goals.

• Employment Support
  One of the primary objectives is to help clients increase income
  by improving employment skills and finding and keeping higher-
  wage employment.

• Effective Teamwork
  CHI staff work closely with property management staff to
  ensure that any behaviors that could endanger a family's housing
  are quickly addressed.

• Money management support
  All CHI clients gain money management skills, helping them
  understand budgeting, credit, and debt reduction. Families also
  receive help determining public benefits for which they qualify.

• Opportunities to transition in place
  Graduating families may remain in their apartment and transition
  to FC's permanent affordable housing program, thereby
  maintaining stability

Foundation Communities is collaborating in the Parenting in Recovery project. This five year federally funded program provides
services for children and parents involved in the child welfare system due to parental substance abuse. Project collaborators include
FC, Travis County Health and Human Services Dept., Texas Dept.

of Family and Protective Services, Travis County Drug Treatment Court, Austin/Travis County MHMR, and Austin Recovery. FC's role is to provide transitional housing and case management support for up to ten families who have completed in patient drug treatment. These families will be incorporated into the CHI program at Crossroads; this partnership is a further impetus for this project.

FC has added new staff position to coordinate all green building efforts including analyzing energy/water use and lighting audits to further increase resource efficiency. They have also launched the Free Minds Project, in partnership with Austin Community College, to offer a college credit humanities course to low income adults.

FC values partners who provide services more effectively than we can. We have formal partnerships with, Heart House, Austin Learning Academy, Caritas, Passages (a program of Salvation Army and the Housing Authority), and Keep Austin Housed (a project of Front Steps).

The corporation has been focused on housing and services. They have a foot in the real estate world, and a foot in the education and social work world. Moreau thinks that this has given them the right sense of stewardship and mission to avoid taking some of the fast growth real estate risks from which some other social housing organizations have suffered. They don't like debt, and are consciously avoiding overleveraging the properties. They want the cash flow to fund services, keep rents low and the properties in top condition – not feed the next or last deal. By doing their own self management, and with healthy property performance, they have not become dependent on developer fee income. They are fortunate to own properties in a growing part of the country, so over the years they have had adequate rent growth.

While they have been cautious about over extending themselves,

Foundation Communities has also been willing to innovate. They like to act first and plan as they go along. Moreau thinks their best programs are the community tax centers, supportive housing communities, and the learning centers that are all adapted ideas from other good programs around the country. They are very focused on green building renovations and using the best practices they can find.

Moreau is proud of developing an individual donor base the past four years. Like most social housing groups in the US, they relied first and foremost on public funding sources – and still do today for all new housing development. About ten years ago they started to successfully add grants from private foundations and corporations, especially to build learning centers. Some of the family foundations pushed them to think harder about individual donations.

When Hurricane Katrina struck, FC rapidly provided transitional housing for 110 high need families. A whole new group of individual and church volunteers became involved in their work, which expanded our donor relationships. Following the "Benvon" model, they started doing a monthly open house at either one of the learning centers or supportive housing properties to get to know new volunteers and donors. The last annual fundraising lunch raised over $300,000 in individual gifts and multi year pledges. Moreau wants to build an organization that will continue to be mission driven. Having so many people volunteer and donate helps root them in the community.

BRIDGE

I first met Don Terner when he was running a housing rehabilitation program in New York City. He had an office in a church rectory on 110st Street. The rehab work was being done by self organized groups of younger people. They were recovering scattered vacant buildings under a program loosely controlled by the city and his office. It was an adventurous program for a person who had a Ph.D. and taught at MIT. However, Don was special.

Some years later, Don worked for the California Secretary of Business, Alan Stern, as the Director of Housing and Development. Stern was then asked to head a Bay Area business group that wanted to do something about affordable housing in the Bay Area. The groups' conclusion was to start a new company with a $670,000 grant in 1982 made through the San Francisco Foundation to address the housing shortage. Alan Stern chose Donald Terner as the Director of the new company.

BRIDGE began operations in 1983. The goal was to develop 1,000 units of affordable housing per year. Its approach was aggressive and opportunistic. It utilized negotiations with local government for land development concessions, density bonuses, reduced parking and other requirements and waivers of development fees. In addition, as a tax-exempt nonprofit it took advantage of purchasing public property at fair-market value before the property was offered for competitive public sale.

Don Terner completed a variety of projects from inner city to suburban, from low rise to a multi story development, from projects for their portfolio and those for sale to owners. On several occasions, I tried to recruit Don to become a member of the Partnership Network but he refused, saying, "Bob, I am not a partnership, I am a homebuilder." He was spurred on by a driving force to accomplish his goal of 1000 units per year.

Don also made the claim that he was building quality affordable housing that would please everyone. Their list of properties indi-

 258

cated that they worked with all sorts of public agencies and private partners, sometimes as the complete owner/developer and at other time, in a supportive role. We once visited Pickleweed Apartments in which they picked up a stalled project, redesigned it, obtained financing, supervised construction and did the tenant selection. BRIDGE Property Management Company operated and managed the project. The combination of city land, tax exempt financing, funds from the San Francisco Foundation, and construction savings yielded dramatically below market rents. We also saw a market rate leasehold condominiums project in which their role is limited to providing complete residential, housekeeping, health, dining, and recreational services. Terner was clear in his use of these resources to help subsidize his other projects.

Don Terner was killed in the plane crash over Croatia with U.S. Commerce Secretary Ron Brown in 1996. He was part of a volunteer trade mission to the Balkans. His accomplishments were immense and his tremendous energy, vision and enthusiasm are sorely missed. The fact that BRIDGE survived is to his credit.

After his death, the Vice President for Management, Carol Galante, who had been with BRIDGE since 1987, was appointed President and CEO. Carol was a determined and exacting leader, and the company did very well during her 11 year run, continuing to develop quality affordable housing. BRIDGE also undertook economic activities to expand social service programs such as child care, family counseling, job training, credit counseling, abuse prevention, and nursing and escort services for seniors. In 2009, Carol left to join the Obama Administration as HUD's Assistant Secretary for Multifamily Housing.

She was succeeded by Cynthia Parker on February 2010. Parker brought 30 years of diverse and relevant experience, most recently as Regional President for Mercy Housing. While BRIDGE has built over 14,000 affordable homes, helped one-fourth of their residents advance to homeownership, provided more than 400,000 square feet of commercial space, and brought new housing to more than 100 California communities, their latest plan calls for doubling their holdings over the next five years.[34] This is quite a goal when one considers the economic and environmental factor that will be faced by the industry. They have to deal with the absence of the redevelopment agencies which were eliminated in 2012. California, just as the other states, is reducing expenditures but still asking that social services be augmented. The San Francisco Mayor's Office of Housing recorded a decline of 50% in federal sources between 2007 and 2012 and a decline of 85% in city/state/federal resources between 2009 and 2012.

BRIDGE sees itself as an organization which strengthens communities and creates opportunities for working families and seniors. Their work begins but does not end with housing. Bridge is a leader and innovator in the mission driven business of effective production, operation and ownership of affordable and mixed income housing. BRIDGE earns the highest degree of customer satisfaction from all stakeholders, including residents, neighbors, investors, taxpayers, private and public-sector partners and employees. It is the go-to developer and owner for public officials, investors and communities seeking an array of housing solutions.

BRIDGE will widen its sphere of operations and be more of a national player utilizing a variety of product financing. While known for its expertise in use of the Low Income Housing Tax Credit, it has acquired skills in other financing areas, such as 80/20 tax exempt bonds, affordable homeownership, master planning, acquisition and rehabilitation, historic preservation and varying levels of service enriched housing. It has been successful in meeting the needs of a wide variety of income groups. Their project at 9th and Broadway, a 250-unit building in downtown San Francisco, will house a mix of residents. Many have special needs and problems related to homelessness. BRIDGE plans to acquirie 3,000 to 3,750 units of existing housing and rehabilitate and/or recapitalize 3,000 more units by 2017.

BRIDGE will also undertake new initiatives such as wrap around service centers, and broaden their experience with master planning and retail operations at scale for diverse populations. With the recent allocation of new market tax credits, they see themselves getting into ownership and operations of large assets in complicated community situations. They plan to create 900 units of new housing in new geographic regions such as Washington and Oregon with new partners.

They will also create an equity fund for portfolio acquisition and soft financing, create a syndication arm, establish a bond fund, develop social capital to support community building and resident services. All of this to be controlled by a performance system based upon business outcomes and individual goals.

<u>LINC Housing</u>

By the 1980's, California experienced an escalating cost of land that would cause homeownership and most rentals to be unaffordable for large segments of the population. Teachers and service sector personnel and young working families in both urban and rural economies were particularly affected. In 1984, the Southern California Association of Governments formed a new nonprofit corporation named the Corporate Fund for Housing (CFH). The board was comprised of government and business leaders who were given the task of determining how the housing question might be addressed. After a short time, CFH formed a new operating entity called LINC Housing. Hunter Johnson was employed as Executive Director. An affiliate company, LINC Cares, was created to deliver service programs.

LINC's mission is to provide housing for people who are underserved by the marketplace. California, particularly Los Angeles, was experiencing tough times. Poverty rates in Los Angeles were above 16%, unemployment above 12.5%, and the number of medically uninsured at about 30%. To date, LINC has developed 7,500 homes in 65 communities throughout California. LINC cares about the quality of design, environmental sustainability and life enhancing resident services. Their housing has varied from new construction, acquisition and rehabilitation of at risk housing, historic preservation and the purchase of manufactured home parks.

REACH

Reach was organized as a Community Development Corporation in Portland, Oregon, in 1982. I visited Portland in 1988 and learned that REACH Community Development, Inc., had purchased and rehabilitated 146 low and moderate income housing units with financing provided by the Portland Development Commission. In addition, rehabilitation work had started on the Mt. Vernon Apartments which provide 57 homeless women with a safe and permanent low cost unit made possible by rehabilitation financing and rental assistance under the Steward B. McKinney Homeless Assistance Act. REACH had also purchased the Taft Hotel to offer residential care to 80 elderly and medically needy persons. Rehabilitation of the building was financed by the Portland Development Commission. In 2006 REACH completed six row houses for first time homebuyers. The project included a number of green building practices including use of non-toxic materials, native plantings, dual flush toilets and small eco-roofs. The hydronic heat system, tankless water heater and a panel roof keeps energy bills low.

REACH has now developed 1,960 units of affordable, quality rental homes for families and individuals in the Portland area and 28 units for first time home buyers. It has continued its purchase, renovation and construction of homes throughout the Portland metro area

The REACH portfolio includes new and renovated complexes, apartment buildings and mixed use developments across the City of Portland. Station Place Tower is located in the Pearl District and includes innovative green features including a rainwater harvesting system, funded in part from a local government sustainability grant program. The Patton Park Apartments, a new 54-unit building for working families and 4600 square feet of commercial space, opened in 2009. More recently, REACH was awarded the "Block 49" project for 209 units of affordable housing in the South Waterfront neighborhood. Forty-two of the apartments are targeted to veterans earning less than $15,000.

The Portland Housing Bureau (PHB) is partnering with REACH. "REACH emerged on top among a very strong group of nonprofit developers," said PHB's director. PHB also announced in February 2011, that REACH and its partners, Human Solutions and Ride Connection, had been selected to co-develop a mixed-use planned project with 120 units of housing and 16,000 square feet of office space.

REACH is looking to expand its region of activities. Together with its partners, it completed in September 2011, the purchase of a prime development site at Orenco Station in Hillsboro, Oregon. Design is underway and securing the financing is in process for a 60 unit, transit oriented housing project for lower wage workers in the Orenco neighborhood.

In addition to development, REACH understands and carries out extensive resident programs in financial education and individual development accounts, eviction prevention, employment and career support, and access to emergency food and clothing.

REACH has published a five year plan to develop, acquire or preserve 1,000 units of affordable housing using sustainable building technologies as much as possible. The organization, with an operating budget of $14 million and unrestricted net assets of $10 million, is financially stable. $1.2 million of their operating budget comes from grants and individual and business contributions.

Dee Walsh was the Executive Director until 2013. She was a great talent and had assembled during her 20 year tenure a very capable staff. She has recently joined the staff of the Housing Partnership Network.

Community Housing Partners (CHP)

The group that would become Community Housing Partners (CHP) began in the early 1970s as a volunteer effort coordinated by the Blacksburg Virginia YMCA, the Cooper House, and the Presbyterian campus ministry of Virginia Polytechnic Institute. At that time, volunteers mostly students and a few faculty members from Virginia Tech and nearby Radford University, focused on home repairs in the New River Valley area surrounding Blacksburg.

By 1975, the organization had incorporated and established its first board of directors. The group continued to focus on addressing substandard housing conditions of low income families in Southwest Virginia, and began expanding the range of repairs performed to include weatherization. The volunteer efforts were led by Janaka

Casper, who was hired to oversee field operations in 1976. Casper would go on to play a pivotal role in the growth of CHP over the coming decades.

The late 70s through the 1980s was a period of significant growth for CHP. Led by Casper, as chief executive officer, the organization benefited from the work and vision of Theodore Koebel, a Virginia Tech professor who served as President of the CHP Board of Directors through 2009. During this time, CHP began constructing single family homes, developed rental housing for seniors with special needs, instituted a rental preservation program, and expanded its weatherization program to areas beyond the New River Valley.

Under Casper's executive leadership, CHP has continued to grow, and has evolved into a full-service affordable real estate development, architecture, construction, and property management business. It now owns and/or manages over 6,000 units of affordable multifamily housing across five states (Virginia, North Carolina, Kentucky, West Virginia, and Florida) and has developed over 250 single family homes in Virginia. CHP has also extended its reach to single family real estate sales by creating its own real estate LLC (limited liability corporation) and establishing a home ownership center that provides homebuyer education programs.

The growth into new affordable housing development did not result in a move away from work in home energy improvements. The organization's weatherization roots have survived as CHP Energy Services, and CHP's recognized expertise in home energy efficiency has led to the creation of the New River Center for Energy Research and Training, a division primarily concerned with workforce training.

CHP's mission is focused on sustainability which they see as both social and environmental. It sees value in creating and strengthening the idea of community. CHP has had a good working relationship with the state Housing Finance Agency and has benefited from a favorable enabling environment. Its increased focus on preservation has lessened difficulties with local zoning restrictions and approvals. They have a long history of success.

Approximately 46% of CHP's $80 million of annual revenues come from housing services. This includes homeownership and resident services, property and asset management, and managing rental income. An additional 33% of revenues come from real estate development activities, including construction and architectural design, and 27% from energy solutions. There is over $9 million in unrestricted cash, and staff of 365.

Wisconsin Partnership for Housing Development

William Perkins, the founding Executive Director of the Wisconsin Partnership for Housing Development (WPHD), after finishing Harvard Graduate School, worked for two years as a housing specialist for the City of Cambridge, Massachusetts. He was assigned to figure out with neighborhood organizations and less well organized residents if the city's plans met neighborhood needs (as perceived by residents, predominantly lower-income residents). If they did not, he was to advocate for changes in the plans. That work resulted in the creation of some of the earliest community development corporations in the Boston area. Perkins then joined a planning consulting firm that did conventional planning consulting, mostly for governmental clients.

Perkins left Massachusetts in 1976 and worked for the Wisconsin Division of Housing for nine years. For part of that time he ran the Division. A key part of the job was to try to get the state housing finance agency to provide loans for home improvement and for home purchase. Both proposals were resisted. The agency could make more money by financing rental housing projects using federal subsidies. They resisted financing programs in central city neighborhoods for being too risky. Under pressure from the Governor and Legislature, bonds were sold to provide capital for the programs, but on the condition that the Housing Division would operate the programs.

Perkins developed alliances and relationships of trust with the City of Milwaukee and other central cities. He also reached out to private lenders to persuade them to originate and service the loans because he believed they could do a better job than a state agency could. The Division of Housing also provided technical assistance and some limited grant and loan financing to community based development corporations.

By 1983, Bill was experiencing his fourth Governor and fifth cabinet secretary running the agency for which he worked. Every time the people changed, they spent a lot of time going over old ground, convincing people to continue good policies that had been initiated by their predecessors. Perkins decided to try creating a partnership among the public, private and nonprofit sectors. The Reagan Administration's demolition of federal housing programs also created both a need and an opportunity to reach out to the private sector not only for capital but also for ideas and expertise. The private sector, except for developers who had benefited from government subsidies, had largely been kept out of community development programs.

Perkins asked the Governor and the Lieutenant Governor, who ran the agency for which he worked, to make the creation of the partnership his responsibility as a state employee. It would be characterized as a state government initiative. They agreed. He spent the next two years planning the Wisconsin Housing Partnership, laying the groundwork for its operation, and negotiating for start up funding. In October 1985 it started operating independently from the state government.

The Wisconsin Partnership for Housing Development expands access to affordable housing opportunities and revitalizes neighborhoods through partnerships among the public, nonprofit and private sectors. It was designed to be self supporting financially, that is, to generate income principally by finding sources of money willing to pay for what they knew how to do, and to create, "programs," or businesses, that could generate income. Perkins did not want to be dependent on foundation or other grant programs, and he thought that if the staff knew how to do the job well enough, they should be able to find people willing to pay for it. Bill also believed that the need to generate income would impose discipline on them to always be thinking about how the work could achieve the objectives of their business partners. By and large, that has worked for the past 23 years. People have used grants only for start-up (for the first 18 months) and as "working capital" for new initiatives and to support advocacy activities which do not generate income. Less than 10% of their operating income has come from grants.

WPHD has developed or been principal development consultant for 800 homes. Development projects have included rental and ownership housing in a traditional neighborhood, single family and condominium projects, infill multi family housing, housing for people with mental illnesses and developmental disabilities, and housing for older adults. The Partnership has provided technical assistance and consulting services to more than 50 nonprofit and for profit developers that have produced, rehabilitated or preserved as affordable more than 1,200 homes. It has also created and managed seven financing programs that provided over $65 million in debt and equity financing to develop, rehabilitate and make energy conservation improvements in more than 2,000 homes.

It has managed down payment assistance programs that have provided $19.6 million to help more than 5,000 low and moderate income households buy homes. About half have received pre-purchase counseling from a network of agencies organized by the Partnership. Almost 40% of the households had incomes at or below 60% of area median, and about 30% have been racial and ethnic minority households. Using funding from the Housing Partnership Network, WPHD provided support for counseling to another 5,000 home buyers and over 400 renters. It has proposed and helped secure passage of legislation that has made more than $63 million in new state funds available for affordable housing.

WPHD has provided technical assistance (TA) to nonprofit developers under contracts with HUD and through fee-for-services consulting. Its technical assistance and consulting includes board and staff training in the development process and neighborhood revitalization strategy design and implementation. Most of the technical assistance and consulting is "hands-on" project-specific work. Part of the agenda is to encourage nonprofit developers to understand the advantages of partnerships with the other sectors. Most technical assistance and consulting to nonprofit developers has been in Wisconsin, but they also worked under contract to HUD in Iowa, Nebraska, North Dakota and South Dakota. One purpose of the business activity is to bring various kinds of financing to affordable housing and neighborhood revitalization that are not available from other sources.

Program development for new financing programs has been supported by grant funds used as working capital or by retained earnings. Program operating costs have always been paid by the capital participants in the programs. They have not subsidized operations of financing programs that they have created and managed.

WPHD created and managed financing programs that have provided predevelopment financing, interim (i.e., construction and holding period) debt financing, intermediate term post construction financing (or "mini-perms"), equity financing by investors earning Low Income Housing Tax Credits, deferred payment forgivable debt financing, and grant financing. They have managed programs that have provided loans for housing development, rehabilitation, energy conservation, down payment assistance, home purchase combined with rehabilitation, and housing counseling.

WPHD considers advocacy an integral part of its mission activities, although it has not been a line of business that generates revenue. Within the definition of advocacy, they include both policy development and legislative advocacy. The Partnership and some of its staff members are registered as lobbyists with the Wisconsin Government Accountability Board and the City of Madison. They strictly observe regulatory limitations on lobbying activity and restrictions imposed by these funding sources. Most of their advocacy activities are at the state government level, although they include advocacy at the federal level and occasionally at the local government level.

In all of their advocacy activities, they have worked as part of broader coalitions of nonprofit organizations and private sector firms, and sometimes public agencies (e.g., advocacy by local and state governments for increased federal resources or changes in the rules governing use of those resources). Often they have played a leadership role in organizing and coordinating those coalitions.

Between 1999 and 2005, the Partnership had HUD contracts to provide technical assistance to Community Housing Development Organizations (CHDOs) in Wisconsin. However, the HUD Milwaukee Field Office did not want them to provide technical assistance for

270

new development projects in Milwaukee. Instead, HUD itself organized and led an "intervention team" to provide support for older CDCs struggling to survive. HUD believed that an emerging new generation of CDCs in Milwaukee should not attempt to take on projects ambitious enough to need the Partnership's development technical assistance. Instead, HUD recruited providers of more basic organizational management assistance to help those organizations grow. HUD asked them instead to focus the technical assistance efforts on CHDOs in other Wisconsin communities that had more capacity and fewer organizational challenges, and that could take on new development projects.

In 2005, after allowing some time for newer CDCs to emerge and grow strong enough to do development, the Partnership began to renew its activity in Milwaukee. Mayor Barrett's election in 2004 and new leadership in City agencies also offered opportunities for more effective housing and neighborhood development policies. WPHD's initial strategy was to provide technical assistance to some of the newer nonprofit developers and to inner-city churches that had expressed interest in housing development. When opportunities to provide technical assistance materialized more slowly than they had hoped, they began to explore opportunities to work as a developer in Milwaukee.

The Partnership had been in the housing development business since the early 1990s. The board of directors saw being a developer in Milwaukee as a logical expansion of their previous roles, if viable project opportunities could be identified. The Milwaukee Department of City Development expressed its interest in exploring a development role for the Partnership that would help implement the city's neighborhood revitalization and affordable housing strategies, particularly in Targeted Investment Neighborhoods.

WPHD was interested in mixed income development projects that would include affordable housing in areas with stronger housing markets as well as projects that could help rebuild weaker housing markets. They had experience in mixed income development in the Madison area and were interested in applying that experience in Milwaukee. They were also interested in exploring joint ventures with for-profit developers in Milwaukee, as they have been doing in other communities.

During the same period in which Milwaukee nonprofit developers were experiencing severe problems, the Partnership designed and managed a successful neighborhood revitalization strategy in Racine built around investment of significant public and private sector funding in a comprehensive program in a single neighborhood. Investments were made in enough properties within a short enough timeframe to rebuild confidence in the neighborhood and restore a healthy housing market.

Wisconsin Partnership for Housing Development secured and managed over $46 million in capital commitments from 25 Milwaukee lending institutions, eight other corporate lenders and investors, and the City of Milwaukee. It created a $7 million revolving loan fund and a Low Income Tax Credit program for the City of Milwaukee in 1986. The Neighborhood Finance Corporation (NFC), created as one result of Perkin's work, was initially capitalized by $15 million in private-sector capital and $4 million in public funds. Since 1989, the NFC has made loans totaling over $150 million on projects involving 3,000 homes.

WPHD has also been a part of a national effort led by the Housing Partnership Network, working in collaboration with LISC, Enterprise and NeighborWorks, to focus on creating the capacity to acquire foreclosed homes, rehabilitate them and put them back into productive use. They have been participating in several different "task forces' working on the foreclosure issue and are working col-

272

laboratively on the issue with LISC Milwaukee and others.
Preservation of Affordable Housing (POAH)

Preservation of Affordable Housing is a mission-driven, entrepreneurial nonprofit organization committed to preserving affordable housing in regions of the U.S. POAH is the work of its Founder and President, Amy Anthony, though she had help from a number of persons along the way,.

I watched her grow from the Director of HAP, a leased-housing organization in Springfield, Massachusetts, in the seventies to become the Secretary of the Massachusetts Executive Office of Communities and Development under Governor Michael Dukakis in the eighties. She has also been President of Council of State Community Affairs and a member of the National Housing Task Force. As EOCD Secretary, she was a member of the Board of the Metropolitan Boston Housing Partnership and assisted its creation with an allocation of 200 Leased Housing units.

Amy Anthony has been a proponent of housing preservation for many years. "Between 1965 and 1990, $60 billion in federal funding was invested to build privately-owned, affordable rental homes for families, the disabled and the elderly. All were built according to the same premise: that the government would underwrite construction and operating costs, and in return the owners would commit to keeping the apartments affordable for 20, 30 or 40 years. As the regulatory agreements governing this compact expired, many owners decided to convert the properties to market rate apartments or condominiums."

The founding of POAH originated in the decision of the National Equity Fund (NEF) to divest itself of 14 properties in Missouri. David Stanley, who would become POAH's founding chairman, led fellow board members Herb Morse and George Latimer in seeking to create a new organization to own these properties. POAH was founded as an independent Illinois nonprofit organization with a 501(c)3 tax exempt status in Chicago in September, 2001. In 2003 the John D. and Catherine T. MacArthur Foundation provided a $500,000 working capital loan and a $2.5 million program related investment (PRI). Both were vital in its success.

POAH's growth over the last ten years to 63 properties in nine States and the District of Columbia, has been remarkable. Anthony and her board and advisors have been innovators and contributors to national preservation policies. They have dealt with owners that were facing massive debts on projects with inadequate operating budgets and poor management. They have purchased properties headed to foreclosure. In their first development, they worked with HUD to inaugurate the practice of assigning Mark-to-Market restructured mortgages to qualified nonprofit sponsors. In their 2007 acquisition of 932 units in 10 New England communities, POAH's staff executed the portfolio purchase by applying measures uniformly across the portfolio rather than property by property. This large-scale practice was used in later multi-property acquisitions.

POAH's property management company has been in business for 25 years. It has now been incorporated into the POAH family. It has recently completed the final phases of a five-year business plan. This represents a major investment by POAH in capacity building including recruiting new members and creating new human resources policies, corporate systems and performance assessments.

POAH, in partnership with the City of Chicago, received a $30.5 million ChoiceNeighborhood Grant from HUD to inspire neighborhood transformation in the Woodlawn Area. It included the redevelopment of the Grove Parc Plaza into a mixed-income, mixed-used community of rental apartments and homeownership units and the new construction of the Woodlawn Resource Center as the cornerstone of the redevelopment area. It will house the Woodlawn Children's Promise Community, the Center for Working Families, and Metropolitan Family Services.

POAH's portfolio reached about 8000 units with the purchase in 2012 of State Street Development and Management Company properties in Massachusetts. The latter comprises 841 units, 537 in three projects in downtown Boston, one in Brewster with 108 units and one in Hudson with 96 units.

The Community Builders (TCB)

I left GBCD, the predecessor organization to The Community Builders, to avoid any question of a conflict of interest during my time with the Court in the Boston Authority Case. Later, TCB, led by Patrick Clancy, went on to become the largest nonprofit urban housing company in the country.

In 1996 TCB made a determination to develop primarily for their own account. Additionally, they have largely limited themselves to develop and manage larger developments that permit them to operate a broad management program that includes extensive resident services. Several years ago, Pat Clancy told me that TCB had $1.3 billion of HUD Hope VI contracts underway. TCB was one of the prime Hope VI contractors in the country.

On his retirement a year ago, Pat said that there were three things of which he was most proud. The first was the level of financial innovation that enabled The Community Builders to shape some extraordinary accomplishments. The aggregation of resources involved in the Boston Housing Partnership projects was a beginning. TCB's role in the creation and development of the Low Income Housing Tax Credit, in the development of HOPE VI mixed-finance program, in the establishment of mechanisms for "porting" Section 8 units to other properties, and most recently, in designing a Quick Start bridge mechanism for use in the Neighborhood Stabilization Program 2 are great accomplishments.

Pat thought their second distinctive contribution has been in the continued focus on how to make affordable residential environments places where families succeed. They did this from their early work at Plumley Village to their development of Ways and Means, now called Community Life, as an entire new practice. Third is the extraordinary investment that TCB made in creating an organization that can function at a significant scale working across a dozen states while in each instance working in an intensive community-based fashion to achieve results that contribute to each neighborhood's long term, strengthening.

I regard Pat Clancy as pre-eminent in the use of the Low-Income Housing Tax Credits and other tax advantages in financing and refinancing housing projects. The developer fees and equity raised kept GBCD going in the seventies, and it was a primary bill-payer for TCB ever since. But TCB also had the ability to take on new challenges. After helping the Boston Housing Authority receive and execute the Orchard Gardens HOPE VI project, TCB went on to do HOPE VI projects in Louisville, Pittsburgh, and Holyoke, Massachusetts. About this time, TCB started to concentrate on larger developments and worked primarily for its own account.

In 2000, TCB was awarded participation in HOPE VI developments in Durham, NC, and in Norfolk, Virginia. Then they were selected for two HOPE VI in Cincinnati. In 2006, TCB completed the first phase of the Oakwood Shores HOPE VI development in Chicago's

Near South Side and the final phase of the New Brunswick HOPE VI Revitalization in New Brunswick, New Jersey, their tenth HOPE VI development. In 2010, TCB received $78.6 million from HUD as part of the Neighborhood Stabilization Program. This grant covered work in 15 States and the District of Columbia.

Bart Mitchell, the new President and CEO who replaced Clancy, writes that work extends from their multi-phased developments in Chicago's South Side and Pittsburgh's East Liberty neighborhood to the $150 million New Charlesview project in Boston. They have an unrestricted cash balance of $7 million. TCB gets the job done on a management overhead rate of about 10 per cent. TCB has developed over 21,000 apartments and homes and currently manages 6,000 units.

Louise Elving, Patrick Clancy, Whittlesey, and Ed Marchant

Whittlesey, Julie Sweeney, Tom Bledsoe, Manuel Muelle

Chapter Nine

The Housing Partnership Network (HPN)

Joseph McNeely, President of the Development Training Institute in Baltimore, asked me to make a presentation at a Housing Partnership Roundtable held on December 10, 1987, in Baltimore. On that panel with me was Kathryn Wylde, President of the New York City Housing Partnership and Arthur Sullivan, a staff member from BRIDGE in San Francisco. Later, Joe reported that our panel was the highlight of the conference. It confirmed for me the general interest in housing partnerships, particularly those well established with business backing. After I returned home, I wrote to Joe and had him send me the list of attendees and their mailing addresses. It was the beginning of my task of running the mailing list.

There were at the time a number of intermediaries in organizations such as the Local Initiatives Support Corporation (LISC), the Enterprise Foundation, the Neighborhood Reinvestment Corporation. But none of these was controlled by its members. When the National Association of Housing Partnerships was formed in 1992, it was designed as a membership organization.

When I accepted the job of Executive Director of the Boston Housing Partnership, both Bill Edgerly and I saw BHP as a model public/private partnership and one that could serve as a standard for a national movement. Some of the partnerships that I gathered for the 1990 meeting in Boston were well established and others still formative. Most had private business connections but the participation from the neighborhoods was still to be worked out. There were a number of themes offered at that meeting. John Zimmer from Pittsburgh said, "There is a real need to work together and try to build coalitions through the whole housing delivery system"; Harry Spence from Boston offered, "Collaboration and partnership are urgently needed because we've made the mechanism by which we respond to these problems immensely more complex than they need to be." And from Marvin Siflinger of Mass Housing Finance Agency, "We must put in place a new institutional infra-structure;" Donald Campbell from the Multi-family Council in Washington, "You need to function as a group"; Zimmer from Pittsburgh, "Management is absolutely crucial"; Tom Fulton from Minneapolis, "The attributes of high-functioning partnerships can be identified, modeled and replicated. We can benefit from knowing what the common elements are that have made them successful." Jim Luckett from Boston, "We want to see the residents use this newly renovated or newly built housing as the launching pad to better their lives, better the lives of their children and ultimately to better the lives of their community. We need to have that broad a vision about what we are doing." The attendees were ready to go to the next step.

A second conference followed in Atlanta the following year. Although we received enthusiastic support at the luncheon from Mayor Maynard Jackson, there were only 40 attendees at the conference and we knew that we had work to do. It was suggested that I incorporate the organization. On my return to Boston, I asked my friend John Bok and his associate David Feinberg of Foley, Hoag and Eliot, to file the necessary incorporation papers with the State of Massachusetts. They had previously submitted a request to the United States Internal Revenue Service (IRS) for a ruling to qualify as a charitable Section 501 (c) 3 organization. The IRS initial determination was that we were a trade association. Feinberg submitted additional information and we received our 501 (c) 3 determination.

The incorporating Board was composed of, in addition to myself, Hattie Dorsey Hudson from the Atlanta Partnership for Neighborhood Development; Lynn Luallen from the Kentucky Housing Partnership; Patricia Massey from the Baltimore Partnership for Housing Development; and Bill Perkins from the Wisconsin Partnership for Housing Development. The initial full Board of Directors, appointed at the next meeting, was a mix of operating people and well regarded business executives. In time, the Board was dealing with technical matters affecting the operations of the members, and it made sense to confine membership to the Chief Executives of the member organizations.

The next conferences were held in Milwaukee followed by one in Baltimore. Both had active partnerships at the time but they lacked sustainability and both were terminated within a matter of years. The Fifth Conference was special. It was held in Indianapolis. While we only had about 50 people in attendance, we had an array of interested parties. Mayor Stephen Goldsmith; William Edgerly, formerly Chairman of the Boston Housing Partnership and now from the Foundation for Partnerships; Irvin Henderson from National Community Reinvestment Corporation; Paul Grogan from LISC; Bart Harvey from the Enterprise Foundation; George Knight from Neighborhood Reinvestment Corporation; Helen Dunlap from HUD; Clark Ziegler from the Massachusetts Housing Partnership Fund and Joe McNeely from the Development Training Institute; Clay Robbins from the Lilly Foundation and Beth Smith from Hyams Foundation; consultants Jim Pickman and Robert Rapoza; scores of partnership heads and others.

With a grant from Freddie Mac, we published a catalogue of sixty-seven partnerships. While this was evidence that NAHP was relatively better known, we were still a long way from being at the center of the national discussion.

Tom Bledsoe, who was the Executive Director of MBHP as well as

Treasurer of NAHP, was busy with both agencies. After a merger in 1991 with a regional non-profit agency that administered 5,000 leased housing units, BHP's name was changed to the Metropolitan Boston Housing Partnership (MBHP), expanding its focus beyond rental housing to meet a continuum of needs from homelessness prevention to homeownership.

MBHP wanted to start a homeownership counseling program but it was unable to access HUD counseling funds due to its limited experience and lack of HUD certification. Through board members that had relationships in Washington, MBHP learned of HUD's intent to administer a portion of the homeownership counseling program through national intermediaries. MBHP identified this as an opportunity for the then NAHP to become certified as a national counseling intermediary and to make these funds available to Boston and other network members. As the sponsor of NAHP, MBHP also saw the potential for this program to establish a role for the network.

In 1995 NAHP became the first HUD certified counseling intermediary and was awarded $800,000. These resources, and others leveraged by this activity, enabled MBHP to create a comprehensive program that includes pre-purchase counseling, acquisition and rehabilitation assistance. It also provided support for families in its leased housing program to buy homes. HPN's initiative was a nationwide network of high-capacity regional housing organizations that partner with local governments and community organizations. Since then, the Housing Partnership Network has won $22 million in competitive grants from HUD, funds which have been used to counsel over 700,000 families and assist more than 100,000 people to buy or retain their homes.

Based on the quality and impact of our local and national delivery system, the Network has received the top competitive score and funding level from HUD on its counseling program. The Network submits a single federal application for counseling funds on behalf of its members, manages the grant awards and provides peer-based technical assistance to participants. In turn, members have leveraged federal support on a 6:1 basis to obtain an additional $100 million from banks, foundations, and state and local governments.

HPN coordinated a national advocacy effort to build Congressional support for homeownership counseling. Working closely with the member counseling agencies in its network, it has provided information and facilitative leadership to encourage its members to educate their Congressional representatives on the importance of the program to their local organizations and districts. HPN is also a leading collaborator with national organizations, including the Neighborhood Reinvestment Corporation and National Foundation for Consumer Credit, to encourage HUD to improve its information collection and outcome tracking. At the request of the House Appropriations Committee staff, HPN compiled legislative recommendations on behalf of its members and the national intermediaries to address the congressional concerns.

The Mark-to-Market program of HUD was the next program jointly sponsored by MBHP and HPN. The Mark-to-Market Demonstration (M2M), was a classic example of HUD devolution and extraction from the subsidized housing world. It presented an opportunity for the NAHP members to acquire skills and knowledge about Section 8 restructuring while earning fees. Utilizing an innovative structure that included members and a private sector firm, Recapitalization Advisors, NAHP created a joint venture with the Metropolitan Boston Housing Partnership that was approved as a financial restructuring entity for HUD-insured multi-family housing.

Raising $1.2 million of investment capital from five local housing partnerships and Recapitalization Advisors, the NAHP/MBHP team successfully bid on a HUD contract to restructure a portfolio of 22 multifamily properties. Building on member relationships in New York and Charlotte, NAHP raised additional capital from Chase and NationsBank to finance a second and a third portfolio. The experience and learning was further spread as NAHP members in Pittsburgh, New York City, Miami, and Wisconsin took on a restructuring role for certain properties.

Through this initiative HPN became the largest Mark-to-Market restructuring entity in the nation and stabilized 46 HUD Section 8 properties in 20 states, preserving 5,000 affordable housing units. The effort generated $3 million in fee income for the Network and its partners. It also established the organization as a leading national expert on Mark-to-Market and a strong voice in Washington for policies facilitating non-profit acquisition of multi-family property.

Tom Bledsoe's work on the Mark-to-Market program had engaged him in challenging discussions with HPN members, and he saw it as an opportunity to build the membership. In 1996, I accepted the role of Chair of the Board and Bledsoe was named President of NAHP. In 1998 he resigned from MBHP and joined the staff as its' full time Chief Executive Officer. Bledsoe had a keen sense of how an organization might be built from the bottom up. The board, now composed of the chief executive officers of the strongest public/private partnership members, would be the driver of an entrepreneurial and innovating organization. There were discussion about this role and the name of the organization. In 2002, the name of the company was changed to the Housing Partnership Network (HPN).

Now with 100 members operating in 37 states, HPN brings together organizations united in a concern for affordable housing and engaged in a wide range of activities including:

- Multi and single family housing development and rehabilitation;
- home-ownership counseling and foreclosure;
- housing-related social services ; and
- charter schools and other facilities

Many HPN members engage in two or more of these areas. Network members have developed and preserved over 300,000 units of affordable rental housing; built, rehabilitated or financed 63,000 single- family homes; and provided homeownership counseling and housing support to 700,000 low and moderate income people. Approximately 80% of HPN members are housing developers. The remainder are lenders, primarily for housing but also for community facilities. A third of the developers also do some form of lending. Most of the developers do their own housing management and provide resident services.

HPN's members:

- Have significant stature and are deeply embedded in the institutional, political, and corporate context of their local community and region
- Operate at a regional scale that is at least as broad as a city and in many instances encompasses a metropolitan area, a state, or a multi-state area
- Have solid records of performance and are led by highly competent professional staffs
- Provide and manage resident and community services directly or under contract
- Involve substantial leadership and participation from the private sector and effective working relationships with public agencies
- Have developed and nurtured an institutional network of local, regional and national organizations - public, private for-profit and

nonprofit - with which they partner and interact
• Have an entrepreneurial approach to exploring new
opportunities and initiatives, and operate their organizations
as substantial business enterprises

HPN is far from simply a holding company or trade association. It
is a dynamic organization that plays an active role in sponsoring and
structuring business initiatives in partnership and on behalf of its
members. Since its founding in 1992, HPN's mission is to:

• promote the spread of innovation and collective learning among
its members
• facilitate business opportunities for its members through
collaborative initiatives
• influence national public and corporate policy impacting
affordable housing.

HPN is a network of members that have their own network of local
relationships. These local relationships are unique and the product
of years of hard work and trust building. They are not negotiable
and cannot be handed off to another player. The members provide
HPN with the local credibility and a comparative advantage when
connected to national initiatives.

HPN identifies itself as a network facilitator among a set of peer
organizations. HPN staff focuses on expanding connections among
the members rather than on the growth and authority of a central
organization. There are five organizing principles that guide how the
network makes strategic decisions, advocates for policy, and inter-
acts with its members.

1. Purpose: HPN supports initiatives that enable the network and
its member organizations to advance their shared missions of

    promoting affordable housing, community development
    and family economic empowerment.

2. Impact: HPN promotes policies and programs that help members address issues important to their communities and that enable the organizational learning and repositioning necessary to foster larger scale impact.

3. Capacity: HPN pursues initiatives that build on and increase the capacity of its local members and that require the support and facilitation of the broader network to achieve success, replication and scale.

4. Financing: HPN and its local partnerships operate as business enterprises and structure initiatives to provide a mutual financial advantage to the network and the member organizations.

5. Policy: HPN prioritizes initiatives that enable the network to shape federal policy in a manner that reflects the experience of its members and reinforces the success of their programs.

The institutional trends that are occurring - devolving federal housing policy, centralizing financing and rapid technological development – create an environment of enormous change and opportunity for non-profit housing organizations. HPN's network is well positioned to identify, design and implement initiatives that emerge from and respond to these sweeping changes.

This synergy is exemplified by HPN's national meetings, which are a microcosm of how the network enables members to leverage their individual capacities to achieve larger impact. Structured as working sessions of directors and senior staff, the honesty and engagement evident in these meetings underscores the special interactive nature of HPN's network. The purpose of the national meetings, and the ongoing interaction of members throughout the year, is to facilitate peer to peer learning and the exploration of new opportunities for collaborative action.

HPN has derived a theory of action that describes how network initiatives are developed. Opportunities or initiatives are originated to which a configuration of organizations can respond. The program is designed to flexibly respond to the complexities of on-the-ground practice and use reflection past experience that may shape new opportunities and roles.

There have been a number of HPN initiatives, including:

Pre-development Fund

HPN completed a Community Development Financial Institution (CDFI) Application in 2000 in which it presented a product need and a business plan. The Housing Partnership Development Fund was created as a lending affiliate and received certification and a technical assistance award from the national CDFI Fund. The Fund offered subordinate acquisition and predevelopment loans enabling members to compete in the marketplace for properties and land.

The Network created this $30 million fund by investing $2 million of equity that leveraged $28 million of bank and foundation capital. A selected group of members leveraged local bank relationships to market the fund and to raise capital from Chase, Citibank, Wells Fargo, Key Bank, Fleet and US Bank. HPN obtained HUD's approval to invest $750,000 of its M2M incentive fees to create a loan-loss reserve and HPN members agreed to invest $150,000 of their own capital in the fund. A variety of loan products were developed and pre-development loans were made to HPN members. While continuing to provide some enterprise level financing, the focus of the Housing Partnership Fund has shifted now to larger scale initiatives that support strategic collaboration among Network members. These initiatives include the Multifamily Stabilization Trust and the CDFI bond guarantees if launched. Proceeds could be used to fi-

nance our members housing development projects.
Single Family Property Disposition

The Network's involvement in the HUD Counseling Program created the organizational relationships and knowledge base to play a leadership role in FHA single family property disposition. In 1998, Neighborhood Housing Services (NHS) of Chicago informed HPN that HUD was considering abandoning its process of giving non-profits the right of first refusal to purchase FHA-foreclosed homes nationwide. Instead, they proposed selling the underlying mortgages to for-profit investors and putting disposition of the properties in the hands of private management and marketing companies.

The Chicago NHS, which was already working closely with the Cleveland Housing Network, asked HPN whether other network members were concerned about the issue. Calls to Miami, Charlotte, Minneapolis and Rochester revealed that HPN's members were some of the largest FHA purchasers in the nation with a strong track record of utilizing the homes for affordable homeownership. Each had been confronting this critical issue on their own and recognized the advantage of working together.

HPN convened an FHA working group and developed policy recommendations for Congress. Members and staff became actively involved in budget deliberations and engaged with congressional staff, FHA Commissioner William Apgar, and senior HUD policy makers. Through network relationships, the collaboration was extended to other national groups concerned with the issue, including LISC, Enterprise, Neighborhood Reinvestment and the National Housing Conference, bringing greater influence and expertise to the campaign. As a direct result of the Network's advocacy to federal policy makers, Congress passed legislation that provides for the bulk acquisition of FHA property by nonprofits in targeted revitalization areas.

In addition to proposing policy changes, HPN worked with its members to develop a risk-mitigation financing program that would facilitate bulk acquisition by nonprofits of FHA homes. With the support of its members, HPN sought and received a $100,000 grant from the Fannie Mae Foundation to develop the technical assistance and financing program.

HPN submitted a proposal to HUD for a $5 million direct loan to leverage a $20 million acquisition fund and demonstration program to assist its nonprofit members to purchase portfolios of FHA foreclosed homes. HUD agreed to implement a demonstration programs with 10 network members. However, HUD failed to approve the direct loan and its half-hearted administration of pilot disposition programs has underscored the need for further legislative support.

Bulk acquisition agreements were successfully negotiated with HPN's members in Cleveland, Chicago and Miami, but other cities decided not to pursue the program due to the high rehabilitation risk and bureaucratic barriers. At the request of the House Appropriations Committee, HPN has proposed legislative amendments that would increase the pricing discounts to non-profit purchasers and earmark a $5 million direct loan to HPN's acquisition fund.

FHA Property Disposition

The Cleveland Housing Network (CHN) was formed in 1981 to provide community development corporations access to capital to develop affordable housing. Focusing on creating home ownership opportunities for low-income families, CHN has rehabilitated or constructed 2400 homes and is the largest purchaser of foreclosed FHA insured properties in the nation.

High FHA foreclosure rates in Cleveland have historically caused neighborhood deterioration and hardship for thousands of families.

CHN has turned this problem into an opportunity by rehabilitating 1000 FHA homes, revitalizing neighborhoods and helping low-income families become first time homeowners.

The Mark-to-Market (M2M) initiative created the knowledge base and institutional capacity within HPN to help members navigate the complex set of financial and organizational processes involved in the restructuring, transfer and acquisition of HUD-subsidized properties. The M2M experience also demonstrated the need for a pre-development loan fund that could help NAHP members obtain the capital and technical assistance to acquire at-risk multifamily properties. Identifying this need out of its practice and the experience of its members, HPN decided to establish a lending institution and to seek its certification as a Community Development Financial Institution (CDFI).

Through an interactive process involving board members and HPN staff, CHN met regularly with Congressional and HUD staff in Washington to shape the federal legislation to protect and expand the role of non-profits in FHA property disposition. CHN collaborated with peers in other cities to develop policy recommendations and to bring in other national allies such as the Enterprise, LISC and NRC.

After passage of the legislation, CHN and the other HPN members pressed HUD to adopt demonstration programs to utilize the new authority. CHN became the first non-profit to finalize an agreement with HUD for the bulk acquisition of all FHA foreclosed homes in targeted Cleveland neighborhoods. It has since expanded it volume of property acquisition and now has a predicable flow of properties into its rehabilitation and sales program.

Multifamily Portfolio Acquisition

Utilizing the predevelopment resources from the loan fund, HPN worked with its most experienced multifamily developers to create a networked property acquisition and technical assistance program. Under this innovative approach, the properties would be acquired directly by the member corporations but HPN would be authorized to operate on their behalf, to coordinate negotiations with the sellers, and to be the focal point in executing the purchase and sales agreements. Through this model the seller would get the practical convenience of communicating with a centralized buyer agent and, at the same time, capable, locally connected buyers would work to deliver the best results and greatest likelihood of closing.

This program was created on the possibility of a large portfolio acquisition from AIMCO, an institutional owner that was selling a large part of their portfolio of Section 8 properties through competitive bids. HPN staff learned of this opportunity and distributed information on the available properties to members, and indicated that AIMCO's aggressive timeline called for quick action.

With extensive use of email and teleconferencing, HPN coordinated a process involving 30 members and other interested organizations and developed a network bid. Participants did the initial due diligence and determined the bid amount for each property, with technical assistance from HPN and Recapitalization Advisors. Members and staff brought in an array of financial partners, including the Enterprise Foundation, the National Housing Trust, Munie Mae, US Bancorp, Piper Jaffray, and the Community Development Trust. Through a collaborative feedback process, HPN submitted the initial bid, handled follow-up assessment and subsequent bidding, and coordinated negotiations of the Purchase and Sale agreements with

AIMCO.
Under HPN's umbrella, twenty organizations bid on eighty-nine properties comprising 10,000 units. Six properties were won. The AIMCO effort also engaged three strong regional organizations that were new to HPN's network. Each has subsequently joined.

Neighborhood Stabilization and Foreclosure Prevention

HPN members have responded to the challenges presented by foreclosure by forming collaborations with local governments and the private sector to develop effective and innovative ways to revitalize distressed communities and foreclosed homes. HPN has helped local efforts achieve greater scale and impact with business support, technical assistance, and new approaches that address such issues as property management, interim ownership, property disposition and home mortgage financing. These best practices are shared through an active peer exchange among members which promotes business collaboration and productivity.

The Network played a key role in making the case for the $7 billion federal Neighborhood Stabilization Program (NSP) which has been the principal capital resource that communities and nonprofit developers use to acquire and rehabilitate foreclosed homes. Working closely with their state and local governments, more than 40 Network members have operated neighborhood stabilization programs – often as the lead player in a collaborative involving public and private partners.

The National Community Stabilization Trust (NCST) was formed in 2008 through an unprecedented collaboration among six leading nonprofits – the Housing Partnership Network, Enterprise Community Partners, NeighborWorks America, Local Initiatives Support Corporation, National Council of La Raza and the National Urban

League. NCST serves as an efficient, large scale vehicle to help community and nonprofits acquire foreclosed homes from financial institutions, with a goal of revitalizing those communities with concentrations of vacant and abandoned foreclosed properties. Tom Bledsoe serves as Chair of the NCST Board.

A new Neighborhood Stabilization and Foreclosure Prevention Initiative was recently funded with a $2.7 million grant from the Citi Foundation. These funds will allow the Network to greatly advance their work in neighborhood stabilization, with grants made to a dozen Network members who are working on innovative, replicable, and scalable solutions to the foreclosure problem. The Network will provide technical support and peer exchange in order to advance new approaches and best practices. Throughout the program, the Network will share learning with the broader industry and policy communities, with a goal of shaping new federal policy responses to neighborhood stabilization.

Another foreclosure vehicle invented by the Network is the Mortgage Resolution Fund (MRF). MRF aims to keep families in their homes and stabilize neighborhoods by purchasing and modifying delinquent notes before foreclosure. By combining federal funds with sources from regulated financial institutions, MRF is designed to purchase delinquent mortgages at a discount and work with servicers and families to properly modify loans to an affordable level so they can remain in their homes and avoid foreclosure. For those households that are not eligible for loan modifications, MRF will provide support as they transition to new housing. MRF is a partnership between HPN, Mercy Portfolio Services, the National Community Stabilization Trust, and the Enterprise Community Partners.

The Community Restoration Corporation

The Community Restoration Corporation (CRC) is a new entity designed to help communities and lenders collaborate when lenders or loan servicers choose to walk away from properties instead of foreclosing on delinquent loans. These "bank walkaways" result in homes being left to deteriorate. CRC addresses this issue by acquiring discounted single-family notes from loan servicers, taking possession of the underlying assets, and then transferring those assets to land banks so they can be demolished, redeveloped or sold. Servicers provide sufficient cash to dispose of the properties in addition to providing the discounted notes. CRC is being piloted in Ohio's Cuyahoga County with funding from the Ford Foundation, the F.B. Heron Foundation and Goldman Sachs.

Housing Partnership Insurance Exchange

In addition to housing development needs, HPN has worked to deliver services to its members. One of these vehicles was a property insurance program. This affiliate called the Housing Partnership Insurance Exchange (HPIEx) provides casualty and liability coverage to 20 Network members who own or manage 50,000 affordable apartments. HPIEx improves operational performance and can contribute to stable rents for residents. This award-winning social enterprise is the first captive insurance company in the country that was created and owned by nonprofit housing developers.

HPIEx was launched in 2004 in the aftermath of 9-11 when insurance companies were raising premiums and canceling coverage. Risk and capital losses were better among nonprofit managers because of their superior operational performance. HPIEx was able to negotiate agreements with international insurance carriers and deliver customers loss control services. In the past years hundreds of millions in dividends have been distributed to the shareholders.

Housing Partnership DIRECT

The Housing Partnership DIRECT provides group buying as a service to HPN members. With neither fees nor investment discounts paid to national vendors, 27 members saved $200,000 on $1.4 million in sales in 2010. The experience has continued to improve over the past two years.

Charter School Financing Partnership

Some of the nation's most productive community development financial institutions (CDFIs) collaborate through the Network to enhance business practices, pursue innovation and develop shared platforms to access capital. Schools are critical part of residential services. Six of our CDFI members (NCB Capital Impact, Low Income Investment Fund, The Reinvestment Fund, Raza Development Fund, the Community Reinvestment Fund and the Housing Partnership Network joined together to create the Charter School Financing Partnership (CSFP). CSFP is a groundbreaking vehicle to access secondary market financing for charter schools that serve disadvantaged students and communities. The U.S. Department of Education awarded the Network $15 million for CSFP to credit-enhance individual charter schools. This financing was being provided through tax-exempt bonds, loans or other financial assistance, including loans provided in conjunction with New Market Tax Credit Transactions. In addition, the CSFP received a $5 million private related investment (PRI) from the Walton Foundation in 2010. Combined, these funds will have enabled CSFP to provide up to $100 million in loans to charter schools. Under the terms of the grant, CSFP will provide a minimum of $90 million in financing to charter schools by 2013, serving approximately fifteen schools with 6,000 to 9,000 student seats. It is anticipated that the grant proceeds will recycle to support additional financing for charter schools by 2015. To date, CSFP has provided an $800,000 credit enhancement to a $5.2 million New Market Tax Credit facility for the Jersey Golden Door Charter School. It has also issued commitments for a $2.8 million credit enhancement and a $1.25 million loan from the Walton Foundation for a $29.3 million tax-exempt bond for three Brighter Choice charter schools in Albany, NY.

Gulf Coast Housing Partnership (GCHP)

After Hurricane Katrina stuck New Orleans, the Network was asked to help. A review of the potential nonprofit developers revealed that there was no existing organization in the area with the necessary qualifications. HPN decided to form a new, well-capitalized Gulf Coast Housing Partnership (GCHP) in 2006 to spearhead the rebuilding of housing and communities in Louisiana and Mississippi.

Building on the experience of successful nonprofit developers, the Network partnered with government, business and philanthropic organizations to create a well-funded nonprofit corporation to serve the Gulf Coast region.. The Network invested $2 million of core equity from its Housing Partnership Ventures Fund to match funds from foundations and a $14 million senior line of credit from Fannie Mae. These funds were critical in giving GCHP the financial capacity to undertake multiple development opportunities to achieve large scale impact.

Kathy Laborde, a highly-regarded New Orleans developer, was hired to serve as President and Chief Executive Officer. Tom Bledsoe chaired GCHP's board. The Board of Directors was comprised of local and national civic leaders, including several Directors of the Network. This unique partnership combined the Network's capital and knowledge of organizational development with Kathy's exceptional real estate track record and partnership abilities.

Although initially managed through the network, our shared goal was to create an independent nonprofit that could be a long-term leader in the region. After a successful launch the Gulf Coast Housing Partnership was spun off from Network management in 2009 and is now a locally- operated nonprofit. Tom Bledsoe has recently stepped down as board chair.

The Gulf Coast Housing Partnership has quickly emerged as the most productive nonprofit developer in the region. GCHP has a production schedule of over 1600 units of affordable homes and apartments serving low to moderate income working families and individuals, persons with special needs, seniors, and the homeless and/ or at risk of homelessness population. It has rehabilitated 535 apartments destroyed by the hurricane, developed state-of-the-art LEED (certified homes in the Lower Ninth Ward with Global Green, and created supportive housing for at-risk and special needs individuals and families in New Orleans and Baton Rouge. Anchored by a new 263-unit mixed-income development, GCHP is carrying out a comprehensive revitalization initiative in the Central City neighborhood of New Orleans that includes new homes, apartments and commercial space.

GCHP is a model response to a crisis that underscores the power and innovation of the Network's social enterprise approach. The two million dollars equity commitment has leveraged more than $235 million of housing and community investments. By combining strong management at the regional level with dynamic national partnerships, we can maximize the impact of public, private and civic leadership.

In July 2009 Louisiana state officials broke ground on a new 61.5 million mixed-income housing development in New Orleans' Central City. Known as "The Muses," the project was developed by the Gulf Coast Housing Partnership in collaboration with a for-profit developer, LDG Development, and is slated to be the first LEED certified multifamily development in the State of Louisiana.

The project's public-private funding structure used $25.7 million in Community Development Block Grants and federal recovery funding to leverage investments by the Housing Partnership Ventures fund, LDG Development, Gulf Coast Housing Partnership and local nonprofit developer Jericho Road Episcopal Housing Initiative. Completed the fall of 2010, The Muses is a model of mixed-income urban living, providing market standard affordable energy efficient housing and quality of life amenities for a range of incomes representative of the city's population.

Multifamily Real Estate Investment Trust

For two years HPN worked to design a social venture investment trust to raise capital, implement shared services, and achieve operational efficiencies. The Housing Partnership Equity Trust is jointly owned by the Network and twelve of its members. The Trust announced its first transaction in 2013 that enabled Mercy Housing Lakefront to acquire and rehabilitate a 128-unit property in Aurora, Illinois.

The Equity Trust will bring a new and quicker source of capital than such traditional subsidies as Low Income Housing Tax Credits. It can cover 95% of the cost of acquisition and rehabilitation. Members can act with the same speed and flexibility as a private cash buyers by eliminating the need to put together a complex financing package before contracting and closing on a property. The REIT allows members to pursue properties that serve a broader range of populations and communities, including workforce housing. Targeted acquisitions will include unsubsidized market assets and expiring

LIHTC properties.

The initial $100 million capitalization is comprised of $3 million from the Network and participating members; a $10 million program related investment (PRI) from the MacArthur Foundation; a $5 million PRI from the Ford Foundation, $17 million in equity from Prudential; and $65 million revolving loan from Citibank. This first phase is just a start. It is projected that $500 million will be raised by the end of 2015. The Network will serve as the managing member of the LLC that controls the Trust, and will hire and manage the staff and service providers.

There are issues with the equity trust that will emerge. It will energize the larger, stronger partnerships and do little for the others. It will be working with non-regulated housing and the owners will have to be careful not to lose themselves in commercial type businesses and draw HPN away from its role of supporting a national movement of regional developers and managers.

Performance Standards

In addition to producing affordable housing, HPN is always in pursuit of achieving best practices and performance on the part of its members. This is critical to success in the affordable housing field as the housing is treated as a capital asset and the value of the well-maintained asset is more fully appreciated. The peer to peer exchanges and workshops have been helpful. Another factor has been Strength Matters. It is a system of performance measures on pioneered technology developed by co-op metrics that are reported and warehoused and made available back to the members. It allows tracking of performance and allows comparisons with peer organizations. Users can see trends in their own business or property operations, compare their performance against others in the industry, and identify areas for improvement. There are 36 participating organizations with over 79,000 units of housing.

The housing world in which HPN operates places a high premium on information and rapid communication. HPN's networked model is made operationally possible by advances in information technology. Using client-server and web based technology, information and program data can be shared and managed from multiple sites. Email and the Internet provide a communication link among organizations engaged in a joint enterprise.

Resident Services

In addition to its role in enhancing operational performance, information technology can be directly beneficial to the residents of the affordable housing managed or sponsored by HPN's members. By connecting buildings and computer learning centers to the Internet and sponsoring technology and skills training programs on site, HPN's members are uniquely positioned to help low-income families overcome the digital divide and access economic opportunities in the new economy.

The Community Builders and others are offering a broad array of measurable activities that are connected to the success of families and children – such things as job readiness, financial couching, and youth development. TCB has done a number of HOPE VI projects. They see their world as providing "a model of mixed income housing communities as a stable platform for long term engagement of low and moderate income families in improving stability, education attainment and quality of life in sustainable mixed income communities." They have generally worked with larger developments. There is a question as to how one does these things in a smaller project community. Clancy may be right in the big developments but it might not be so in smaller communities. The State of Massachusetts in now proposing a reorganization of its State Public Housing Authorities which would reduce its 240 housing authorities into possible six agencies. The local agencies are arguing that they have relations with the Towns that are irreplaceable. But costs are the key and solutions need to be found that permit savings in the such things as procurement, certain maintenance functions and accounting, and allowing the local site office to stay in touch with the residents and be a player in the community.

Peabody Trust Caring for Londoneers since 1862

Lord Richard Best looking over Earswick Housing

1993 Dutch study group including Schaaper, with poster, and Catau in upper right

Martien Schaaper and Whittlesey

304

1995 Dutch study group hosted by the Whittleseys with van Moolen and Johan Dunnewijk in rear

2003 study group on the terrace at Lord Richard Best's Office

Terrace houses on Princess Road in Kilburn Park

Paddington Church's Elder housing in Kilburn Park

306

Council housing in Kilburn Park

Thamesmead under construction in 1969

Peabody Trust Housing in London

Peabody Trust Housing for mentally disabled

Broomley council housing involved in transfer

Broomley council housing involved in transfer

Right-to-buy house

Childcenter in Brent council housing

1925 social housing in the Netherlands

Bajlmermeer prior to its rebuilding

New development site in Tilburg

Elderly housing in Tilburg

Kitchen and community room in elderly development in Tilburg

Regional housing waiting room in Tilburg

WonenBreburg new elderly development

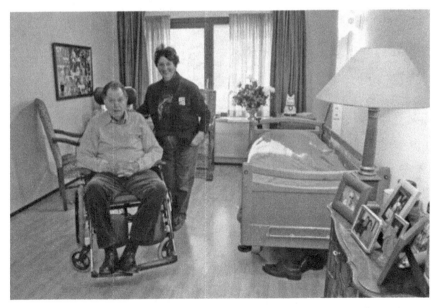

Resident with service attendant

Building with exterior cladding for energy savings

Enschele elderly housing in 1995

Pathmos project area

Woonplaats Housing for homeless

Tilburg school children awaiting transport

Independent living homes next to shelter housing in WonenBreburg

Chapter Ten

A View from Abroad

My three years in Bournemouth as a child and my military service Europe during the World War Two had given me an interest in England and the Continent. Louise and I did an exploratory trip visiting 14 cities in Europe in 1962. I became a member of the International Federation of Housing and Planning and attended its annual conferences in Budapest in 1985, The Hague in 1988, Japan in 1989 and Berlin in 1991. I attended my first National Federation of Housing Associations (NFHA) conference in London in 1984 and subsequent conferences in 1989 and 1990.

I discovered that the work of the Boston Housing Partnership was analogous in a number of respects with the role of the Housing Corporation in the United Kingdom. BHP was the primary funder of the community development corporations. The Housing Corporation was the primary funder of the housing associations. My knowledge of European housing systems led to exchanges with a number of British and other housing officials. I became the tour guide in Boston for groups of foreigners, including two groups of Dutch housing officials.

There are a number of countries with well-organized and funded social housing systems. We could surely learn from their experience. The history and financing of the housing associations in England and its choice of housing associations as the primary provider of social housing is noteworthy. England allowed rent control to marginalize private for-profit rental housing and then favored social housing by local government. When local government housing encountered problems, the national government decided to support the nonprofit housing associations. It provided capital grants over a twenty-year period and thereby developed a network of financially capable social enterprises that could be the primary producers and managers of their social housing.

The UK has been several decades ahead of the USA in recognizing the potential of the nonprofit sector. A number of other countries have also utilized nonprofits much longer than the US. France enacted a housing law in 1903 which included a provision that businesses allocate 1% of their revenue for workers' housing. In 1901 the Netherlands passed its first major housing bill. Nonprofit organizations in the Netherlands now own and manage 35% of all housing and 75% of all the rental housing in the country. Their experience is useful when one considers options for our social housing here in the USA.

The story of social housing in the UK dates back to the twelfth century. The first formal recognition that there should be established practices to address housing for the poor originated in the sixteenth century poor laws. In 1572 in the 14th year of Elizabeth's reign laws were enacted to provide for the collection of taxes. In the 39th year of her reign, the poor laws were rewritten to include an authorization to local government to erect "working houses for the poor" and that the churchwardens erect "convenient houses of habitation" on "wastes and commons for the impotent poor."[35] These were the almshouses, some of which exist today, that became part of England's social safety net. A more structured system of care of the poor in England began in the eighteenth century. This included in addition to the care of elders and the homeless, provisions for schools, dispensaries and hospitals.

The industrial revolution came to Britain decades before any other country in Western Europe. The country was transformed from a largely rural society to a predominately urban one. By 1860 it was the richest county in the world, with a per capita income 50% higher than that of France and almost three times that of Germany.[36]

On the other hand, the poor in the cities suffered. The cities attracted workers from rural areas as well as immigrants. Housing overcrowding was common and many families lived in underground cellars and deserted buildings. Clean water was frequently unavailable and dark and dank living conditions were ideal breeding grounds for disease. A report on an area in Manchester in 1843 indicated that there was only one toilet for every 212 people. Newly built housing was frequently of poor design and obsolete within decades. Back-to-back housing in which the buildings had party walls on three sides andwindows only on the entrance side with a communal out-building for the whole block was a health and environmental disaster. It took decades for such housing to be replaced. In 1913 200,000 people still lived in back-to-back housing in Birmingham, a city known for its industry and civic pride.[37]

In 1835 the Municipal Corporations Act greatly enlarged the responsibilities of local city government. Subsequent acts assigned to local government responsibilities for housing the poor among other things. Some cities made significant progress in addressing the most serious municipal problems and others did not. In 1868 and again in 1879, Parliament enacted laws that not only empowered local governments to demolish slums but required that they be responsible for building replacement social housing.[38] A commission in 1885 reported on the appalling conditions in which so many were living in London. Rebuilding old housing areas, addressing health concerns, providing adequate housing for the poor would all remain serious problems.

The most common form of commercial market housing in the late nineteenth century was terrace or row housing with a backyard, washhouse and privy. In some situations developers were able to crowd in more units and build at lower costs for families with modest income. Built for single family occupancy, these two- to four-room houses would be occupied by two or more families. In time demolition of much of this housing was often essential, through adequate replacement housing was in short supply. Over the last half of the century, England prospered and people became more and more enamored with the idea of owning a single-family house with a garden. However, most of these were for the middle and upper class.

Better housing was often built in "Garden Estates". In the City of London there is a good example. Bedford Park built in the 1870s and 1880s, became the best known symbol of both the garden estates and the aesthetic movement. An advertisement for a house indicating the developer's sense of accomplishment was headed –

> BEDFORD PARK, CHISWICK, W. THE HEALTHIEST PLACE IN THE WORLD. Close to Turnham Green Station, Trains every few minutes. A Garden and a Bath Room with Hot and Cold water to every house, whatever its size. A Kindergarten and good Cheap Day Schools on the Estate, and a School of Art. Also Church Club (for Ladies & Gentlemen), Stores, Tennis Courts, &c."[39]

Most of the houses are two- and three-story architect-designed Queen Anne style homes. The houses have a variety of windows in the street facade and interesting details and surrounds around the entrance door and windows. Bedford Park was developed by a mysterious fellow name Jonathan Carr. He had the wisdom to employ good architects but his business skills were modest and he was not financially successful. However, the buildings have worn well over the years.

Louise and I stayed in a friend's two-story terrace house and found the neighborhood very pleasant. A nearby corner house was on sale for 1.8 million pounds. Those like the one in which we stayed on St Albans Avenue were selling for four to six hundred thousand pounds.

Philanthropic and institutional landlords were busy in the late- nineteenth and early-twentieth century. They were driven in part by the faulty notion also held in America, that modest return on borrowed funds could by itself make affordable housing financially viable. But unplanned high maintenance and other operating expenses have been the undoing of many philanthropic housing schemes.

There were some interesting examples of philanthropy. In 1862 Lord Shaftesbury, a well-known social reformer who championed both limiting factory workers hours and public health reform, persuaded George Peabody, the American financier, to create a fund for affordable housing for the people of London. It was then the largest philanthropic gift in the history of the country. Over the next 30 years Peabody Trust built and rented 5000 flats to needy families at affordable rents. It now has more than 20,000 homes.

The Peabody Trust was a model for others. The Guinness Trust, launched in 1890, was noteworthy. It operated across the Country and now owns and manages 60,000 homes. Octavia Hill, renowned reformer for better health and child care, for education, housing and prisons, came on the scene in the 1860's. She campaigned against large clearance programs that displaced the most needy families and the construction of blocks of flats that she considered oppressive and difficult to manage. She advocated purchase of rental properties by investors who could then turn the properties over to her for rental to the poor.

Octavia Hill introduced good, tenant-oriented management and repair together with strict requirements for rent payment. Over the following decades, she managed some 15,000 properties. Her work was widely acclaimed and influential in bringing in government regulation of slum landlords.

There were shining examples of model villages for workers built by the Cadbury and Rowntree Trusts, both supported by the English love of chocolate. I visited the Rowntree village of New Earswick on a visit to the see Lord Richard Best, then Director of the Rowntree Foundation. Originally built in 1902, it was still serving as a model community with its own primary school and community "folk hall" in which a variety of community organizations met. There were also "garden city" developments in England inspired by idealists such as Robert Owen and Ebenezer Howard.

The government enacted laws that allowed housing associations to acquire slum clearance sites but limited financial incentives to become landlords. The existing housing societies and trusts were well known, but they were seen as conservative and not capable of undertaking larger-scale operations. By 1914 120,000 homes had been created by philanthropic organizations, including 50,000 or so by housing associations.[40] Only 20,000 new units would be built by local authorities (governments). In 1914, 90% of the housing stock was rented from private, generally small, landlords. Just 10% were owner occupied. These ownership ratios were to change dramatically after World War I.

The War was catastrophic for the United Kingdom. Six million of its citizens were involved directly, and the country expended vast resources to continue the fight through 1918. In 1915 the national government passed wide ranging rent control because of shortages of rental housing in the cities, in factory and ports areas, and where the troops were housed. Rent controls were continued after the War. One of its most significant impacts starting with the War was a precipitous decline in the number of households renting from private

landlords - a loss of over 30% in the following twenty years.
Britain turned to local government for the dominant of new rental housing. Government had become a dominate player in people's
lives during the War. Continued government enterprise was supported. In 1919, Parliament passed an Act calling for 500,000 new council homes, most to be "planned cottage estates" that featured single
family homes.   However, local governments were not effective in
meeting the goal. They built only 213,000 homes, and the program
was replaced by a new one with construction costs shared by tenants
and local governments.

Housing designs called for more spacious rooms with consideration
for light and air. By the late 1920's, the "garden estates" homes started to be replaced by large-block housing. Soon there were more flats
than homes built as rent levels on those were lower.[41] After the 1930
depression, the government assigned localities additional responsibilities to rebuild whole neighborhoods, manage rent controls, and
provide housing for the very poor. A million units were built by local
governments during the thirties, much of it on sites where Victori-
an- era housing was condemned or demolished. Four million people
would be displaced.[42]

In the same mid-war years, large numbers of moderate-income families did achieve the popular dream of a single family home. This
was facilitated in some measure by attractive mortgage loan programs provided by the building societies. Home ownership grew
from 700,000 to 3.5 million homes by 1939, about 25% of the housing stock. One and a half million homes were newly built and the
balance acquired from rental housing owners. The row house design
of much of the investor- owned housing stock made sale to individual buyers practical. Single- family home ownership also increased
dramatically again after World War II, to 45% in the mid-sixties and
over 70% in the eighties.

I can recall coming through London's Hyde Park in June of 1945 on furlough from my company in France. There were a variety of speakers on soapboxes announcing that the Conservatives would be thrown out and that a Labour Government would be elected. My cousin, with whom I had lunch, doubted these claims. She believed that war hero and Conservative Winston Churchill would be reelected. He was not. Clement Atlee and his Labour Party brought in extensive new social programs.

One of Atlee's proposals was to set up a national housing corporation to sponsor the construction of social housing on a mass scale. Large housing developments of modern design were planned. The corporation idea was soon abandoned in favor of development by local authorities that "already had extensive planning powers, a major role in public health as it related to housing, and were the only bodies that could enforce closing and compulsory purchase orders on negligent private landlords."[43]

Over the decade of the 1950's public authorities would build 65% of 2.5 million dwellings. Over the following two decades, 42% of the 5.8 million new dwellings were built by local government agencies.. Over 40% would be flats and 12% high rise building. Much of this new housing, particularly the high rise buildings, would prove to be less desirable and difficult to manage.

New building construction systems were used, a number of which proved to be faulty. England's damp climate was too damp for thin-wall concrete construction. The government had pushed the new systems and felt obligated to pay the costs of demolishing buildings that failed. Maisonettes, a particularly British design of two-story flats in blocks with balcony access, were a failure and unpopular. I Bristol concrete, I saw maisonette buildings waiting to be demolished.

On that same trip I visited the Thamesmead Project along the Thames River in Southeast London and observed the casting, building, delivery and placement of the large prefabricated concrete components. I also saw rejected and damaged components awaiting removal. It was clear to me that there was little promise in utilizing such a cumbersome system involving heavy equipment in lieu of the more traditional systems put together by masons and carpenters. The aesthetics were not that attractive. The Thamesmead project never got beyond an initial phase. Much later, I saw what had been finished incorporated in a new planned redevelopment scheme implemented by Gallions HA. The older prefabricated section looked a little out of place but better in its new surroundings.

Problems of mismanagement and resident discontent caused council housing to be increasingly more controversial. It developed a reputation as housing for the marginalized members of society. Building failures did not help. Just as a significant portion of urban public housing in the USA was overwhelmed by the social disorder in the sixties, council housing started to have "sink hole" estates. Smaller local governments lacked the professional skills and financial expertise required for running real estate operations and providing adequate resident services.

In 1974, a time when local governments owned over 5 million dwellings, the Government amalgamated local governments, reducing their number from 2000 to 400, thereby achieving administrative economies of scale.[44] It meant, however, that the scale of operation of the larger local governments was greatly expanded. A number had over 40,000 dwellings and some more than 90,000. Local governments were demolishing, constructing and leasing thousands of dwellings per year. There were difficulties in all aspects of these programs. Supervision was often inadequate, contractors did shoddy work, there were labor disputes and tenants were inconvenienced and often disillusioned with the results. Families did not like high rise living and there were issues with racial inequities. There were protests with political consequences. The exception to all this was the New Towns, but they had different goals and were predicated on serving working families and offering employment opportunities.

The central government had to address the issues of consumer dissatisfaction, design and construction standards, and the running expenses of council housing. Who should council housing serve and at what public cost? Government's role in social services had expanded considerably in the 1930s. Local authorities lacked a distinct administrative framework for delivering housing services although they did for education, health and physical infra-structure.

Since World War I, municipal governments had pooled council housing costs with other running expenses. It was not by itself a cost center. Council rents were set by the local authority on fairly subjective criteria and as long as they were reasonable, the national government subsidy continued. Any shortfall had to be made up through local taxation. The local authorities had powers to give rent rebates to low income tenants. The extensive inventory of cheaper old housing was used to cross subsidize the more expensive newly built housing.

In 1972 the national government instituted control of council rents. They had been set by the localities to keep rents low for political reasons, resulting in inadequate revenue to maintain and repair the buildings. Rents were increased and pressure was put on the local authorities to repair and improve their existing stock. A universal rent rebate system was also instituted.

The new regime was controversial and opposed by the residents.

Andwas repealed in 1975. However, the government continued to control rents and operating subsidies. Vacancies increased in estates in economically deprived areas as well as in some of the new unpopular estates. There were rising revenue deficits. In 1977 the Homeless Persons Act created a new obligation on the part of local governments to house homeless people. Council estates became heavily occupied by poor families and those formerly homeless. In 1965, one in ten council tenants was receiving rent rebates. By 1975 it was one in five.[45]

Margaret Thatcher's Conservative Party won elections in 1979, '83 and '87. One of Prime Minister Thatcher's major programs was reform of council housing. The Conservatives viewed council housing in the hands of local government as a monopoly run by landlords who lacked incentives to do a good job.[46] They also saw that local Labor Party officials were winning elections on the credit they received for providing low-rent housing. Proposed changes included privatizing council housing by extending the right-to-buy for council tenants, reducing development by local government and supporting private investment in neighborhoods.

Virtually all council tenants after three years of residency could purchase their unit on very favorable terms. Flats were discounted as much as 70% of value. Local governments were required to provide a mortgage loans at favorable terms. Right-to-buy was not required of housing associations at the time but would be later on a more limited basis. The houses purchased tended to be the best houses in better estates. Buyers were generally moderate-income households.

The program was a great giveaway and further concentrated low-income households in council housing in impoverished areas. The inventory of council owned housing was reduced by 1.2 million homes sold to sitting tenants, about 20% of all council stock. Funding for new council housing development was curtailed.

The severity of the so-called sink-hole estates, while not as deplorable as Cabrini Green in Chicago, was great. The designs were seemingly out of character with one's image of the English single family home. The 1986 Audit Commission report found 85% of council-owned dwellings in need of repairs and improvements. A number of programs were directed at improvement of both projects and their management. I visited Brent in London to see their troubled estates. One was Chalk Hill, a four-story complex of concrete buildings with large circular stairway sections at the corners between the blocks. The community center was burned out and in ruins. The estate when new had been used as housing by American GIs during the War. I spoke to a resident who had lived in the development for seventeen years and raised her nine children in the development. She descried how the estate had become ugly and mismanaged. She said that the architect who had designed the project came back recently to see the project, saw its forlorn state and thereafter committed suicide. I turned to the policeman who came by, and he confirmed her story. On a recent visit in 2004, I saw that the estate had been totally rebuilt.

While difficulties with council housing became increasingly apparent in the sixties and seventies, there were also troubles in the private sector. By the 1960's, the substantial decline of private rental housing demanded a response. By the time rent controls ended in 1957, many private investors had sold their properties to home buyers. The tax benefits for home ownership put private rental housing at a competitive disadvantage. Private-sector rental housing dropped from 90% in 1914 to about 30% in 1960. There were scandals about private landlords taking advantage of families who had no alternatives and were living in rundown flats awaiting repair, sale or demolition. The government began looking for an alternative to "the private landlord" that would have flexibility, initiative and social responsibility as well.

In the early 1960s, the Ministry of Housing launched an innovative scheme with the National Federation of Housing Societies (now the National Housing Federation). It was to be the beginning of an increased role for housing associations. Under a pilot program, the government provided capital for middle-income family developments which would be created and operated "without subsidy or profit." The program was a success and became the basis for launching a much larger program in 1964.

In the Housing Act of 1964 the british government proposed a new Housing Corporation for the purpose of funding a "new sector" of housing for middle-income families. Ownership of the housing would be by a housing association that could get a loan from a building society equal to two-thirds of the development costs, and the corporation would then provide the remaining one-third. Developments would have rents based upon the costs of the building loan plus operating expenses. Alternatively, the corporation might be a co-ownership corporation was popular in the Scandinavian countries. The Housing Corporation was charged with registering housing associations eligible for the program and providing monitoring and advisory services. In 1964 there were about 1,000 associations that collectively owned approximately 100,000 homes, just a fraction of the total stock of 17 million dwellings in the country. In four years the Corporation registered over 850 associations.

Within the next few years several things became apparent. The grants required to make the HA developments financially sound required that the Corporation put up an increasing amount of money, sometimes well in excess of 50% of development costs. Even so, the rents were not affordable for most lower- income families. Not until the 1972 Act were rent allowances for low-income tenants introduced for both housing association and private housing similar to the rent rebates common in council housing.

In the 1970s there was a substantial increase in interest rates that made development of rental housing more difficult. Co-ownership housing as allowed in the 1964 Act was slow to take off but did provide higher percentage loans and gave co-owners the benefit from mortgage tax relief. Co-ownership subsequently had difficulties as down-payments for new buyers became too high.

On the basis of an inquiry report submitted in 1971, the Government enacted the Housing Act of 1972 with purposes to rationalize the variation in the housing associations, expand the role of the Housing Corporation giving it the central role for financing developments together with a greater supervisory role, and the introduction of "fair rents" set by the Independent Rent Officer. These rents would be higher than council housing but well below the market in keeping with the Government's support. However "fair rents" did not provide adequate operating revenue and associations frequently had to turn to local government or philanthropy for help.

The Housing Corporation looked for changes necessary "to consolidate and streamline the (voluntary) movement if it is to realize its full potential." The Housing Corporation's position was that the full potential of the "established" housing associations had not been realized.[47] It accepted the task of encouraging and promoting the capable associations to increase production, and became responsible for financing developments in which rents would be "fair rents" as in the private market and ensuring that associations would receive adequate subsidies. The National Housing Federation, argued for more generous subsidies and greater consideration of how associations might fulfill their charitable purposes.

New legislation in 1974 introduced the Housing Association Grant (HAG) and Revenue Deficit Grant for eligible expenditures on qualified projects. The HAG was a tool to expand the development work of the associations while still charging "fair rents." The grants were a single capital grant at completion for 85% to 100% of capital costs. The program had wide political support. HAGs were intended to make the voluntary sector a major player in the housing system. This system was in place for the next 14 years. New housing associations were formed, some community based.

Housing Associations were regarded as supportive of the new urban policies for sensitive and more transparent neighborhood regeneration and could now take on acquisition and rehabilitation schemes of urban properties. Much was premised on the ability of housing associations to work with local governments. The work of the associations was intended to complement council housing, providing more choice of tenure. The grant program required that 50% of housing selections be from the local government's waiting list and in cases where the local government had provided the land, an allocation of 100%. Associations were encouraged to provide homeownership opportunities and to serve special groups such as the handicapped and homeless.

Housing production by the associations increased significantly in the 70s and 80s reaching 35,000 dwellings per year in the 1977-9 period. Paddington Churches in London had about 200 social homes in 1969. By 1980, it had over 6000 homes. By the end of the 80's, the associations had become the primary developer of social housing. By 1990 eight housing associations owned more than 10,000 homes, and 124 owned more than one thousand. From 1969 to 1990 housing associations built more than 400,000 new dwellings.

The grant program over the 70's and 80's also saw the net worth of the associations increase significantly making them credit worthy borrowers. This, in addition to the implied backup provided by the

Housing Corporation, put them in a position to borrow against their entire portfolio of assets as a normal private developer might. This is different than in the US where each housing development insured by FHA or using tax credit subsidies must be financed as a single business entity. This requirement restricts the use of assets as collateral to finance other activities.

Public expenditures in the UK became a central issue in the 80's and this put pressure on government budgeted amounts for social housing. The 1988 Housing Act changed the Housing Corporations' financing program, requiring that housing associations obtain a significant portion of project funding from conventional private sources. Housing associations set their own rents under "assured tenancies", a new national rent regulation regime that allowed increases in rents on the renewal of the lease.

I recall a meeting of the NFHA in Bournemouth at which the head of the Housing Corporation suggested financing developments with a conventional mortgage loan for 70% of costs and a 30% grant from the Housing Corporation. Representatives from Shelter, the national advocacy group, and others saw this ratio as impractical and hurtful for low income families. The Housing Corporation was overly optimistic. The eventual formula for London was about a 55% grant and the balance from private institutions.

Conventional financing with market interest rates caused the rents to go up. This increased the cost to the government for rental assistance payments to residents. This relationship between higher rents as the result of increased private financing and lower rents achieved through the government grants allowed the rational decision between the costs of grants and costs of housing benefits. Included in the mix was the increased production of housing made possible by the capital grants.

The Housing Associations developed relationships with financial institutions. They frequently established lines of credit with multiple institutions secured by part or all of their assets. This gave them operating flexibility and an ability to respond quickly when building opportunities came along. Creditworthy associations supported and monitored by the Housing Corporation became effective producers. In the 80's, the Thatcher government reduced council housing production to a level well below that of housing associations. Local governments received funding approval for 54,000 homes, and housing associations were approved for 171,000 homes. The ascendancy of housing associations as the primary developer of social housing had arrived.

What I found impressive was the level of funding that was provided in the late 80s. The HAG funding program of the HC in 1988 was 1.8 billion pounds. In a country which had one-fifth the population of the USA, that is a lot of money for housing. HOME, our program for assisted housing production, was funded at a level of $1.5 billion dollars that year.

Over the years, housing associations, as well as private for-profit developers, discovered the benefits of mixed-tenure occupancy, i.e., having both rental and ownership units in low- and moderate-income developments. In some cases a housing association joined with a private developer that built homes for sale and cross-subsidize the rental apartments that were owned by the association. In other cases, the housing association would do it all. Having for-sale units in a scheme made planning approvals more likely and more feasible.

Beginning in the eighties, shared ownership was introduced. A new homeowner would buy and finance with a mortgage of 25% of a dwelling's value. The association would then rent that shareowner the other 75% portion. The homeowner could thereafter purchase additional equity ownership until she/he owned it all. On the sale of the unit, appreciation in the value of the unit was shared. The appreciation in shared ownership developments was an important revenue source for the associations. It took banks some time getting accustomed to these partial ownerships but in time they became standard transactions.

The Thatcher government had a goal of privatizing council housing to the degree possible. In the 1985 Housing Act was a provision that allowed local authorities, with the approval of the residents, to transfer their council housing to a new landlord. The government saw these transfers as a means of obtaining private financing for physical improvements using the asset value of the existing housing stock as collateral. Transfers were also a means of getting in new management where the existing management was failing. By 2008, 214 transfers had been completed with over 900,000 dwellings.

Housing Associations have had a history of providing a range of resident services but there are limits as to what is financially possible. Large associations with substantial revenues have more flexibilities in meeting the costs of services. Housing associations have in many cases initiated affiliated enterprises to provide job training, care services for the elderly and child care.

Over the last several decades the UK has modified funding priorities. It seeks to improve the effectiveness of housing production both in meeting housing needs and protecting the environment. HAs must accept tenants from local government waiting lists as a requirement for obtaining the housing grant. There is a growing need for housing for families living on low paid employment and for key workers (public employees such as teachers, police and firemen). Further, it wants to utilize grant funding for social housing as part of a broader investment strategy in regeneration of communities. Funding is available to both housing associations and private sector developers. The government recently named 115 or so housing associations that are financially capable as qualified developers. The government expected housing associations to be leaders in these undertakings, in many cases in partnership with local government and other private for-profit and nonprofit organizations. More recently, the government has funded a production program in London with a group of housing associations for the creation of 15,000 homes

In response to reduced grant amounts, HAs have been allowed to raise their rents to 30% of 80% of the average local market rent. But this is a problem for associations whose rents are geared to the needs of low- income families who are close to the limit of the housing benefit. This will put financial pressure on the associations at a time when they are increasingly the government's response to the need for social housing.

Social housing serves an increasingly poor population with more social problems. 62% of HA tenants are not in the labor force. Older and younger tenants predominate. A recent study by the NHF indicates that only 17% of the general population wants to live in social housing.[44] The government wants to improve the political standing of the HAs but that has not been easy. The HAs produce about 20% of new housing units. Private homebuilders are not significant contributors and they are frowned on for their destruction of green space.

The HAs are shifting away from the past public sector culture to a more entrepreneurial approach. They are seeking ways to improve business efficiencies and methods and to make better use of human resources. As they acquire more skills at financing and debt, they can spend more time on management and consumer satisfaction. The future for housing associations depends on their success builders and managers with a record to prove it.

Regulations by the Housing Corporation have been criticized as too focused on organizational and financial details and not enough on performance and serving tenants' interests. It is of paramount importance that their estates not be seen as home for marginalized populations. They are developing performance measures that can substantiate their success as capable, caring and efficient business enterprises. This includes their role as sustainable community agents. Their independence has raised questions of accountability and "value for money.'

There are issue about the effectiveness of large organizations, say with more than 10,000 units, as compared to more locally connected associations with fewer dwellings. A large association, such as Affinity Sutton, with management of over 50,000 units operating through local offices throughout the country, raises questions about delivery of quality services. Surveys of resident satisfaction are common as well as extensive performance monitoring. A recent inspection by the Audit Commission found their services to be good but indicated that more had to be done relative to diversity.

There is an organization of smaller associations (less than 6,000 dwellings) that argues that smaller organizations can be more locally oriented, more informed about community needs and better connected with local government. Yet the economic and environmental quality of housing locations vary tremendously and services reflect these differences.

Over the years HAs have generally been seen as better managers than the councils but at modestly greater costs. Improved services and more involvement of residents has always been a goal. There have been questions of who should regulate the housing associations. The National Housing Federation has viewed registered social landlords to be "among the most regulated groups of organizations in existence."

In 2008, the Housing Corporation was merged with another agency called English Partnerships into a new agency called Homes and Communities Agency. The regulatory function was transferred to a new agency called the Office for Tenants and Social Landlords. The new Conservative government has reversed some of the changes. Of the 4 million social housing dwellings in the UK, about half are owned and managed by housing associations. This will increase as new transfers of council housing occur.

With the prominence of housing associations, first as an alternative social housing provider and now as the primary producer of new social housing units, there is an ongoing debate about their effectiveness. Neighborhood regeneration programs require a myriad of social services, and it remains unclear to what degree these services can be part of the social housing system. The housing benefit program is universal but always encounters regulatory problems and budget restrictions. Reduced public expenditures are likely.

Will housing associations continue to have access to private capital that they need? Over the last three decades, it is clear that housing associations have become creditworthy and have raised major amounts of private investment capital. But will this continue? The UK has a goal of three million newly built units by 2020. Some of these will come from an increased private for-profit sector but the lion's share will have to be from the housing associations.

The National Housing Federation represents 1,400 Housing Associations. David Orr, the Chief Executive, is an articulate spokesman and thoughtful leader. He has had to withstand the recent revisions in regulations of the HAs. He wants them to be more freestanding but knows that they will continue to need public support. The large HAs are becoming more independent as they carve out niches for themselves. For a number of organizations, mergers may be the route they will follow.

Some looks at individual housing associations follow.

Peabody Housing Trust

Peabody Housing Trust was founded in 1862 by a grant from George Peabody, an American banker and financier. The purposes of the organization are to provide rental housing for people who are unable to afford the usual open market rent; the provision of supportive housing and care for those who need additional help; provision of low-cost home ownership; and the delivery of community regeneration activities. It was to work solely in London.

Some years ago I met George Barlow, the President of Peabody, and other officers at a variety of Housing Federation meeting. I visited their organization's headquarters and discussed their operations. Barlow, and his deputies, had an architectural staff and other skilled people who not only worked for the organization itself but did work as consultants to others. It was clear that Peabody had a special sense of their residents. I can recall seeing signs in front of their buildings that said "Peabody Trust working for Londoners since 1862".

Peabody provided a variety of resident services. Barlow took me to lunch at an elderly center and we also looked at a block of housing that they had under renovation. As an older association, they had a lot of properties that date back to the early 1900s. Peabody's board is satisfied that through the provision of affordable housing and the delivery of community regeneration activities, it is creating social and financial opportunities for its residents and other consumers in London.

Its current Chief Executive, Stephen Howlett, has Peabody focused on regeneration, particularly in East London near the site of the Summer 2012 Olympics. It has an ever increasing number of younger and older tenants and its communities are becoming more diverse. It also delivered 113 new homes that met the development requirements with the Homes and Community Agency. It believes it is well-positioned to take advantage of the new flexibilities around tenure, rents and allocations.

With the help of its endowment, Peabody operates with a surplus and is clearly sustainable. It has been assigned an Aa2 credit rating by Moody's and has raised 150 million pounds from the bond market. They have indicated their desire to grow by the purchase of 1,230 homes from The Crown Estate. Their goal is also to build about 300 new units of each year.

Like other housing associations in England, Peabody is concentrating on and is working with their repair contractor to make further improvements.

Gallions Housing Association

I had an opportunity in 1969 to visit Thamesmead, the new planned development for 60,000 Londoners on a 1,000 acre site along the Thames River in Southeast London. I saw Phase 1 being built. The site plan included provisions of varying sizes of family dwellings in four-story terraced and high-rise tower concrete buildings. The designers planned for a first-class public transport service that could minimize the need for the use of the private car. 17,000 homes would be connected to residential open spaces that would be linked together to form a green covering of the entire development.

The Thamesmead project was the work of the Greater London County Council. In 1985 Margaret Thatcher shut down the Council and the project reverted to the local Thamesmead Government. The project was managed by Thamesmead Town Ltd. for thirteen years. The concrete construction system had been abandoned and the operation of the housing by the Town's Housing Association was below standards. On July 1999 the residents of Thamesmead voted to turn their housing over to a new Registered Landlord.

I met Tony Cotter, Chief Executive of the Gallion's Housing Association, through my work with the Housing Partnership Network. Gallions Housing Association was formed in 1999 and was registered a social housing landlord by the Housing Corporation in 2000. It accepted transfer of the properties of the dissolved Thamesmead Town Ltd. with the intent of providing the people of Thamesmead with the best possible housing services into the future.

The Housing Partnership Network visited Gallions in 2008, and we found the Association upbeat with improving services and new social programs. Tony Cotter had been with the Town as a Housing Services Director since 1996. He led much of the work on the transfer and on the formation of the new Gallions Housing Association. He became Chief Executive of Gallions in May 2000. One of Tony's interests is Quality Housing Services (QHS), of which he is a founding member. It is an established and successful quality accreditation system in the social housing system in the UK. QHS does the quality control monitoring for Gallions.

Tony is proud of the results that Gallions has achieved. They collect 98.7% of their rents and have a rent arrears of less than 4.5%. They have contracted with Axis Europe to do their maintenance and repairs. The performance measures indicate that Axis Europe is contributing to the net surplus of the Corporation. The Corporation continues to provide strategic delivery of effective neighborhood and community services, including community renewal and community safety programs. The Association is a developing partner with the Homes and Community Agency and is working on a 680 new homes funded in part with a 51 million pound Housing Grant.

Gallions makes a genuine effort to keep their residents involved with informed contacts from their staff, meetings, announcements and publications. They care that maintenance calls are handled quickly and the work is done as promised. They are checking that their notices and letters are accurate. They are still not satisfied with their consultancies with residents and they are working to improve it.

Gallions now operates over 5,000 units. It has several regeneration developments programs involving building demolition and relocating of families. It makes an effort to make sure the existing residents are well informed. It also has a broad program of neighborhood fix up which is carried out with residents. One of their housing project was designed and built by a Dutch firm that operates very efficiently; they are looking at other green initiatives.

AffinitySutton

AffinitySutton is one of the largest housing associations in the UK. In 1995 and again in 1998, I visited Keith Exford, Chief Executive Officer of Broomleigh Housing Association (now part of Affinity-Sutton Group). Exford described the transfer by the Bromley Authority of its 11,000 dwellings of council housing to a new independent housing association. It was the first metropolitan large scale voluntary stock transfer in the country.

Bromley is a conservative middle-income town and its properties were in relatively good shape. Broomleigh had narrowly won the residents approval for the transfer after promising improved maintenance and repairs. The tenants were promised that they would be included in high-level decisions.

Existing management staff came with the real estate. The board, however, was new. It determined after a period of operations that new operating leadership was necessary if the potential of independent private sector management was to be realized. Exford was brought in as Chief Executive Officer. One of the first things he did was to arrange a 136,000 pound line of credit from banks secured by its assets to refurbish old and build new dwellings. Broomleigh was the first housing association to receive an A- rating from Standard and Poor.

Within a few years, Exford and staff had transformed the Broomleigh Housing Association into a conglomerate called Affinity Homes Group. It was a combination of Broomleigh Housing Association, Downland Housing Association, Mid Sussex Housing Association and Grange Management. Downland Housing Association, formed in 1964, had participated in the co-ownership housing program that existed under the Housing Act of 1965 and found that the Right to Buy legislation of 1980 allowed their residents to buy the properties in which they lived. They lost a substantial portion of their management revenue.

Investing their sales revenue from the Right-to-Buy tenants, Affinity enlarged their role in ownership and management of housing for the disabled and for those with learning disabilities. In a number of cases they took on management of properties that they did not own. In fact, between 1985 and 1989, their managed rather than owned properties increased from 25% to 50%.[48] As Mid Sussex Housing Association, formed in 1990, and Grange Management, formed earlier in 1982, were the remaining pieces of Affinity. Downland Affinity became a Housing Corporation preferred partner with a commitment to build 1200 new homes a year.

One more important private investor was William Sutton who made a fortune as a common carrier which was later expanded into a variety of enterprises including soft-drinks. He had more than 600 branches when he died in 1990. Under his will, 1.5 million pounds were provided for the building of houses for the working class, a bequeath that was in dispute for thirty years. The trustees did build several estates while the will was contested. It was not until 1927 that The Sutton Dwelling Trust was fully authorized. During the mid-war years, the Trust built 17 estates in which 32,000 residents lived.

There was a keen competitive interest in showing that construction biddings was efficient. In 2005, Affinity and the Sutton Group, both of whom had been exploring possible partners, submitted a joint funding bid that would have economies of scale, volume procurement, national coverage and opportunities to deliver new homes at competitive grant levels. The proposal was very successful. The two groups, now managing 49,000 homes, merged in 2006. Shortly thereafter, they obtained approval of a 250,000 pound bond issue that secured their immediate operations. They now manage 53,000 homes nationwide.

The council transfer program has occurred in a number of ways. In most cases, the entire inventory of a council is transferred. In other cases, the inventory is divided into several new entities. There are continuing transfers of individual estates. In 2008 two developments in Lewisham in South East London with 130 homes were transfered to the Broomleigh Association . The residents were promised improvements and the vote in favor of the transfer was 92%. In cases where the existing authorities stock is in bad repair with vacant units, a grant from the government is required.

England has experienced a boom in house prices with the average house price exceeding the average national income by ten times, and by thirteen times in London. The present Cameron government has introduced an austerity program that cuts the level of government spending including in the housing program, cuts the level of

344

housing benefits, and requires local governments to do more with less. AffinitySutton has turned to its foundation to augments it social services to its tenants. It has demonstrated the ability to get private financing for its projects but, it will also have to raise rents and develop non-government sources of revenue. AffinitySutton sees itself going back to the market for new financing for its on-going construction program.

Hexagon Housing Association

I met Tom McCormack in 1984 when Tom was finishing his work at the Massachusetts Institute of Technology and he was working for one of the CDCs in Boston. When he went back to England, he worked first for Saint Pancras Housing Association and then as a Regional Director for Sanctuary Housing, before accepting the position of Chief Executive Officer of Hexagon Housing Association in Southeast London. We have become increasingly good friends over the years.

Hexagon has in excess of 3,750 units, more in keeping with the size of HPN's nonprofit housing corporations. The stock has an estimated value of 340 million pounds. There is an active Board which has responsibility for a system of internal controls which review the effectiveness of the association's operations. In addition to review of new development and new business, the group has a comprehensive system of performance reports which are reviewed monthly by staff and quarterly by the board. The board also approves the annual budget, a three-year corporate plan and 30-year financial forecast.

Hexagon's objectives and strategy for 2011-2014 are to put residents at the heart of what they do; to change the ways of working to achieve maximum efficiency; to ensure that Hexagon continues to grow in a sustainable manner; to respond to the needs of the diverse communities they serve, to implement chosen management and sustainability strategies, and to communicate clearly to stakeholders. Hexagon has a variety of housing types and sizes. They plan to build around 70 new homes a year, with 35% having three bedrooms or more. The company has a four-year development program with lines of credit with a number of banks. They spent 29 million pounds on developing properties, of which approximately 11 million was grants. Rent arrears are about 4%, within the top quarter of housing associations. They now contract out about 50% of their repair work. They earned 2.9 million pounds per year surplus.

Hexagon has concerns about new government program requirements and has taken steps to meet them. They have cut back on the number of sale homes they will build and increased the number of homes they will sell. They do not want to cut all of their development business because they would loose the skills and the funding agency will penalize them when things get better. They do not like the plan the government is sponsoring but anything they build now will be paid off in twenty-five years and they will have the asset. They will not raise the rents on new three- and four-bedroom apartments the local government will continue to refer to them as residents, which the welfare system supports. But they will raise the rents on new one- and two- bedroom up to the 80% level.

The primary concern for the associations is the impact of people failing to pay the higher rents which will now be made by the government to the residents who will then pay the landlord. Hexagon will continue to fund the Hexagon Academy to provide residents with a range of supports from work placements in the office, care homes, construction placements and one-to-one guidance. They are currently giving attention to community affairs and will continue to fund neighborhood initiatives to the degree possible.

Hexagon is working on green sustainable efforts such as voltaic plates on the roof to supply light for the halls but they do not have the resources to undertake pioneering new designs. The measures that they use to monitor operations are standard aides used by the industry and they are satisfied that they are on top of management costs.

Housing Associations in The Netherlands

A second European social housing model that was capitalized by the government operates in the Netherlands. Its system is ahead of ours by forty years and has similarities with the British system. I encountered it through the International Federation of Housing and Planning. Martien Schapper, an attendee at the National Federation of Housing and Planning meeting in 1980, took Louise and me through several Amsterdam neighborhoods before returning us to our hotel. I saw him at several meetings later and he was also one of a group of Dutch housing officials who came to Boston on a visit that I planned for the National Wonengaad (NWR) in 1993.

Schapper and I became very good friends, and he was my host on several subsequent trips to the Netherlands. He was a wonderfully generous person. On my visits we would travel from his office in Baarn to projects and places of interest. I had dinner with Yuebe and Martien at his eleven-foot wide house in Amsterdam. The house lots were laid out in the sixteenth century. The house had a glass storefront in which he displayed pottery pieces made by his friends for sale. Tragically, Martien died suddenly and I was left without a key friend and colleague.

The Netherlands has an old and well established social housing system. It comprises portfolios of rental and mixed use properties owned by nonprofit housing associations. The HAs are also involved in other types of real estate development, including homeownership and commercial properties. Generally, HAs have a narrower programmatic focus than nonprofits in the US. The population of the Netherlands is about 16.5 million with 7 million dwelling units. It is a very densely developed country with about 20% of the population of foreign backgrounds, that is people born abroad and people who were born in the Netherlands of whom at least one parent was born abroad in a non-western country. This number is estimated to increase to 30% in 2050. Unemployment is modest at 5 -6%, the housing vacancy percentage is low at 2 – 2.5%, and the country is one of the richest in the EU.

The average useful floor space of a unit is about 900 square feet. About 70% of the housing stock consists of one-family dwellings, the remainder is multi-family apartments, including 6.7% in highrise (more than four stories) apartment buildings located predominately in the larger towns and cities. 80% of the housing dates from the period after 1945, which makes the stock relatively young. The 1901 Housing Act recognized HAs as "private companies with social goals". About 50% of all housing is owner occupied and 35% is social housing. The latter does not have the stigma that most affordable housing does in this country. It is home for a broad intermediate group in addition to low income households.

HAs were introduced in the Netherlands in the mid-19th century, encouraged by churches, unions, and factory owners. They grew in numbers and recognition during World War 1 and the years following. The number of organizations increased from 300 in 1914 to 1,350 in 1922, a period of housing shortages and high demand. In those years, housing associations built about 90% of new social housing and the local authorities about 10%.

In the twenties and thirties the local authorities commissioned about 30% of new social housing and more than half up to 1965. During these years the HA movement matured politically and the role of the HAs (there were two groups, Protestant and Catholic) were discussed and resolved in the findings of the De Roos Commission, that made housing by the HAs preferable. Its report recommended that the HAs should develop their independence and build and retain their own capital base. In the seventies, urban renewal had priority and a significant portion of old stock was renovated or replaced. The housing associations participated, frequently with substantial financial support from government.

Project financing was generally with government loans and later bank loans with a guarantee from either the local government or the State or both. Consulting with the existing tenants was a critical part of these programs. By 1980, the politics of the housing situation had been ameliorated and the government wanted to substantially reduce it involvement in the sector.

In the 1990's the big step was the mutual cancellation of the remaining state loans which the housing associations were obligated to repay and the future subsidies that they were promised to receive. This made the reallocation of responsibilities complete. The HAs, now well capitalized with help from government, were to be independent and were to finance their operations predominantly from their own resources. Today, they are diversified developers that are politically strong and well capitalized. They are independent organizations that are regarded as the "third sector," sitting between government and the private market. Virtually all of the affordable housing being produced is developed by nonprofit associations.

Two financing institutions were created when the subsidies were cancelled — the non-profit and independent Social Housing Guarantee Fund and the quasi-public Central Housing Fund — to provide financing guarantees and oversight for all HAs. Virtually all HA loans are backed by the Guarantee Fund, which has recourse to a portion of HA's equity and also to the central and local governments.

All the HAs pay a small annual amount to the Fund. The return on investment is projected on a 50-year timeline from cash flow, property sales, and other business income. Private lenders provide loans and credit lines to organizations, not generally to the real estate projects. The Central Fund provides financing and management restructuring assistance to troubled HAs.

Rent controls exist throughout the Netherlands and the rent level is calculated on the basis of size and physical attributes of the unit. The Netherlands has a system of housing allowances for those eligible. In excess of a million households receive rent assistance. It is the largest single state housing budget item at EUR 1.5 billion per year. About one-half of WonenBreburg households in southern Holland receive a housing allowance. The housing associations are now dealing with control measures to ensure performance. There has also been a contracting out of functions such as maintenance work and service delivery. In the nineties, the national advocacy groups were reorganized into one agency called Aedes to serve all the associations.

There is a shift in HA culture from a more public and regulated orientation to an entrepreneurial model that encourages professional management and private sector business practices. HAs are working to develop new business models and income producing ventures. There are two corporate forms for a housing association: an association or a foundation. Companies have drifted to the foundation form as the business activities and the scale of the organizations has increased. There are an increasing number of affiliated or partnering companies that have been created and incorporated into the HA's company structure.

The Netherlands is facing substantial budget constraints that will impact the associations. There is a reduction in the grant amounts but that only effects individual projects. The more critical issue is the requirement that 90% of the new rentals must be at or below EAU 652 per month.

WonenBreburg

One of the members of the second study tour that I arranged in Boston in 1995 was Johan Dunnewijk. He was then the Director of SVW, a housing association in Tilburg with 10,000 units. Two mergers later, his agency merged with an association in Breda to form WonenBreburg with 29,000 units. We have maintained contact and become good friends.

In 2000 Johan brought his wife, his two sons and his brother to visit and view the fall New England colors. Louise and I had visited with Johan and his wife Helen in Tilburg. He has been a great help in understanding Dutch housing. Dunnevijk worked as a consultant to NWR until 1990 when he became the Chief Executive of SVW in Tilburg. In 2003, he became Chief Executive of WonenBreburg. They are one of the biggest housing associations in the Netherlands. They are famous for building joint retirement housing and medical facilities.

WonenBreburg has 260 employees. They have to pay the rate negotiated by Aedes with the labor representatives. Their politics has been made more difficult because officials of a few HAs have violated the regulatory agreement with the government and this has given the associations a bad name. There is now a tendency on the part of the government to see the associations as too independent and wealthy. The size of the sector is too large by the EU regulations and it wants to see a reduction in the number of social units from 2.4 million units down to about 1.6 million units. This will produce a surplus for the associations and the government intends to tax the HAs. Starting in 2014 HAs must pay some part of the cost of the housing allowances. While Dunnewijk and officers of other HAs are protesting these regulations on occupancy by low-income families, they are making adjustment to comply.

Woonplaats

Fons Catau was a member of the first study tour to Boston in 1993. On a subsequent trip to Holland in 1995, I visited Fons and he showed me his housing. He then had about 6000 units. He told me at that time that 10,000 units would be as far as he wanted to go. I called Fons about a year ago and discovered that his organization had about 20,000 units.

Dutch housing associations have frequently worked in partnership with other associations. The Pathmos project was one of the main reasons for the expansion of Fons' group. The Enschede People's House Corporation had nearly 5,000 homes in Enschede but did not have the financial strength to fix the properties. Fons' group, Woonplaats. had more than enough. The two organizations merged. Over a seven year period a total of 1000 homes were renovated. 200 homes were demolished and the sites rebuilt with new housing and supportive facilities. Neighborhoods and others organized and the developers discussed their plans with the groups. Because tenant in one area had little concern for the wishes of other areas, the developer worked on small scale projects. That individual choice and small scale approach are now standard for his organization. Fons' association took over a national organization which was developing elderly units in a number of areas. This qualified his organization to have units in many areas except Amsterdam. They have renovated many units in partnerships with other organizations. A number of his projects are in the eastern part of Netherlands where the population is quiet poor. Forty percent of his residents are receiving rent allowances from the government. In anticipation of difficult times, their company has reduced the construction of new units from 600 to about 350 per year.

The financing of developments is with the banks, insured by the Guaranty fund. They use sales proceeds of houses and profitable activities to earn a surplus. They have built schools, health facilities and other public improvements but these have to link with their housing. They have projects with mixed incomes but Fons says that they do not put low- income families in the same buildings with middle income families. It makes for trouble.

Both the UK and the Netherlands have systems of independent private credit worthy housing associations that manage their own affairs. However, both systems need public support and rely on financial support from government. They get their funding at rates below the national rate.

Currently, the housing associations in the UK and the Netherlands are facing cutbacks in project funding. In the Netherlands, because social housing is considered public ownership, the associations must reduce their ownership position. But the financing systems, both more than twenty years old, remain. In both countries, there is a housing allowance program. It is the key element that guarantees the contining presence of social housing.

Chapter Eleven

The Future for HPN

The Housing Partnership Network, is now twenty years old. It started with 26 partnerships and now has 100 members from 37 states. The member organizations have collectively developed, rehabilitated or preserved 340,000 affordable homes and own 189,000 affordable, rental units. They have also counseled in homeownership and financial literacy over 750,000 families. HPN's work and the recognition of its accomplishments by the public, however, are just beginning. Its members need to build on their accomplishments to date as well as fashion new solutions to meet the challenges of tomorrow.

The United States has lacked a comprehensive private social housing program and has only marginally focused attention on the potential of the nonprofit sector. The 1959 Housing Act, which included grants for the nonprofit elderly housing, was the initial step in private social housing. Service coordinators were added and some remarkable elderly housing organizations were formed. The federal government added a family housing program for nonprofits in 1961 with below market insurance rate (BMIR) financing, but the projects were scattered, often in "one-shot" developments and much of it was unsustainable. SECD's Demonstration Program was of this vintage. Among other things the SECD contract did not mention "housing management." HUD's insurance processing saw the operating budget as what was left over from rent revenue after paying off debt service on the mortgage loan. It is not surprising that the rents were too low to cover adequate management services.

The Housing Act of 1968 contained a target to build 26 million homes in ten years. It never met its goals. In 1973 President Nixon authorized a moratorium on new housing commitments, and in 1974 initiated block grant funding to the states and local governments. Along with block grants came the Section 8 leased housing allowance program. This was an important tool that resulted in a number of projects in the 1970s. But the inflation factor in the funding of the 100% Section 8 projects led to excessive unit costs, and the program was shut down in the 1980s.

During 1960s and 1970s, the development of numerous community development corporations (CDCs) occurred. They were mostly focused on a neighborhood, and few became major developers. The Neighborhood Reinvestment Corporation was formed, but it was primarily an instructional agency focused on a neighborhood strategy.

The Local Initiative Support Corporation (LISC) and Enterprise Corporation were initiated, but they were largely focused on roles of their own selection. The Community Reinvestment Act, designed to encourage commercial banks and savings associations to lend in all segments of their communities, was passed in 1978. This did lead the banks to become more engaged in community revitalization but never served as a primary bank program.

Private housing partnerships were being formed twenty-five years ago but with little coordination among the new organizations. The Housing Partnership Network has ended that isolation but the task of capturing the public's imagination on what HPN has and can accomplished is still unfinished business. HPN members must increase the scale and coverage of their operations as well as meet publicly endorsed performance standards and make their activities transparent to residents and the general population at large.

I suggest that the scaling up of HPN members needs to happen in four areas: (1) housing development, both multifamily rental and homeownership, and special collaborative projects with partners; (2) development of a respected and accepted performance rating system; (3) resident programs as an understood component of the services delivered; and (4) the counseling program and single family ownership.

In the absence of an adequate equity grant program, developers, investors and the Congress turned to tax benefits to support housing development. This meant that nonprofits had to form affiliate for-profit corporations that could do the project and receive the contributions from the third-party investors. Congress became concerned with abuse of the tax shelters, and in 1986 the federal tax code was revised. The nonprofit developers that had become skilled in the use of the tax benefits protested the proposed changes. In response, Congress created the Low Income Housing Tax Credit. It was recognition of the continuing need for subsidies and has been over-subscribed. Its value was recently increased and tied to changes in the cost of living. It is a wasteful way to make grants but is off-budget and does not have to be appropriated each year.

The problem remains that the LIHTC yields only 40% of what is necessary for project financing. The HOME and Community Development Block Grant programs are frequently used in conjunction with the tax credits but still fall short. LINC Housing's $25 million dollar project in Compton, California, had $10.3 million dollars of Low Income Housing Tax Credits and $3.4 million dollars of HOME funds. The first mortgage was for $1.5 million. It took ten other public and private funders to make up the balance required. That would have made our European friends go crazy. The HAG program gave the HAs what they needed over and above the bank loan. The loan program is curtained currently in the UK, but the HAs now have the equity to borrow using their own balance sheet.

The Bipartisan Policy Center (BPC) Housing Commission issued its report in February 2013 recommending a number of things, two of which were to expand the value of the LIHTC by 50% and to provide a public "guarantor" to insure the timely payment of principal and interest in these housing markets. It would only be triggered after all private capital ahead of it had been exhausted.

The guarantor would be independent of all other agencies. It would have powers to qualify borrowers and servicers. It would raise fees on its activities and set standards including loan limits and would be responsible for establishing an affordability threshold that would primarily support the development of rental housing that is affordable to low and moderate-income households. Its purposes are similar to the guarantee fund in the Netherlands, but it is cluttered with protections against risk and regulations that restrict its application. At a time when the Congress will be constrained in increasing costs to the government, both of the BBC recommendations will be in question.

The need to package together five to ten sources of financing in addition to the credits is horribly complex and burdensome. All these bits and pieces are tied to one piece of real estate. Commercial developers as well as housing associations abroad, have demonstrated the advantages of financing the company and not the project. This would require good accounting that can separate the costs in a reliable way.

HPN is in the business of developing good accounting systems. These can be used on preservation, rehabilitation and projects on which the investor tax credits have expired. In many cases, projects will be implemented through partnerships with for-profit firms. Performance standards would be a part of any proposal and would be required of all partners.

The practice of having owners set up individual financing entities for developed projects arose from the presence of FHA insurance. But it also came in with the real estate basis calculation of the LI-HTC. It is hard to imagine how this could be changed. However, projects that are no longer insured by FHA, that do not have credits, or those funded by a grant such as the Section 202 program, could be held in a portfolio and administered accordingly. This would produce administrative savings. It could also allow for a reallocation of subsidies to projects that needed them. When dealing with portfolio transactions, the ability to transfer available rental assistance among properties would be helpful.

Another possibility for social housing is the transfer of public housing in selected situations. Public housing authorities now have a program of transfer to private housing but it has been rarely used. The Moving to Work program could be modified to serve this need but it would not approach the UK model.

There are additional inefficiencies in current programs that can be modified. There exists a possibility that some budget tradeoffs can be made. For example, a number of housing experts have suggested that savings in the home mortgage interest deduction in the personal income tax could be used to support social housing. Others have said that the allocation of the Section 8 subsidies could be better focused on the families with the greatest need. This is also a time for rewriting the rules. The government wants the private sector to accept a greater share of the risks and costs of social housing, but there are limits as social housers require some measure of financial help if the lowest income groups are to be served.

Enterprise financing provides increased flexibility in financing projects. Size is a big factor. Allowing owners to raise private debt at the enterprise level will allow owners to raise larger amounts of capital and then deploy this capital to those properties in their portfolio with the greatest need and investment opportunity. They could finance groups of properties for the short- and long-term depending on the owner's schedule. Flexible debt will allow developers to move more rapidly in purchased existing projects. The housing associations in the UK and the Netherlands are demonstrating the effectiveness in flexible financing of portfolios.

It is assumed that the state housing finance agencies and special lenders, such the Massachusetts Housing Partnership Fund, could be persuaded to provide flexible financing. In time one would hope that the customary commercial banks and financial institutions would also follow. Such financing would support the issuance of bonds and other marketable securities. Mixed-income developments would be more common as developers move to be more self-sufficient.

For-sale units in housing developments also improves financial viability. HPN members could introduce shared ownership to the mix. There will be an increase in the complex developments in which partners from a variety of disciplines join. These partnerships are frequently committed to programs that offer educational, training and recreational opportunities. Most will bring in their own funding but some will want the housing partner to own the entire development and lease the space. The Network has members who could do this. BRIDGE in California is doing a complex project with the state Department of Transportation. The New York Housing Partnership is doing a number of projects that combine social housing with a variety of other uses. These experienced partners have access to financing for their own part of the work. Cross subsidies among programs or developments might occur but under appropriate management decisions and controls.

HPN has among its members CDFIs. There are a number of ways

in which the capacity of CDFIs could be enhanced. CDFIs could be members of the Federal Home Loan Bank System. There is the CDFI Bond Guarantee program to provide a source of long-term, patent capital. The savings in rent subsidies could offset most of the federal expense. One could imagine a special program of selected CDFIs that pooled their resourses and combined with a substantial one-time grant from the federal government, could provide funding for approved members of HPN. These would be the high-performing nonprofit organizations which would be approved by HPN.

A new section of the National Housing Act might include criteria for participation and performance standards. It would be a role for HPN in conjunction with others in designating these provisions and accompanying regulations. The government's risk would be mitigated by combining it with the capital equity grants and contributions. The project would be focused on providing below-market rents for eligible low-income families. In cases of trouble projects, the prequalification of developers and oversight by the Network would facilitate corrections in the event of failure. A new section in the Housing Act would give the program more definition and political presence and help ensure continued funding when established.

Preservation of the existing affordable stock is another source to be considered. There are individual scattered-site developments as well as portfolios owned by for-profit corporations that were created on the basis of covenants to maintain the affordable units for 20 years, at which time the developers could opt out. The federal government has an interest in putting these projects in the hands of new owners to maintain their affordability. Preservation of Affordable Housing (POAH) has acquired about 8,000 units of such housing. These purchases require analysis of the characteristics of the development and whether the project is viable. Sometimes there are subsidies which can be utilized. The big issue is cash flow. Some purchases can take advantage of reserves that are held by the owners and can be accessed by the new owners. At a time when money for new projects will be limited, preservation may be worth investigating.

There is a history of trouble with for-profit development. Developments such as Kynes Lynne created by Corcoran, Mullins and Jennison in Lynn, Massachusetts, continue as an exemplary projects. But a number of for-profit projects have a limited sustainable life and are available at the end of the tax credit or regulatory period. These are likely projects for purchase by a nonprofit. They need to be refinance to save the public subsidies or lose the property as subsidized housing

The counseling program is the oldest program of the Network and one which has proven itself to be very valuable. Half of all the rental housing in the US is single-family homes and that suggests a number of ways in which the Network can be involved. The foreclosure problems which the banks and financial institutional investors encountered needed special attention. The Neighborhood Community Stabilization Trust was launched in a number of locations and scattered site single family housing involving First Look and preferred purchase were started. The RETURN Initiative will enable members operating in distressed markets to acquire REO properties and manage them in portfolios of scattered site rental housing. There are a number of problems associated with management of scattered site rental housing. Programs will require money and experimentation to prove their value.

Social housing is an appropriate name for HPN housing because it serves as an element of a comprehensive community plan supported by the entire society and largely addressed through private nonprofit organizations. The nonprofit has a tax exemption and is prepared to accept certain restrictions on its revenue in return for the necessary funding required to meet its goal of providing good housing to people who cannot afford the market costs. The cost of these expenses is a question. Some developments can pay for services and in others the owner/landlord has to have local government or philanthropic help. The size of the organization makes a difference with the larger landlord doing better.

Resolving this issue is best accomplished under a plan involving the government and the nonprofit sector. The Network is the major private sector player representing high-performing housing nonprofits. It has now arrived at a point in its development that it is ready to take on a leadership role in pursuing a federal mixed-income housing program that will provide rental housing for a wide section of the general population with some of that housing permanently allocated to serve the poor.

The US lacks strong civic cohesion and support for welfare programs is difficult even in such an immensely wealthy country. There are generational problems as costs are transferred from younger workers to the retired, the sick and those receiving public assistance. Where social programs are intended to be comprehensive and cover every citizen, the government role is crucial. Owners of the property have to have enough units to provide the economies of scale. We saw this factor influence the sustainability of operations of small CDCs. I suggest that the country is ready to support a distinct role for the major nonprofit organizations, but their activities have to be transparent and competently run.

The state of Massachusetts is attempting to close down housing authorities that have less than 800 units. SECD's eighty-three units in the South End were not viable. HPN's experience says that a nonprofits needs 750 to 1,000 units to be sustainable. In addition to scale, organizations must have a monitoring system that indicates quality of operations at each site.

If one assumes the ultimate goal is that a percentage of housing in the US be social housing in the hands of highly qualified non-profit organization's that are credit-worthy, have strong performance records and net worth sufficient to obtain financing for on-going operations from commercial banks and investors, the Network has made a good start. But it must continue to expand its reach and influence. A large proportion of American households own their home or can afford the rental of a standard apartment. The poor in most cases cannot. Thomas Jefferson's idea that all men are created equal, is neither self-evident nor correct. In fact all men are created unequal with very diverse economic opportunity. Without some form of assistance, the poor live in substandard housing associated with health and safety risks.

The dilapidated flats in rundown buildings, the tin shacks and mud huts occupied by the poor in cities and rural areas of the world, illustrate the inability of governments to solve housing problems. The occupants of such housing in developed countries are frequently unorganized minority or ethnic groups with inadequate political power to demand change. These differences are exasperated by the nature of our competitive society, which generates winners and losers. Achieving a decent home for all Americans was one of the great challenges of the 20th century, and it remains unfinished business today. The members of the Housing Partnership Network should continue their housing work on the basis that in time they will fulfill the promise of becoming a key central player in community development in this country.

HPN Membership List by State

Chicanos Por La Causa	Phoenix, AZ
Raza Development Fund, Inc.	Phoenix, AZ
Abode Communities	Los Angeles, CA
BRIDGE Housing Corp.	San Francisco, CA
Eden Housing	Hayward, CA
LINC Housing Corp.	Long Beach, CA
Low Income Investment Fund	San Francisco, CA
MidPen Housing Corp.	Foster City, CA
National Community Renaissance	Rancho Cucamonga, CA
South County Housing Corp.	Gilro, CA
Tenderloin Neighborhood Development Corp.	San Francisco, CA
Mercy Housing	Denver, CO
Rocky Mountain Communities	Denver, CO
Housing Development Fund	Stamford, CT
Community Preservation & Development Corp.	Washington, DC
National Housing Trust/Enterprise Preservation Corp.	Washington, DC
Atlanta Neighborhood Development Partnership, Inc.	Atlanta, GA
Chicago Community Loan Fund	Chicago, IL
Heartland Housing, Inc.	Chicago, IL
Hispanic Housing Development Corp.	Chicago, IL
IFF	Chicago, IL
Neighborhood Housing Services of Chicago	Chicago, IL
Indianapolis Neighborhood Housing Partnership	Indianapolis, N
Community Ventures Corp.	Lexington, KY
Federation of Appalachian Housing Enterprises	Berea, KY
Housing Partnership, Inc.	Louisville, KY
Gulf Coast Housing Partnership	New Orleans, LA
Neighborhood Development Foundation	New Orleans, LA
Boston Community Capital	Boston, MA
HAPHousing	Springfield, MA
Housing Assistance Corp.	Hyannis, MA
Massachusetts Housing Investment Corp.	Boston, MA
Metropolitan Boston Housing Partnership	Boston, MA
Planning Office for Urban Affairs	Boston, MA
Preservation of Affordable Housing	Boston, MA
South Shore Housing	Kingston, MA
The Caleb Group	Swampscott, MA

The Community Builders	Boston, MA
Homes for America, Inc.	Annapolis, MD
Montgomery Housing Partnership	Silver Spring, MD
St. Ambrose Housing Aid Center	Baltimore, MD
Great Lakes Capital Fund	Lansing, MI
Metro Community Development	Flint, MI
Aeon	Minneapolis, MN
CommonBond Communities	St. Paul, MN
Community Reinvestment Fund, USA	Minneapolis, MN
Family Housing Fund	Minneapolis, MN
Greater Metropolitan Housing Corp,	Minneapolis, MN
Greater Minnesota Housing Fund	St. Paul, MN
Minnesota Homeownership Center	St. Paul, MN
Project for Pride in Living	Minneapolis, MN
Southwest Minnesota Housing Partnership	Slayton, MN
Regional Housing & Community Development Alliance	St. Louis, MO
Mississippi Housing Partnership	Jackson, MS
The Housing Partnership	Charlotte, NC
DHIC, Inc.	Raleigh, NC
North Carolina Community Development Initiative	Raleigh, NC
New Community Corp.	Newark, NJ
New Jersey Community Capital	New Brunswick, NJ
Homewise	Santa Fe, NM
The Housing Trust of Santa Fe	Santa Fe, NM
Nevada HAND, Inc.	Las Vegas, NV
Affordable Housing Partnership of the Capital Region	Albany, NY
Common Ground	New York, NY
Greater Rochester Housing Partnership	Rochester, NY
Housing Partnership Development Corp.	New York, NY
Long Island Housing Partnership, Inc.	Hauppauge, NY
Neighborhood Housing Services of New York City	New York, NY
New York Mortgage Coalition	New York, NY
NHP Foundation	New York, NY
Settlement Housing Fund	New York, NY
The Phipps Houses Group	New York, NY
Cleveland Housing Network	Cleveland, OH
Homeport	Columbus, OH
National Affordable Housing Trust	Columbus, OH
National Church Residences	Columbus, OH
Ohio Capital Corp. for Housing	Columbus, OH

Community Action Project of Tulsa County	Tulsa, OK
REACH Community Development, Inc.	Portland, OR
ACTION-Housing, Inc.	Pittsburgh, PA
HDC MidAtlantic	Lancaster, PA
The Reinvestment Fund	Philadelphia, PA
Omni Development Corp.	Providence, RI
Community Development Corp. of Brownsville	Brownsville, TX
Covenant Community Capital Corp.	Houston, TX
Dallas City Homes	Dallas, TX
Housing & Community Services, Inc.	San Antonio, TX
Tarrant County Housing Partnership	Fort Worth, TX
Community Development Corp. of Utah	Salt Lake City, UT
AHC, Inc.	Arlington, VA
Community Housing Partners	Christiansburg, VA
NCB Capital Impact	Arlington, VA
Wesley Housing Development Corp.	Alexandria, VA
Champlain Housing Trust	Burlington, VT
Bellwether Housing Trust	Seattle, WA
Capitol Hill Housing	Seattle, WA
Wisconsin Partnership for Housing Development	Madison, WI
Religious Coalition for Community Renewal	Charleston, WV

366

Notes

1. Kathleen Dalton, *Theodore Roosevelt, Alfred A. Knopf*, New York, 2002, page 426
2. Raymond Moley, *The First New Deal*, (Harcourt, Brace & World Inc., New York, 1966) page 199
3. Michael Katz, *In the Shadow of the Poorhouse*, (HarperCollins USA, 1986), page 25
4. Katz, *In the Shadow of the Poorhouse*, page 37
5. Katz,. *In the Shadow of the Poorhouse*, page 35
6. Katz, *In the Shadow of the Poorhouse*, page 53
7. Katz, *In the Shadow of the Poorhouse*, page 34
8. Katz, *In the Shadow of the Poorhouse*, page 43
9. Sydney Fine, *Laissez Faire and the General Welfare State*, (University of Michigan Press, 1956), page 181
10. Fine, *Laissez Faire*, page 236
11. Roy Lubove, *The Struggle for Social Security*,
    (Harvard University Press, Cambridge, 1968), page 49
12. General George Steinberg, Committee on Building of Model Homes,
    (President's Homes Commission, Washington, DC, 1908), page 4
13. Fine, *Laissez Faire*, page 325
14. Arthur S. Link and Richard L. McCormick, *Progressivism*,
    (Harlan Davidson, Wheeling, Illinois, 1983), page 42
15. Gail Radford, *Modern Housing for America*,
    (University of Chicago Press, Chicago, 1996), page 44
16. Home Ownership, Income and Types of Dwellings, (President's Conference on Home Building
    and Home Ownership, Washington, DC, 1932), page 198
17. Radford, *Modern Housing*, page 53
18. Arthur Schlesinger, Jr, *The Crisis of the Old Order*, (Houghton Miffin Company, Boston,1957), page 173
19. Kent Colton, *Housing in The Twenty-First Century*,
    (Harvard University Press, Cambridge, 2003), page 173
20. Nancy Altman, *The Battle for Social Security*,
    (John Wiley & Sons, Hoboken, New Jersey, 2005), page 27
21. Frances Perkins, *The Roosevelt I Knew*, (The Viking Press, New York, 1946), page 113
22. Katz, *In the Shadow*, page 224
23. William Leuchtenburg, *Franklin D. Roosevelt and the New Deal*,
    (Harper and Row, New York, 1963), page 133
24. Frances Perkins, *The Roosevelt I Knew*, (The Viking Press, New York, 1946), page 283
25. Edwin Witte, *The Development of the Social Security Act*
    (University of Wisconsin P, Press, Madison,1963), page 47
26. J. Douglas Brown, *The Development of the Social Security Act*,
    (Princeton University Press, Princeton, New Jersey, 1972), page 188
27. Radford, Gail, *Modern Housing for America*, page 181
28. Arthur Schlesinger, Jr., *The Crisis of the Old Order*,
    (Houghton Miflin Company, Boston, 1937), page 363
29. Lukas, J. Anthony, *Common Ground*, (Random House, Inc., New York, 1986), page 166
30. Boston Redevelopment Authority Memorandum
31. Jayne E. Shister Affidavid June 4, 1976
32. Judge Garrity, Decision July 25, 1979, page 36
33. Garrett, Patricia, *Memorandum* dated July 14, 2008
34. BRIDGE *Five Year Plan*
35. Schweinitz, Karl de, *England's Road to Social Security*,
    (A.S.Barnes & Company Inc, New York, 1961), page 27
36. Asa Briggs, *The Social History of England*, (Book Club Associates, London, 1983)

37. Norbert Schoenauer, *6000 Years of Housing*, (W W Norton and Company, New York) page 295
38. Anne Power, *Hovels to High Rise 9* (Routledge, New York, 1993) page 174
39. Hamilton Jackson, title on coloured lithograph, 1882
40. Anne Power, page 175
41. AffinitySutton, *Building on our Heritage*, 2011, page 9
42. Anne Power, page 182
43. Anne Power, page 187
44. Anne Power, page 200
45. Emms Peters, *Social Housing, a Europen Dilemma?*
    (School for Advanced Urban Studies, Bristol, England, 1990), page 31
46. Anne Power, page 218
47. The Housing Corporation, *The First Twenty-five years*, page 19
48. AffinitySutton, *Building on Our Heritage*, page 25

368

INDEX

370

Printed in the United States
By Bookmasters